Goodbye Bad Guys

BCACT TO THE RESCUE!

The experiences of a compassionate animal abuse task force who fought for the animals and put their abusers behind bars.

As told by Capt. Andi Taylor, BCSO

To Kate J. Kuligowski

Author—Dog Writers' Association of America Best Book 2014

D1601652

Proceeds will be directed to NMDOG, a 501(c)(3) and BCSO animal welfare activities.

ISBN: 978-0-692-75967-7

Library of Congress Control Number: 2016912100

THE GUYS™
PUBLISHING
COMPANY

905 Maverick Trail, SE, Albuquerque, New Mexico 87123
wkkjk1027@gmail.com

Design and typesetting by Julie Melton, The Right Type
Cover photo by Helga Carter
Sheriff photo on page 8 by Sean Weaver
Photo on page 10 by Helga Carter
Photos on pages 6, 7, 8, 9
courtesy of NMDOG and Capt. Andi Taylor, BCSO
Printed in the United States of America

"Each remarkable individual of our highly successful Bernalillo County Animal Cruelty Task Force will never forget their rewarding experiences with the hundreds of animals we encountered; and those animals whose lives we saved will never forget the kindness of our team members. This is our story."

– Capt. Andi Taylor, BCSO

Author's note: clarifying "quotes"

Because many of these touching stories are told by Captain Andi Taylor, her text is indicated by italics, without quotation marks. Quotes from other individuals are in regular text with quotation marks. Background information, statistics, news-making stories and a few observations of my own are in regular font, no quotes.

This book is not intended to provide legal or official advice. Its information and procedures are subject to agency policy and review by the communities, counties, state and federal prosecutors, lawmakers or other legal advisors. Although the research involving laws and incidents reported in this book was thorough and ongoing, government entities constantly change, amend or create new laws.

TABLE OF CONTENTS

DEDICATION

TO OUR INTER-AGENCY SQUAD: BCACT

"Every life is important. In instances of animal cruelty and neglect, animals should no longer be seen as 'just animals' but should be regarded as living beings and provided the care and respect appropriate to those who have been victimized. Our task force's achievements demand and inspire justice for all animal victims in Bernalillo County, and we salute them."

– Matt Pepper

The compassionate and brave members of BCACT:

Back row L to R: Deputies Kyle Hartsock, Lee Madrid, Todd James, Jesse Cash, Felipe Haynes, Boyce Berry; BCAC Director, Matt Pepper; Officers Pete Smiley and Pat Trujillo.

Front row: Deputy Laura Dailey, Captain Andi Taylor, NMDog President Angela Stell, BCACS Officer Brittney Nelson.

DEDICATION

INDIVIDUALS OF BCACT— MAKING A DIFFERENCE

BCSO Deputies: L to R: Capt. Andi Taylor, Deputies Aaron Schwartz, Daniel Portell, Unidentified, Deputies Laura Dailey, Felicia Romero. Not shown: Sgt. Amy Dudewicz, Detective Donnie Hix, Detective Sam Ungaro.

NMDOG VOLUNTEERS: L TO R: Tina Holguin, Mychele Moody, Angela Stell, Jennifer Toennies, Belinda Archuleta, Tonya Munding Dixon and, of course, JoJo (NMDOG Mascot).

DEDICATION
SOME OF OUR SUCCESSES

Because of the selfless commitment of BCACT, these innocent, battered and abused animals are now enjoying new lives in the safety of new and loving homes. Not only did we make a difference in their lives, but they definitely made a difference in ours!

Angela Stell and Matt Pepper with Casey Jones, before and after rescue.
See Chapter 20

Capt. Taylor calms newly rescued Ferdinand.
See Chapter 6

Sheriff has a new life, free from chains.
See Chapter 19

Pearl enjoys outings with new owner.
See Chapter 4

A recovering Romeo poses with Angela Stell,
BCACS Officers Pete Smiley and Shawn Clark.
See Chapter 4

BCSO Deputies Jordan Seay
and Dominic Howe hold rescues
Ringo and Starr.
See Chapter 20

NMDOG'S award-winning mascot, trainer and companion, JoJo has a "cool" moment.
See Chapter 4

INTRODUCTION

GOODBYE BAD GUYS
BCACT TO THE RESCUE!

Humanitarians and pet activists have long prayed for an action that was a sure-fire means to reduce the abuse of animals. This is it!

BCACT, Bernalillo County Animal Cruelty Task Force, is an amazing inter-agency animal cruelty task force, masterminded by Capt. Andi Taylor of the Bernalillo County Sheriff's Office. Through its creation, the county's sheriff's deputies, animal care officers and NMDOG were determined, by working together, to lessen the numbers of animals suffering from abandonment and abuse in New Mexico.

Although this book is centered on experiences of law enforcement and animal care officers, it is primarily about saving the lives of abused pets, their heart-breaking as well as heart-warming stories, and how laws throughout the United States have failed them. It addresses events, policies, and procedures in both law enforcement agencies and animal control facilities throughout our country.

Enforcement of animal codes in some communities was lukewarm, and the judicial system was usually too busy, unequipped and uncommitted to deal with pets. Their tragic stories as experienced by BCACT came to their rescue were the result of animal codes and statutes that were without teeth, leaving these animals unprotected from the violent behaviors of humans of all ages. As these stories encompass animal cruelty incidents in all parts of the United States, these chapters will not only prove enlightening for pet owners and pet activists alike, but hopefully inspire them even more to continue their dedication and efforts to strengthen these archaic laws with lenient penalties.

BCACT's celebrated success is due to its concentrated cross-training and its unscheduled sweeps through those neighborhoods with a high-call volume of animal neglect and abuse complaints. Sporting a no-nonsense "boots-on the ground" philosophy, this dedicated team has saved the lives of hundreds of abused pets and arrested their abusers along with a slew of other criminals on unrelated charges. Their credo is, "Where you see evidence of animal abuse, open your eyes: there is more." They have accomplished this feat without costing the taxpayers any additional monies. Remarkable!

Forget about the Avengers' and the Guardians of the Galaxy. These are actual people having actual encounters of white hats VS black hats: the good guys against the bad. Their fight against animal neglect and abandonment reveal heart-breaking and moving stories: real stories, real life.

Your Community's Guide To Stopping Animal Abuse

Peppered with the stories and details of the conception, planning, formation, training and missions of an animal cruelty task force such as BCACT, these chapters detail each of the steps necessary to improve or establish this inter-agency team in your community. It can be easily adapted to all regions of the United States. These chapters:

- Clarify federal, state and county animal abuse laws.

- Dissect, compare and evaluate animal codes and programs from every state, including D.C., as to humaneness, strengths and weaknesses.

- Provide examples of model animal ordinances.

- Explain how to successfully combine two government agencies to collaborate on this task force.

- Outline the lecture information necessary for the safety and enlightenment of the future members of your task force.

- Includes the safety implications on the community of said animal abuse violations.

- Lists resource and reference materials recommended by BCACT.

Definitions of Acronyms

AACC	Albuquerque Animal Care Center
AAS	Aztec, New Mexico Animal Shelter
AAWD	Albuquerque Animal Welfare Department
ADBA	American Dog Breeders Association
AFF	Animal Farm Foundation
AHAA	Animal Humane Association of America
AHANM	Animal Humane Association of New Mexico
AKC	American Kennel Club
ALDF	Animal Legal Defense Fund
APD	Albuquerque Police Department
APNM	Animal Protection New Mexico
APRI	American Pet Registry, Inc.
ASPCA	American Society for the Prevention of Cruelty to Animals
AVMA	American Veterinary Medical Association
BCACS	Bernalillo County Animal Care Services
BCACT	Bernalillo County Animal Cruelty Task
BCSO	Bernalillo County Sheriff's Office
BSL	Breed Specific Legislation
CARE	Companion Animal Rescue Effort
CKC	Continental Kennel Club
CYFD	Children, Youth and Families Department
GDS	Guard Dog Site Permit
HARC	The Hoarding of Animals Research Consortium
HEART	Humane and Ethical Animal Rules and Treatment
HSUS	Humane Society of the United States
IACP	International Association of Chiefs of Police
MCASP	Multiple Companion Animal Site Permit
NCOVAA	National Coalition on Violence Against Animals
NCRC	National Canine Research Council
NIBRS	National Incident Based Reporting System
NMCADV	New Mexico Coalition Against Domestic Violence
NMDOG	New Mexico Dogs
NMDPS	New Mexico Department of Public Safety
PAW	Pre-adjudication Animal Welfare Program
PETA	People for the Ethical Treatment of Animals
SNAP	Spay Neuter Assistance Program
SPCA	Society for the Prevention of Cruelty to Animals
SPCC	Society for the Prevention of Cruelty to Children
UNM	University of New Mexico
USDOJ	U.S. Department of Justice

CHAPTER ONE

WHO, WHERE AND WHY

"Pets are living proof that in our often ugly and violent world, good still exists."

– Unknown

WHO

Each remarkable individual of our highly successful Bernalillo County Animal Cruelty Task Force will never forget their rewarding experiences with the hundreds of animals we encountered; and those animals whose lives we saved will never forget the kindness of our team members. This is our story.

It was only a weekly meeting of our animal cruelty task force, but I could not contain the tremor of excitement in my voice. "We've done it," I announced, tears of joy streaming down my face. "Our animal cruelty team has made a really big difference! Stats say that reported animal abuse has been curtailed by 40%, in only three years! Dogs are no longer chained! Residents are becoming more aware of their legal responsibilities as pet owners. And our team was responsible for saving hundreds of animals from abuse and painful deaths."

Overjoyed, hugging, choked up with the enormity of our accomplishment, we shared flashbacks to some of our most horrific rescues...the hope we held and the tenderness we displayed as we lifted into our arms a critically injured animal while transporting it for veterinary care. In these three remarkable years, we had relocated hundreds of abandoned, abused or neglected pets and issued an impressive number of citations for animal, child, elder and domestic abuse, and well as other related crimes in Albuquerque's unincorporated South Valley.

Our BCACT is the acronym, Bernalillo County Animal Cruelty Task Force. Our mission is the rescuing of abandoned and abused animals through collaborative efforts of Bernalillo County Animal Care Services (BCACS), New Mexico Dogs (NMDOG) and Bernalillo County Sheriff's Office (BCSO), the third largest law enforcement agency in New Mexico. Not only has it been a rewarding and challenging adventure for our dedicated deputies, BCACS officers and the volunteers of NMDOG, it has also been hailed by both our community and our county as a successful and major undertaking. In comparison to those similar animal cruelty task forces in Los Angeles and New York, the organizational requirements of BCACT are simple, and involve uniting the talents of two county agencies and not necessitating the incorporation of a national humane association.

Masterminded by three capable and compassionate community leaders, this county team's goal was two-fold: to greatly improve the existing, painful statistics of pet abuse in their beat while improving the safety for those residents. The task force members of Capt. Andi Taylor, BCSO, Matt Pepper, Director BCACS, and Angela Stell, President and Founder of NMDOG became heroes in a present day world, racked with physical violence and indifference. Their team is making a difference—a big difference!

Everyone enjoys a touching, feel-good story about a rescued abused or abandoned animal now residing in a new loving home. The humane actions of the newly formed BCACT, continually brings media raves throughout regional newspapers and television stations. Its humane accomplishments pepper the social media. BCACT has provided a much needed "fix" to New Mexico's embarrassing, calloused and indifferent approach to animal abuse and a boost in public relations for Bernalillo County, for New Mexico! Best of all…what a saving grace for the animals!

WHERE

Ranked as one of the most dangerous states in America, New Mexico's violent crime rate, for the third year in a row, was in the top five. Although its state and local taxes per capita are the nation's 17th highest, this beautiful state has the highest percentage of its residents in poverty, possibly attributable to its 2016 ranking as 46th in public school education.

The state of New Mexico, officially recognized as "The Land of Enchantment" is blessed with unequaled beauty and weather. Travel magazines paint it as a paradise for skiers, mountain climbers, art lovers, cowboys, UFO buffs, and for those who wish to explore our caves, ice caverns, bottomless lakes, white sands and Indian ruins. Rich in history, its support of three different cultures sets it apart as a destination for art lovers of all mediums.

However, the state's laws (or lack of) have not protected its many treasures and have allowed it to become rampant with poverty, crime, ignorance, homelessness, and child, domestic and animal abuse. New Mexico is ranked second highest in the nation for teen alcohol. Drug deaths are rated second in America. Our state's teen suicide rate is twice the national average.

New Mexico ranks 46th in the nation in child homelessness. According to the National Center on Family Homelessness, our state had 22,463 children 17 or younger living in abandoned cars and structures, condemned properties, tent cities, neighbor's basements, porches and tool sheds, parks, campgrounds, arroyos, beaches surrounding rivers and lakes, as well as under railroad crossing bridges. Officials have mentioned that there is not much hope for our homeless children or families, as the waiting list for that public housing managed by Albuquerque Housing Authority exceeds 3,500 names.

Within this breathtaking state with so much unmet potential lie the beautiful, rugged lands of 33 counties. Bernalillo County encompasses an enormous 1,169 square mile region in the central part of New Mexico. As the most populous county of the state with 673,460 residents, it is blessed with near-perfect weather: high altitude, low humidity and 167 brilliant blue, and sunny days. Most (555,417) make their home in the sprawling 189.5 acres of Albuquerque, the state's largest city, resting plumb in the middle of Bernalillo County and protected by its own police force.

Legally the authority of our Bernalillo County Sheriff's Department (BCSO) extends throughout the entire county, including into Albuquerque as well as its other surrounding, smaller communities. But like many other communities, the delegated jurisdiction accepted by the county sheriff's department lies mostly in those locations outside those inner city and town limits, the unincorporated areas of the city. Incorporated jurisdictions within the county, such as Albuquerque and Los Ranchos have legal authority, and can occasionally can present sticky issues for the sprawling Bernalillo County. Cooperation is essential between those five surrounding counties with which it shares geographic boundaries as well as those incorporated cities within.

The configuration of rural and agricultural land which BCSO must serve is divided into three commands: north, east and south. Boundaries of the sheriff's command are bundled between the Sandia and Manzano Mountain ranges on the east and the petroglyphs and the inert volcano escarpment on the west. Its southeast boundary is Kirtland Air Force Base, serviced by military police; its southwest boundary is the Isleta Pueblo, policed by tribal law enforcement.

Occupying great significance in Bernalillo County's landmarks is the famous Rio Grande, which shares the same classification of the Nile, as an "exotic" river because it flows through a desert. It is of geological interest to note that New Mexico's Rio Grande lies within the Rio Grande Rift Valley, which means it is bordered by the system of faults. Ten million years ago these faults were instrumental in lifting the Sandia and Manzano Mountains. While this was occurring, it was lowering the land where the narrow and often drying Rio Grande now flows, a natural drainage basin through central New Mexico.

Its demographics support three cultures, but its more than 70 ethnicities create a unique Southwestern blend for a county with a majority (47.9%) of Hispanic residents, many boasting ancestral families established before statehood.

Dotting the mesas and mountains surrounding this country are ten pueblos: Acoma, Laguna, Isleta, Cochiti, Santa Domingo, San Felipe, Santa Ana, Zia, Jemez and Sandia. Theirs is a Southwest presence dating back more than two thousand years when their ancestors roamed the pristine wilderness as hunters, farmers and traders. About 1,500 years ago, these early tribes joined together to establish permanent settlements, villages which are termed pueblos. Each is considered a sovereign nation and practice different languages, customs, feast days, ceremonies and laws. Although they continue their traditional styles of fine arts and sought-after crafts reflecting their unique culture, in this 21st century, many also operate busy casinos. Unable to adjust to life outside their pueblos, they are seriously impacted by unemployment and substance abuse.

Toss these residents into a still-active wild-west cowboy culture with a mañana attitude. Fuse with the scientific research and technology at Sandia National Laboratories (born during World War II's Manhattan Project). Stir in the sage of the University of New Mexico. You have created a unique diversity, a one-of-a-kind: Bernalillo County, home to all of these, and whose notorious South Valley is home to BCACT, whose brave members have saved hundreds of victimized animals since its inception in 2012.

I began this endeavor as lieutenant in the Bernalillo Sheriff's Department South Area. My beat was actually known as the South Valley by county residents and was home to nearly 50% of unincorporated Bernalillo County's population. It is located on the southwest side of the county, away from the Albuquerque's breath-taking skyline and its majestic mountainous landscape on the east. Across the drying river bed of the Rio Grande, this flat, dry and often desolate landscape consists of agricultural and rural lands and mostly constitute the unincorporated areas of South Valley, extending all the way to the Isleta Indian Pueblo, 13 miles south of Albuquerque. The government of this pueblo, situated on an ancient Rio Grande channel, employs their own tribal sheriff and under-sheriff.

Within its boundaries lie interesting and diverse neighborhoods. Historic Atrisco, established in 1703 by settlers who built their haciendas on the banks of the Rio Grande. Some of Albuquerque's original families still reside here, lending an air of stability, history and establishment to this diverse area. Seldom do our visits encounter their neighborhoods. Fast forward 400 years to this area being the chosen location for scenes over a ten year period from two television series, "Breaking Bad" and "In Plain Sight."

Los Padillas neighborhood, four times the size of Parajito, is a neighborhood under siege, plagued by menacing gang activity: narcotics trafficking, human trafficking, property crimes, domestic violence, child abuse and animal fighting.

Parajito Mesa is a small and forgotten South Valley neighborhood, whose greatest concerns continue to center around the unavailability of both water and electricity. This location received no county services, as the residents are perceived as "squatters" on private land. Their pioneer life has generated "do as I want" individual pioneer attitudes in regard to their lifestyles, living conditions and scattered illegal building developments with a mish-mash of unplatted paths, carved into the hard caliche by the continued use of residential vehicles. There exist no dedicated streets.

The Rio Grande drainage ditches intersecting this land are used as roads or trails by automobiles and horses alike (the ratio of horses to cars is one to five). Some intersect and run through the middle of a "street," and because they are lower than the streets, these ditches offer low visibility, providing perfect escape routes for criminals. Often chases result in the deputies backtracking a mile or more in order to cross the ditch to reach the other side of the road.

Surprisingly, a great number of its other roads are unpaved (just caliche) and flood when there is a rare accumulation of moisture from rain or snow. Not only do these valley 'streets' lack signs and lighting, but the numbering system of their homes is usually random and follows no pattern. Sidewalks are few and far between.

It follows that our South Valley is also burdened by its deprivation. Statistics tell it best. Because its average income is lower than 69.9% of America's neighborhoods, it is not surprising that the South Valley has a higher rate of childhood poverty than more than 88% of American neighborhoods. More than 80% of its high school students are eligible to receive free or reduced lunches. The graduation rate of the South Valley's only high school was listed as only 66.3% and its ill-prepared students scored a graded "F" on the nationally administered SBA and PARCC tests. As long as those stats and demographics remain bleak and untended to by our government officials, many of these downtrodden, neglected South Valley residents have developed a greater-than-average tendency to turn to crime.

And, to further increase the dangers in that rugged territory, the South Valley is definitely gun country with no background checks for gun show purchases. Records reveal almost 50% of our state residents have a firearm in the home; the national average is 29%.

WHY

"...it would also be mistaken to view other living beings as mere objects subjected to arbitrary human domination."

– Pope Francis

But clouding their beautiful, incredibly bright blue skies, their sought-after high desert landscape and climate exist ugly statistics that unfortunately label the county of Bernalillo (incorporated and unincorporated together) as one of the worst locations in America for both child and animal abuse and abandonment. Once the animals are rescued from abusive situations or are found homeless on the streets, the BCACS officer cannot transport them to the county shelter, as its present impound capacity is very limited and not compliant as long-term residence kennels. Its new facility is expected completion by 2017.

An existing arrangement allows the County, at the tune of $350 per animal, to transfer dogs and cats from BCACS to the Albuquerque Animal Welfare Department (AAWD) facility. This cost includes all medical care including spaying or neutering and microchipping, kennel boarding, food, adoption services and permits. In 2014, that number was 2,666, of which 1,629 were dogs, and only 14% of those were reunited with their owners. A disproportionate number those impounded were Pit Bull Terriers/crosses. AAWD was able to provide live exits for 84% of Bernalillo County 2014 impounds. "Live exits" refers to animals who have been adopted, reclaimed, transferred or are "change-of-hearts."

Recently BCACS entered into another supplemental contract with Aztec, New Mexico Animal Shelter (AAS) for $96 (including 180 mile transportation) per transferred dog, considerably less than their contract with Albuquerque. Because of Aztec's close network arrangement with rescue groups in nearby states, most of these transfers have found homes.

Federal dictated standards for kennels include humane handling, housing, ventilation, space, sanitation, shelter, veterinary care and nutrition for those abused and neglected impounded animals. In keeping with its minimal standards for its animals, the state has allotted NM Animal Sheltering Board no authority to investigate shelter complaints even though overcrowding is a constant in most public and private New Mexico shelters, thus higher rates of euthanasia. This needless condition (needless, because our laws and ordinances do not seriously address basic care for our pets) also accounts for the many more-than-average number of New Mexico 501(c)(3) organizations with hard-working, dedicated and selfless members who foster the abandoned and abused of our state.

Inspections of animal shelters are included in <u>Virginia's</u> **code 3.2-6502.**

This state allows their veterinarian and representative to conduct inspections of public and private animal shelters, and inspect any business premises where animals are housed or kept, including any boarding establishment, kennel, pet shop, or the business premises of any dealer, exhibitor or groomer, at any reasonable time, for the purposes of determining if a violation occurred.

Another animal sheltering dilemma most states also face is that of caring for pets associated with a domestic violence case. Companion Animal Rescue Effort (CARE) network, created by Animal Protection New Mexico (APNM), has limited resources and is able to meet the needs for but a few who need temporary housing for these pets, as does Red Rover's SAF-T program. These programs give the victim peace of mind, so that when relocating from their abuser, they can be assured that their pet is in safe lodging. Tragically, in New Mexico, 71% of domestic violence victims who have pets report that the animal had been threatened, injured or killed by their abuser. APNM also partnered with New Mexico Coalition Against Domestic Violence (NMCADV) to yearly seek appropriations from the New Mexico legislature to support the animal lodging facilities for victims of domestic violence that are the result of this partnership.

Regardless of the hard lobbying and rigorous networking by APNM for more humane statutes, not all of their efforts are successful. New Mexico legislation has failed to recognize, much less tackle, the repeat-faction of animal cruelty, alarming in New Mexico, and a problem which could be addressed with an animal abuse registry software program in all states and their communities. Currently, the only method available to gather statistics on abuse are from daily media articles which are catalogued by national animal humane organizations. These reveal a ghastly number of animal cruelty cases, increasing in number, but even sadder is the fact that most cases are never reported, and even fewer are released to the media.

Because New Mexico statistics of animal cruelty and abandonment are so overwhelming, and are also increasing in occurrence, Capt. Andi Taylor, BCSO, decided in 2010 to be a guiding part of a Bernalillo County project that would greatly lessen these numbers through pro-active team-policing. She would make a difference and her BCACT would serve to other rural and incorporated areas as a successful example of how easily they, too, could make a difference.

CHAPTER TWO

BECAUSE OF ANDREA

"You can't lead the people if you don't love the people. You can't save the people if you don't serve the people."
                                                                    – Cornel West

"No! No! Please call me Andi. No one knows me by Andrea," she insisted.

This is the success story of a determined, compassionate team and the tireless efforts of their commander, Capt. Andi Taylor, Bernalillo County Sheriff's Office, New Mexico, to establish and maintain an animal cruelty task force Bernalillo County Animal Cruelty Task Force, BCACT. Its actions would change and save the lives of victims of animal, child and domestic violence and bring to justice to those responsible for these heinous crimes. These pages speak not only of fulfillment, disappointment and heartache, but also of courage, change and success. They detail the remarkable results of the compassionate endeavors of BCACT. They also reveal a very personal side of their commander, Andi, a force to be reckoned with—a woman to be admired, a woman who believes in the positive powers of teamwork.

As Andi begins our interview, she confiding her reason for working so diligently to form an animal cruelty task force: her undaunted deep respect for all animals.

Any time that I observed them suffering needlessly because of neglect or abuse, I was deeply saddened...to the point of becoming physically ill...that I was powerless to make a difference in their lives. Maybe that explains why, for most of my life, I had this strong prod, like a 'Jiminy Cricket conscience,' that I must choose a path in which I could use my short time on earth to make a difference for all of our world's creatures.

And since the 2012 formation of BCACT, the Bernalillo County Animal Abuse Task Force, she has—and she continues—to make that difference. Loyal, quick, competitive and determined would only partially describe this perky and attractive female officer in her crisply pressed sheriff's uniform, worn with great pride. Strong and focused, her thick, long brown hair pulled back in a soft ponytail, she leaves no doubt in our conversations that she is a 'straight shooter.' As we speak, it is obvious that this lovely captain feels it an honor to be serving in the sheriff's department. She is fiercely protective of her deputies and anxious to tell my readers about BCACT, its formation and its successes.

My childhood experiences had a tremendous impact on my present life as a law enforcement official and were a major catalyst in my formation of BCACT. Those early years were spent in the delightful and beautiful rural countryside in Columbus, Warren County, located in the far northwest corner of Pennsylvania, less than 25 miles from New York State.

My older sister, Holly and I were living the dream of every child: an enchanting acreage of woods filled with towering trees, forbidden caves to explore, a 'crick' to follow, mountains to climb, an awesome assortment of woodland creatures to admire, and Mother Nature's mysteries to ponder. Our mom had always taught us to respect all living creatures, and this environment had preponderance: furry, feathery, slimy, scaled, crawling, slithering, walking and flying. It was our very special classroom—to study, appreciate and to be in awe. Although it was calming with no evidence of human destruction, unknown adventures lurked everywhere. Sometimes the sheer magic of it was so intoxicating that I could not control my urges to peek under rocks, bark, blossoms and leaves—to study Mother Nature's creatures as they hopped, slithered, flew or crawled, then disappeared, quietly and completely.

But on those occasions when our father went into the woods to hunt, Holly and I would convert the rusted hollow poles of our swing set into our megaphones and strain our small voices to holler-out warnings to the resident wildlife. "Run!" "Hide!" "Watch out!" We had laryngitis and sore throats for the whole week, but it was well worth it.

Adjoining our 100-year-old house on our sizeable property was the fenced-in grave of a Civil War drummer. We intended no disrespect but Holly and I, along with our buddies (all boys), could not resist incorporating his wandering ghost into numerous scary stories at Halloween, assuring shrieks and shivers, "Ohhhs" and "Aahhs" from the new kids in the neighborhood, especially if we had a full moon or waxing gibbous moon, illuminating the grave—eerie! Providing the absolute perfect horror setting for more ghoulish October tales was the second story of our very old wooden home. It was poorly lit, poorly heated, with walls, floors and ceilings that creaked, scratched, moaned and breathed; unexplainable shadows appeared, moved and disappeared.

Holly and I took delight in the fact that our corny Halloween stories could be told all year long and we didn't even need to visit a fabricated haunted house—we had our very own. But we were never brave enough to hold our story hour in our unfinished, spooky, dark and dreary, moist and smelly basement. It served as a shelter during Pennsylvania tornado warnings and became a refuge for our family when, in 1985, a strong tornado swept through our Allegheny Mountains, downing 90,000 trees and carving out a path 2/3 of a mile wide. That was reality...actual terror!

Seven years later, our move sent us back to Mother's roots in Albuquerque. Although we missed the many adorable and magnificent wild critters who roamed on our Pennsylvania land, our new residence in the north valley served as a sanctuary for an assortment of abandoned, but loving cats. Also included in our menagerie was one dog: our neighbor's actually, a small black Shih Tzu-cross, Bear, who, though quite old, held his own around our many spunky cats, especially our over-assertive female Calico kitty, Bunny.

One cat with which I had the greatest attachment was a very scrawny, short-hair, black and white rescue, Buddy, who had wandered onto our front porch one morning and collapsed...no tags, no collar. We fed, fawned and petted until, in no time, he bounded back with an ample physique filling-in his broad-boned frame. After a few months of living with a bunch of adoring females, he assumed the role of male guardian of Mom, Holly and me. Each evening, he made his rounds, traveling from bedroom to bedroom to check that we were all 'tucked in' before retiring, then cuddling up in his own overstuffed pillow in our kitchen. Later we acquired, Max, a handsome, loving, long-haired orange and white Persian, gifted to me on my 14th birthday by a classmate and admirer, Max, not orange and white, but handsome and thoughtful.

But in the following years, my teens, I am embarrassed to admit that I was considered rebellious, bitter and angry, giving my sweet mom a great many premature gray hairs. I try to explain away these tumultuous times as my reaction to previous difficult and troubled years, during which our pets served as my only confidants, my non-judgmental companions. Holding them tightly in my arms, I could not hold back my tears of confusion and sorrow as I whispered, again and again, my special vow to them, 'Once I become an adult, I promise to be there—for the animals, with the proper authority to make a difference.'

Now I was maturing to an age where I should begin to honor that long-ago, but still-lingering childhood vow. With this unkept promise and best-forgotten, sad memories weighing heavily on my conscience, I was determined that, after graduation from Valley High School in 2000, I would get my life together, change its direction, allow my scars to heal and shed those friends whom I *allowed to be a bad influence and spark my overly adventurous spirit. It was time for me to demonstrate some semblance of character and take those first steps of my accepted journey to make that difference. Law enforcement had to be my chosen path in honoring that vow—to lessen the violence in Albuquerque, particularly that which causes the unnecessary suffering and death of the 'innocents—children and pets.'*

With a scholarship to Marquette University in Milwaukee, Wisconsin (their slogan is 'Be the Difference'), the new 'responsible me' began freshman studies in criminology and psychology. With its beautiful tall trees and historical buildings, this was not at all like Albuquerque's geography. I was in awe at the 93 acre campus and the excellent professors and teachings of this private, Jesuit school. Lake Michigan was just a mile away. But, I decided to return home, to Albuquerque, the ensuing year to attend University of New Mexico (UNM) on a leadership scholarship.

I planned to room with my dear friend from high school, Amber—beautiful and bright, happy and humorous, capable and composed, with lots of strong character. One of her most awesome qualities, besides her total honesty, was that she was comfortable in her own skin, being who she was, not being part of the crowd, but being her own person. Admirable! A current resident of Albuquerque today, Amber and I still enjoy a strong, special friendship.

Amber and I rented a small apartment near the campus and began our hurried schedule of classes and cramming. We had only been living there a few months, when I happened on a small, excruciatingly skinny, short-haired cat, abandoned and ravenous. Yes, pets were forbidden in the apartment lease, which is usually the case around the University, but I could not just callously leave her to starve or get hit by a car, and I could not find anyone else to take this frightened feline—yes, I tried! The obvious reality was that we, no I, really needed a cat. We became covert pet-owners and made the same mistake that most pet owners make: we fed her table scraps from the kitchen table. So, every time we walked into our tiny kitchenette, surprise, this new kitty was on our café table, loudly demanding food. Her name became a chant. 'Get off of the table, Mabel,' we snickered.

I was devastated when some selfish snitch revealed Mabel's presence in our apartment. We'd broken the terms of our lease by harboring a pet and ruffled the feathers of our no-nonsense landlord, so he retaliated by giving us pitifully little time to find a new home for Mabel—or for the three of us—our choice. We were fortunate that a friend of Amber's, an engineering student, lived in an apartment complex that was pet-friendly and he was eager to adopt our fantastic, roly-poly Mabel. Now she was free to push away curtains and press her little pink nose against the window panes. No longer hidden behind curtains and background music, she could openly meow her opinions and demands.

I consulted the university want ads, seeking an affordable apartment that did allow pets. Amber brought a precious six-month-old Siamese kitty, Lola, as a housewarming surprise as we celebrated my move into my new room: dark, cold, cramped and leaky but within my strained budget. For the last 16 years, after enduring my stress to excel and graduate from both the university and sheriff academy graduations, Lola still accepts me as her human. Even more demanding, intolerant, finicky, and bossy in her older age, she has earned my first greeting snuggles as I enter my home after work.

Lola pretends to barely tolerate our energetic but laid-back, ten-year-old American Pit Bull Terrier, Vic. However I am aware that 'She doth protest too much,' for I often find her curled up next to Vic's tummy, sleeping. In spite of a knee replacement, Vic continues his daily regimen performing Rocky sprints up and down the 15 steps to our second story. His two surgeries for maxillary cancer have dramatically changed the shape of his mouth, leaving this funny-faced dog with an adorable Elvis smirk. These welcoming, loving animals serve as my personal stress-relievers on those days when I return from the field, saddened by the animal abuse and human violence I encountered.

The December 2000 evening I graduated from UNM was a major stepping stone in my life and my future. My excitement (and relief) were overshadowed by my stress, as my exams for acceptance in Bernalillo Sheriff's Department were scheduled the following day. It is not an immediate process as it also involves a polygraph test, a psychological evaluation, a physical agility test, background checks, a personal integrity questionnaire, an oral board interview and two written examinations.

Four months later, April 17, 2001, marked my first day at Bernalillo County Sheriff's Department Regional Training Academy, then located on Kirtland Air Force Base, New Mexico. For the next harrowing six months, my life was a blur. My days began with a three mile run, 45 minutes of intensive strength conditioning, followed by six hours of classroom instruction: laws, ordinances, codes and policies of Bernalillo County, Albuquerque and New Mexico, investigative skills, officer safety, victim first aid, emergency vehicle operation, ground control exercises, weapon safety, arrest techniques, and community communications.

My body ached with all this strenuous training, and my head was swimming with this overload of technical information. By the time I graduated I would have been exposed to more than 1,000 hours of training.

Some of the most professional advice for policing in the neighborhood came from my wise and compassionate drill instructor, my mentor, Capt. Edward Mims. He was relentless as he emphasized to his class of stressed-out and frustrated cadets, 'These intense mental and physical preparations cannot be properly utilized unless you, as a sworn officer of the law, exercise discretion, responsibility and respect for all mankind, for all beings. We are not in law enforcement to judge. Honesty can never be compromised. Patience and kindness are of the essence.'

These teachings are still my credo. I hope they will remain a polarizing factor in any future and stressful encounters, a constant in my chosen career. And, just in case I stray, Capt. Mims, as my supervising officer at BCSO, will have no compunction in jogging my memory. He is not shy in reminding his deputies that we are here, primarily, to serve the citizens of our community. He exemplifies what law enforcement should represent.

"YESSS!" I yelled as I forcefully thrust my fist into the air. "YESSS!!!" I had done it! What a memorable and melodramatic celebration took place, October, 2001 at my Academy graduation! All of my family, lifelong friends, and neighbors cheered loudly and proudly as I walked across the stage, head held high and big smile, disguising both the shaky knees and butterflies in the tummy. But my eyes were bright with the promise of my future, an honorable and courageous profession with the Bernalillo County Sheriff's Department.

Every day, since celebrating that graduation, I have been grateful for these past 15 illuminating and fulfilling years that this job has afforded me: a definite means for me to achieve my dream and to make a positive difference in the many lives I touch daily in my South Valley.

And every day since that graduation, this complex and determined woman has skillfully juggled her long working hours as Commander of Bernalillo County Sheriff's Department Criminal Investigations Division to include her daily regimen of boxing workouts with a trainer at the gym. Her hefty resume with BCSO speaks to the fact that this lady is no lightweight. Possessing a Master's degree in forensic psychology, Andi has served as Field Services Director and Watch III Patrol Commander. She was also a member of Region 1 Narcotics Task Force, DEA Task Force, and a supervisor of the Gang Unit. Because of these (and more) outstanding accomplishments, she qualified for attendance at the 250th FBI National Academy. She was into her second year as director of BCACT when BCSO Lt. Andi made Captain.

My first assigned beat would be in the South Area Command Substation in the Field Services Division accompanied by a veteran Field Training officer responsible for guiding me through unknown and often perilous and shaky situations. After serving in two other commands, I returned to my first beat, my present beat, the unincorporated area Bernalillo County stipulated as the South Area Command, where BCACT was conceived and became.

The South Area demographics and rural land use are contributing factors to the fact that this mañana community holds the infamous reputation of the county's highest area of crime. Greater than 70% of reported crime, mostly drugs and gangs, in the unincorporated Bernalillo County occurs here.

This was my beat, an area responsible for 1,500 more calls than any other county patrol area, some generated from the tougher neighborhoods, proven to harbor suspected drug cartels visiting from Mexico, whose money-laundering and drug ventures often hide behind ranching and farming. They are also bold enough to launder these illicit-gained monies through dogfighting operations.

I still suffer nightmare flashbacks of my first domestic violence call that year. It was close to midnight on a particularly cold and windy winter evening. Although my partner and I were aware of that these are uncertain and possibly volatile calls, we were not prepared for the gory scene that we encountered when we entered the family's small stucco home.

A battered wife lay in her own blood, crying, suffering from multiple stab wounds she had received from her domineering angry, very physical and verbally offensive husband. And although it was evident that she was suffering from her wounds, she shook her head at our repeated inquiries, recanting, 'No! No! He did not mean to hurt me. He loves me.'

After making sure than an ambulance was en route, we began our interviews of those present: husband and wife and a small frightened four-year-old daughter, too quiet, unresponsive. After making sure that both mother and child were safe, we inspected and photographed the crime scenes more carefully, taking copious notes and gathering evidence as we moved from room to room. But as I entered their daughter's room, my knees gave out. I could barely catch my breath. Five small kittens had been slaughtered, their skulls repeatedly slammed against the wall. They lay lifelessly in a heap, bleeding out on the pink flowered rug. A sixth kitten whose skull had also been crushed in the same manner, had survived, and lay, mewing softly, bleeding, suffering, dying on the floor. I scooped him up, cradled him and hummed until animal control arrived to humanely euthanize him.

Although I was shaking with disbelief at such raw cruelty, I confronted the family, as calmly as I could, about this horrifying scene. The wife was injured and crying so hard, that it was difficult to follow her ramblings. Her husband had used the kittens, in front of her daughter, to coerce her into performing certain sexual favors. I tried to hold back my anger and repulsion when we spoke. That scene of violence overcame all my training and my judgment. I simply could not contain my disgust and wrath as I approached the father, who was leaning casually against the kitchen counter, a smirk on his face. I let down my guard and my raw emotions took over. I was hurting, bad.

In a high pitched scream and an outburst of uncontrolled rage, I demanded. 'What kind of demented monster are you to do this to your family and pets?'

Whoops! I had made an unprofessional, incorrect and dangerous assumption that the handcuffed father had been restrained, so I was unprepared and shocked when suddenly low guttural sounds emitted from his throat as he lunged at me and tried to bite my face…unsuccessfully. A scream wedged in my throat. I softly moaned, 'Our civilization is not!'

*The father was charged, according to New Mexico Domestic Violence Crimes Statute **30-3-11** with aggravated battery against a household member. Because these injuries caused great bodily injury with a deadly weapon, this is a third-degree felony, punishable by a three year prison sentence and a fine up to $5,000.*

Although the rates of domestic violence in New Mexico rank among the highest in the nation, there exists one excellent state law to protect the victims. In cases such as the above, of aggravated battery, the officer responding can press charges. By taking the responsibility of pressing domestic violence charges out of the hands of the abused, the victims are safer and under less pressure by their violent partners who intimidate their victims to not press charges.

That evening I rededicated myself to strive harder for a quicker completion of the formation of a county animal cruelty task force, but this would not come about until Matt Pepper, with dreams similar to mine, joined Bernalillo County Animal Care in 2011. Together, in September 2012, we announced the formation of Bernalillo County Animal Cruelty Task Force, termed BCACT. Its boots-on-the-ground encounters have been credited with saving hundreds of domestic and farm animals as well as the charging and convicting of these monsters whose violence takes, ruins and changes so many innocent lives.

Regrettably on most days, law enforcement personnel are intertwined with the horrific deeds of civilized man. In spite of Andi's exposure to these horrendous actions committed by and to mankind, she has not yet been jaded by their continuing occurrences. She seems to have that rare talent to dissect her experiences in a non-judgmental and analytical manner, still adhering to her weary hope that most people's lives are intrinsically decent.

Comfortable with herself, thrilled to be serving as a captain for the sheriff's department, she is not only career-oriented but fiercely protective of her deputies and of her department. As she starts to describe the strong bonds, kinship and camaraderie in the sheriff's department, the opening is perfect for me to pop the inevitable question to a female deputy. I query, "Most people are curious about whether or not there can really be equality in the treatment of the females in a macho-dominated law enforcement career, the 'brotherhood of the blue'..."

Andi's response came instantly and with a big grin. *I challenge their questions with one of my own. Wasn't it Eleanor Roosevelt who believed: "No one can make you feel inferior without your permission."?*

I literally glow as I proudly reply that I have never felt like a 'woman' in this progressive and unbiased department. No department member has ever made me feel "less than" for being a woman. To the capable, open-minded members of BCSO, I am an individual who chose a career in law enforcement and I am accepted, not according to my age, nationality or gender, but according to my abilities.

My greatest responsibilities lie with the residents of the South Valley. In order to best serve the residents of any neighborhood, you must be interested in their lives and be aware of their demographics: occupations, ethnicities and ancestries of its residents. I am a Valley girl myself and am part of the unique composition of this neighborhood. I strive for my life to make a positive difference in the many lives I touch daily in my South Valley. And although I work hard not to disappoint them (or myself), I realize it is none of my concern how I am regarded, as an individual, by these people. It will not change my professional standards or how I treat others.

A whopping 46.5% consider their heritage as Mexican, not Hispanic. More Spanish ancestry individuals (3.2%) live here than most neighborhoods in our nation. And, it is also notable that 14.8% of our residents were born in another country. It would not present an accurate picture to say that the most common language spoken here is English (in 50% of their homes), because more than 49% speak Spanish. Do not expect to hear the structured Spanish you were taught in school. Many of the words of the language spoken here are considered to be variants of Mexican-Spanish slang, usually indigenous to their region of New Mexico. Some refer to it as Spanglish, some Chicano.

Out of respect for these residents, I have but a 'working' grasp of their language, key words and phrases. But this knowledge is also important in case of an actual crisis, a situation will not be hampered by a language barrier.

When I return home each evening after work to my own pets, my own home, I am indeed a grateful woman. I am appreciative and humbled by the love in my life, my family, my friends and my pets. I am thankful that I am a major player in the difference BCACT is making. Working with, not separately, to reduce the rate of violence and related crimes in the South Valley has brought the neighborhood and my officers together with a strong feeling of accomplishment.

As a featured speaker at a variety of law enforcement and social services forums, I leave my audiences with this invitation:

Our unique BCACT has proven its success in eradicating animal cruelty and related crimes. It can serve as a role model for such a task force in your town. My deputies and I urge you to consider incorporating this accredited program into your community's law enforcement agency, and would be honored to give our presentation to them. Integrating the specific needs of your community, we can be helpful with other presentations to your city council, mayor or other governing body. We want you to be able to proudly boast your community: "Coming soon to our neighborhood...an innovative law enforcement program that will attack crime and curb our animal abuse. Join us as we share with you this new undertaking."

Please contact our task force to schedule a presentation or to enlist our help in establishing an animal cruelty task force in your community. We hope you will give BCACT some serious thought. All animals deserve better than an indifferent approach to the law. Scores of abused animals across America have waited a long time for their community to protect them from existing abuse and torture. It's your time to make a difference. We at BCACT look forward to your request.

Captain Andi Taylor
Commander, Criminal Investigations Division
Bernalillo County Sheriff's Department
400 Roma NW, Albuquerque, NM 87102
Email: ataylor@bernco.gov
O: (505) 468-7621   C: (505) 263-7652
www.bernco.gov

CHAPTER THREE

BERNALILLO COUNTY CARES

"Bernalillo County Animal Care Services is committed to providing the highest level of services and protection to both citizens and the animals of our community by effectively and humanely enforcing the ordinances as they pertain to animal care and the public's health."

– BCACS Mission Statement

Matt Pepper served in the prestigious position of a board member of the National Animal Control Association, and, since 2011, he was also the tireless and diligent director of BCACS. He began working with me on the formation of BCACT soon after his hiring. The conditions in Bernalillo County Animal Care were strained and stressful as his department was allotted very limited funds for helping the many county innocent animals, victims of neglect and abuse. The animal facility and administration operated from an old but attractive fire station in the South Valley, on which were built but nine outdoor pens for the dogs. Improving this situation with such limited funds required that Matt draw from his knowledge of 13 years of management experience in animal care and control in both private nonprofit and public municipal shelters. He did so with a cautious, conservative but caring manner. He made Bernalillo County proud.

His staff of 12 included officers, a project coordinator and field supervisor. Matt proudly boasted of their dedication and respect for animals, which did not end with their working hours or even with retirement. "One of our newly retired officers was returning home in heavy morning work-traffic when he spotted three newborn pups on a dirty dog bed in the middle of a busy intersection. Dodging traffic and the rages of disgruntled drivers, he scooped them up, wrapped them in a blanket, and delivered them to our veterinarian for care and fostering with NMDOG.

"Two of our officers discovered Wrangler, a Hound-Beagle cross encumbered by a chain weighing more than half of his own body weight. After receiving medical care and socializing, Wrangler found his niche. As the constant companion to his delighted adoptive Colorado dad, they not only were a team at home, but also on daily visits to job sites and weekend hiking trips. Their bond was an excellent example of 'Who rescued who?' (sic), as Wrangler's new owner had been mourning the loss of his Coonhound companion of 13 years.

"Bernalillo County Commission held a special ceremony to honor two BCACS officers for 'going above and beyond the call of duty.' While off-duty, Officer Brittany Nelson jumped into the shallow, cold waters of the Rio Grande to rescue two puppies tied to a garbage bag, inside of which she found her five litter mates, dead. On her personal time, she bottle-fed these two back to health and into the care of a new, loving, forever home.

"Also recognized were the brave actions of Officer Shawn Clark, who also ventured into the frigid Rio Grande waters to save a frightened Chihuahua who was stranded on a sandbar and likely to drown. After removing his dress shoes and socks and rolling up his good pant legs (he was on his way to a birthday celebration), Shawn thought he could just wade into the usually fairly shallow. What a shock when he fell into a sinkhole! But this remarkable, muddy man emerged with a smile, clutching this little shivering dog, intent on licking the mud from Shawn's cheeks.

"That's my crew!" Matt beamed.

Each of their 14 fleet service vehicles, which must cover the many miles of rough terrain of unincorporated Bernalillo County, is equipped with a rope stick, cat pole, nets, snappy snare, leather gloves, bite gloves, animal cages, transfer cages, bungee cords, Hazmat suits with latex gloves, stretcher, goggles, human first aid kit, camera, dog and cat food, treats, and bowl as well as water and water bowl. Many officers provide their own often-needed towels and rags. The officers carry on their own person pepper spray, an asp baton, slip leash and a Leatherman tool. These officers are always, eight hours a day, on animal cruelty duty and encounter a wide variety of happenings, always hoping for a happy ending to a usually tragic call-out.

Matt was aware that the wording of BCACS's booklet of county animal care codes could be confusing. It listed a variety of specialized permits and licenses totaling 14 and offered senior discounts on some. He explained further, "But most important, our pamphlets did not appropriately represent the true spirit and compassion in our community nor did it fully protect the animals that we shared it with. Although we focused on the zero tolerance chaining code and the tethering in the open bed of pick-ups, we began the process of reviewing and amending the entire ordinance."

In November 2012 Matt unleashed, in state-wide press releases and live presentations to acquaint the county dog owners with two new important ordinances. Effective August, 2013. **Code 6-53** *would make it unlawful for animals to be in open beds of a truck unless in a crate fastened to the truck. Citing studies proving the cruelty of tethering, he presented BCACS's new zero-tolerance, no-chain* **code 6-43.** *This was not just the strongest tethering ordinance in the state, but it offered the healthiest protection for county animals, the majority of which had been burdened by ropes, chains and other tethering devices for most of their lives. For a year, whether walking a neighborhood or attending a Little League game, BCACS utilized these community gatherings to educate the county's pet owners about alternatives to chaining and the dangers involved in transporting animals, untethered, in the bed of a truck.*

BERNALILLO COUNTY ANIMAL CODES ENACTED AUGUST, 2013

Sec. 6-43 Restraint of Animals
It shall be unlawful to tether a companion animal as a form of confinement.

Sec. 6-53 Animals Transported in Vehicles
Animals carried in the open bed of a truck must be in a crate that is securely fastened to the truck.

Although his position dictated long and tiring hours, Matt, whose office was always short of staff, could still muster up enthusiasm as we discussed the steps necessary to form an inter-agency animal cruelty task force. He had spent his entire career protecting animals from cruelty. He wanted to do more for these animals; I wanted to do more for these animals. So we proposed joining the talents of our agencies to form BCACT.

Because this idea of an inter-agency task force was a new concept to us, it took the two of us many months to construct the organizational and training guidelines and content for our proposed task force, (complete with state certification hours) and submit them for departmental and state approval. Those planning and operational plans of BCACT are detailed within the following pages.

Matt recognized that, to be successful, we would still require the services of one more agency: a private 501(c)(3) rescue organization that would go into the trenches with BCACT. "I know you have not yet met, but I have worked with one group that will fit the needs of our animal cruelty task force," he remarked, "and that is NMDOG, whose founder, Angela Stell is unrelenting with seemingly boundless energy and a deep respect for all life. Her organization is the Cadillac of dog rescue in New Mexico."

A reminder from Matt. "Let us not forget the kitties of our county. The most often received feline complaint is, 'My cat always comes back home, but...' and we hope this time it will also. BCACS must continue to educate cat owners, repeating our warnings that our county is full of dangerous predators: nocturnal owls with wing spans up to five feet, bobcats, hawks, fearless coyotes and more...all hungry. This does not include fatalities due to our speeding traffic, careless drivers or at the brutal hands of gang initiates. By allowing your cat to explore the outdoors, you could be responsible for its violent death. Cats are perfectly content to live indoors (which is the legal, humane approach)."

Within two years, Matt would leave BCACS and accept another position as President/CEO of Michigan Humane Society which would better utilize his many talents. He has instituted programs similar to BCACT in Michigan. Although my deputies and I were saddened to see such a devoted animal activist leave our ranks, at the same time, every member of BCACT was proud of what he had accomplished for the abused and neglected animals of Bernalillo County. Matt's innovations and his special respect for animals are permanently woven through the policies of BCACT, a powerful blow against the animal abusers of Bernalillo County.

In the fall of 2014, Bernalillo County welcomed Matt's competent replacement, Misha Goodman, who had held similar positions in Los Angeles and Iowa City. She also served as an elected officer of National Animal Control Association for ten years. BCACS' participation in BCACT offers her a unique leadership opportunity.

CHAPTER FOUR

NMDOG:
DOWN IN THE TRENCHES AND
ACROSS THE STATE

"Rescue is not about finding a dog a home; rescue is about finding a dog the perfect home."

— Angela Stell, founder, president of NMDOG, recipient of APNM Milagro award

New Mexico's most powerful, on the scene, dog rescue, NMDOG was founded by animal activist, Angela Stell, dedicated to dogs and fiercely determined to bring about permanent change in the lives of those most abused. When approached by Andi and Matt, Angela was elated to join BCACT's war on those who violate their animals with a boots-on-the-ground approach.

Andi and Matt chose NMDOG as their third musketeer because Angela's Bernalillo County based rescue group, already familiar with the South Valley, operated with an in-the-trenches, on-call response. But, although NMDOG provides the safety-net for many of the broken and sick animals seized by BCACS, it is not a shelter. Following a veterinarian exam with treatment, if indicated, and a behavioral evaluation, the dog is placed by NMDOG in a temporary foster shelter or in the home of one of their volunteers, where, if necessary, the dog can be socialized or undergo rehabilitative training. NMDOG's accepting the responsibility to make those arrangements for kenneling these rescued dogs is due, in part to the limited space in BCACS' present facilities.

Angela explains further, "Our work is often fairly dangerous, so we only have trained, tried and true volunteers in the field. Chained dogs typically lack socialization and are very territorial of their area. All of our dogs are in various stages of behavioral rehabilitation, so it is key to have folks that understand the boundaries and special needs of each dog."

Once those steps are completed, then comes the final, joyous, tail-thumping occasion for this once-damaged dog: forever placement in the perfect home. Without the immediate and financial care of NMDOG, many of New Mexico's dogs would be placed in our cities' overcrowded shelters. Too often these volunteers are called upon for heart-breaking help: tenderly removing the lifeless body of a dog whose help arrived too late, or carefully removing those puppies from an unwanted litter whose lives were cut short.

With a solemn tone, Angela lowers her voice and her eyes. "Sometimes all we can give these dogs is a dignified end."

An all-volunteer, foster-based, 501(c)3 organization, their mission to unchain and to attend to the abused and forgotten, is accomplished on a daily basis by the selfless and caring volunteers of NMDOG. Operational funds come from donations ('key-in' their upbeat website for rescue information and SOS alerts). These cover expenses for the veterinarian traveling New Mexico to assist county officials, and boarding of the animals. NMDOG is credited with improving or saving the lives of thousands of New Mexico dogs, a feat that fills the souls of their volunteers with fulfillment and an unequalled respect for Angela, their leader whom they admire and emulate for her selfless dedication, often spending her personal funds and a double-time week to help those dogs who so desperately need immediate care.

NMDOG's active role with BCACT assures a safer, more loving environment for pets who are not cared for properly by their owners due to either financial restrictions or indifference. Throughout the year, not only does NMDOG help the county to distribute the free certificates for their Spay Neuter Assistance Program (SNAP), but they also distribute donated doghouses, straw, food, leashes, harnesses, bowls and toys to these outdoor pets, often chained, ignored and without shelter.

Angela describes their most difficult season. "New Mexico's harsh, cold months demand long hours, requiring our volunteers to push their energies and resources to the max during our Winter Outreach with BCACT. As bone-chilling cold winds sweep through the plains and mountains of the state, our dedicated volunteers observe the importance of their mission as dogs drag their thin, half-frozen bodies to the donated straw or doghouse for warmth.

"Sometimes it can be all smiles. On Thanksgiving, Christmas Eve, New Year's Eve, and Valentine's Day, NMDOG selects a specific community to service, and provide to those pet-homes most in need, whatever supplies they require to survive through the winter months."

Angela describes the shock of these residents when NMDOG descends upon a community in one of their outreach missions. "Dog guardians are temporarily confused, sometimes turning confrontational until they realize NMDOG has arrived with help—free help for their pet. Our genuine concern for their dog as well as our gentle approach with the dog guardians often causes a change in their attitudes, allowing them to see our humane actions in a new light: to help both the dog and the family. This is where our kindness, patience and respect create an educational opportunity for the pet guardians to recognize the need for change in the approach they use in caring for their dog.

"We are unyielding and steadfast in our primary mission of unchaining New Mexico dogs. In support of BCACS's zero-tolerance chaining animal code, we volunteer alternatives to chaining. For approved families, those that will allow our services and adhere to our fencing agreement, we construct secure chain link fencing and dog runs along with dog houses.

"All this for only their promise of no-chaining."

Dubbing their pilot program UNchain BernCo, NMDOG obtained a large grant in 2013 from Humane Society of the United States (HSUS) and Lowell Foundation which resulted in the their providing humane containment of 23 dogs vs at-the-end-of-a-chain by December of that year.

She beams at this accomplishment. "That seems like a mere drop in the bucket when you think about it…and it truly is. There are hundreds more that need our help, daily, just in BernCo alone. This is why I get up in the morning and do it all again and again and again."

Angela is quick to compliment the compassionate attitude of a trade class at Carlsbad High School, who, as an ongoing project of the Skills U.S.A. program, construct doghouses each year for low-income families in their neighborhood. This year numbered 30 from scrap lumber. Carlsbad C-Paws director, Victoria Morse, proudly commented that this project had taught her class the importance of providing shelter for animals, rather than tethering the dog outside without protection from the weather.

These dedicated NMDOG volunteers also join BCSO and BCACS in their unannounced sweeps of high call neighborhoods. And because of their availability and know-how, NMDOG is on speed-dial for many other rescue organizations, county and rural animal control agencies, as well as

BCSO and BCACS. They reach out across our plains to scenes of hoarding, dogfighting, and to the chained, starved and abused canine victims.

Such a dog, a small brown, black and gray Heeler-cross, was Cub, missing his rear leg with the tibia bone fully exposed. His right leg, with the tibia also exposed, was dangling. Using these exposed bones as stilts, he had been wandering on the eve of Valentine's Day, determined to find help and was walking on a county road. Cub was sighted by a Good Samaritan who immediately contacted Animal Welfare Coalition of Northeastern New Mexico, and they, in turn, called out to NMDOG. Cub was transported to an Albuquerque emergency veterinarian clinic. They surmised that in order to free his crushed and gnarled hind legs from a snare trap, Cub must have chewed off the lower part of these legs. Recognizing that this dog's miraculous trek was special…a living example of the agony caused by steel leg-hold traps, NMDOG recognized his incredible will to live and pledged to give him their all—they did and then some.

Their endless admiration and support of this tough little fellow paid off. Although both legs were amputated in 4½ hours of surgical procedures by Petroglyphs Animal Hospital, and the bullets removed (Oh, yes, he was also shot), Cub was tenacious in his training with the new prosthesis (designed and donated by Kevin Carrol of Disney fame, and associated with Hanger Clinic, a nationwide company in designing and supplying prosthetic devices.) All the many generous souls who became involved with his rehabilitation are amazed with that his adjustment to his new life, which includes not only his prosthesis and new cart, donated by the Oscar Foundation, but also a new and forever family, that of his veterinarian at the Canine Physical Rehabilitation Center of New Mexico.

The intense investigations by San Miguel County Undersheriff Anthony Madrid which followed this heinous incident revealed twists and turns that caused the case to remain open. Excruciating encounters such as Cub's with a steel trap occur yearly on public and private lands and result in the deaths of thousands of innocent animals every year in those states that allow the cruel, tortuous snare traps, which is basically all except Massachusetts, Colorado and California, who ban recreational and commercial snare traps. Arizona only bans these traps on public lands.

One news-worthy heated debate occurred in Montana in 1997 concerning the lenient laws which led to the death of a pet dog, Buddy from a Conibear 220 "humane-trap" which exerts an impressive 90 pounds of pressure per square inch. In response, Montana Trappers Association proudly and boldly displayed their stance by sponsoring a state highway billboard, which proclaimed, "We Montanans Reject Animal Activists." This, in short time, was vandalized with black paint.

Although the phones of our NMDOG volunteers stay busy, some of their rescues are simply by chance, such as that of Pearl and Romeo, a doggie fairy tale.

Angela expounded. "Unsocialized and used only for breeding, Pearl, a neglected, white Bull Terrier with one black eye, lived her life, lonely and tethered in the South Valley. She had but one friend in her small, very limited world: an emaciated, but exceptionally handsome Mastiff, Romeo, also chained a few feet away. Pearl was determined to free herself from her mire of mud and feces up to her knees. A proven contortionist, Pearl had previously used her Houdini moves to extricate herself from her chain so many times that her angry owners banned her to a small, dark, dingy pen located on the opposite site of the property. Their rationale was that if she could no longer see Romeo, she would not try to get loose to be with him.

"Romeo was so adversely affected by Pearl's removal that he refused food and water, lay his head in the feces-laden dirt and mourned. Disgusted by Romeo's reaction, his guardians did not attempt to rectify his loneliness, but labeled him expendable and chained him just off the property to let him die, alone without sustenance or shelter. His frail body developed open, oozing wounds as well as a severe case of mange. He was also losing his vision…and his fight. He had given up.

"One freezing November day, when my volunteers and I took a wrong turn while on the way to a fencing project day, we came across a dying Romeo. By phone we apprised Andi of the situation. After she arrived, she provided the authority we needed. To the rescue: NMDOG. Just in the nick of time, we were there to provide warmth, food, substantial medical care. Romeo's transformation was like a butterfly emerging from a cocoon. He gained weight, grew back his fur, was treated for his failing sight.

"Romeo's proud new family has provided this wrinkly guy with his own cozy chair near the fireplace, where he gracefully lounges until bed time and then sleeps peacefully at the foot of their bed, knowing that when morning comes, they will still be there for him, for always."

Andi remembers the terrible ache in her heart as she drove away from NMDOG's rescue of Romeo. *I knew Pearl would suffer a horrific fate if she were left alone and we did not intercede, so a few hours later I returned with one of my deputies. I voiced my concerns with her owner, who had a lengthy criminal history and was heading back to prison. He indicated that his hesitancy in relinquishing her was because of the attention she brought, as a rare dog. He liked that people thought she was expensive. Eventually he came to the conclusion that, because no one could care for her while he was 'away,' he would surrender her to NMDOG through BCACS.*

It was past midnight, so until the next morning, Pearl made herself at home, curled-up in a blanket on the back seat of my patrol car. Still on duty, I was called to the scene of a horrific residential fire that claimed the life of a small child. Choked-up with emotion, my investigating deputies came intermittently to report. While they sat in my back seat, Pearl was silently cuddling next to them, absorbing their pain, their sadness at this tragedy. Some buried their heads in her fur and cried. She became their therapy dog. I believe that Pearl came into our lives that evening to help the deputies grieve the loss of innocence. A career in law enforcement is very difficult, and it is often necessary for us to push back our emotions. Pearl was a reminder that there is good in our world.

Our loving Pearl now spends her days with her doting and fantastic family on the California beach, living the life of unconditional love and happiness that she has always deserved.

Another NMDOG rescue, simply by chance, was that of Mr. Pickles, abandoned within yards of Angela's residence in the South Valley. His body screamed of a painful life. Most of his body was covered with tale-tell scars of past wounds: puncture wounds, cuts, abrasions, broken limbs and mange. Angela was appalled at his condition. "His top canines had been ripped out. Although his badly damaged body spoke of years of cruelty, this guy did not hold grudges against all humans. He was tender and loving. After completing extensive medical care and rehabilitation, he was placed in an always family, where he was able to fill the deep void left by the death of their two older pitties. Mr. Pickles not only discovered the security and permanence of a new family, but he also was recipient of a new emotion: love, and a new behavior: tenderness."

Angela spoke of many other heartwarming rescues. Craigslist on the Internet displayed a photo of a very young and thin pup at the end of a short, heavily rusted chain. The caption read, "Owners wish to be rid of this dog."

"I have a special distaste for those who dispose of their animals on Craigslist, so I wasted not a second in responding, 'NMDOG will be happy to oblige.'

"She was such a happy dog that NMDOG named her Smiley after talented and compassionate BCACS Officer Pete Smiley, who left our world too soon."

Angela was delighted with her new ward. "Her blindness in one eye did not deter Smiley's exuberance, wagging tail and desire for human contact. After lengthy medical care and positive conditioning, Smiley was progressing so well that she was invited by Animal Humane Association of New Mexico (AHANM) for a Karen Pryor Academy clicker training demo.

"Soon after she met her forever family, an Albuquerque policeman, his wife and children who were all in agreement. 'Smiley is incredibly perfect… without flaw. We are grateful for NMDOG's continued efforts for the sake of the animals.'"

With a name that reflects their charge, NMDOG reflects the tenacity, dedication and fortitude of their founder, Angela, whose less-than-perfect childhood taught her that those three qualities are necessary for survival in this tough world. Her inspiring story is the result of her immediate bonding with a stray: a remarkable Black Labrador Retriever blend, JoJo. Their by-chance meeting, which was really the rescue of Angela's life, occurred during the early 2000's, a decade in which many of our young Americans were without jobs or direction and losing hope.

"As I was driving deep into the heart of the South Valley, a big black dog darted in front of my car and stood! While I was busy swerving to miss him and bring my car under control, he was running up to greet me, dragging the heavy chain attached to his neck. Our eyes met and locked. We immediately connected. He jumped right into the passenger seat. Once we were in a safer location, I removed the chain and examined my new furry friend, discovering that he really didn't have much fur, due to mange. His jutting ribs, backbone and hip bones were indicative of severe malnutrition."

From their first meeting, it was obvious these two were a forever pair, and thus began their adventure of learning first-hand about how to help other animals that were in need of rescue, but it was also a perfect example of "Who rescued who?(sic)"

Angela's deep love and respect for JoJo intensified her need to save the abused. "By working with JoJo, I have become the rescuer that I am today. He has been an extraordinary teacher, and as our mascot, he was a direct participant in the rehab and recovery of hundreds of the dogs we have rescued. JoJo came into my life to rescue not only me, but hundreds of New Mexico animals who need our help: the chained, abandoned and forsaken pets. He has been active in the training responsible for changing their behaviors from frightened and quirky to bouncy and playful. He acts as our four-legged team mate when NMDOG seeks for missing, injured and trapped dogs.

"JoJo's determination to train me has taken years, but each time I observe his actions and reactions, I learn. His heroic actions were recognized with the 2015 APNM Milagro Animal Award for exceptional intelligence and courage for inspiring the founding of our NMDOG.

"The example of NMDOG's accomplishments as partners in BCACT is especially invigorating for those who are weary from years of rescue in unincorporated rural areas of our country, seeing no hope, no strong legislation or enforcement in sight. Forming such a pro-active, inter-agency animal cruelty task force in your community is a proven method to provide a more humane existence for many of your community's abused, abandoned, chained and forgotten pets."

The closing suggestion of this incredible leader was far reaching. "It is my hope that every community will prioritize the welfare of its animals. The success we have seen in Bernalillo County as a result of our BCACT partnership with BCSO and BCACS has had far reaching implications: a deeper feeling of community between law enforcement and residents, a more proactive approach to the abuse and neglect of our most vulnerable citizens and a deeper understanding and respect of the risks and challenges of and by our partner agencies. And at the end of each mission, our purpose is being fulfilled—To serve and protect New Mexico's dogs.

"This certified win-win example of community and law enforcement teamwork, BCACT, can easily be modified to meet the needs of most communities."

CHAPTER FIVE

COMBINING FORCES

"Alone we can do so little; together we can do so much."

– Helen Keller, deaf-blind American author,
political activist, educator, humanitarian

Angela, Matt and I harbored no doubts. Joining together the authority of NMDOG dedicated volunteers and the authority of my county sheriff deputies with experience of his animal control officers was a winning combination. Our new task force could not fail in making monumental strides in fighting the high incidence of animal cruelty in Albuquerque's South Valley. Once we completed a practical structure and smoothed a few organizational burs in the program, our sheriff could make his official endorsement of this idea.

Matt and I recognized that although our two law enforcement jobs were inherently different because of the type of beings victimized, our daily calls of the sheriff's deputies and animal service officers were often intertwined. While responding to animal abuse calls, an officer from animal service would often encounter child abuse, domestic violence and drug sales, while my deputies would, in the investigating of a felony, observe animal cruelty. We were almost oblivious to the necessary hundreds of hours of preparation because we were organizing for the animal—for a program that would make a difference.

Putting the duties of our team in perspective, Matt expounded, "Whether a victim is an animal or a person, victims are victims and violence is violence. None of it should be acceptable in our community. It is incredibly important that officers don't see animal cruelty as just animal cruelty, a horrible enough crime as it is, but as violence."

MISSION—**"BCSO deputies recognize that animal abuse/neglect is proven by academic studies to be associated with other family violence as well as other crimes such as gambling, guns and drugs. BCACT's success has proven to be the perfect example to relay that message to other law enforcement and social agencies."**

– Bernalillo County Sheriff Manuel Gonzales

Our shared goal for both BCSO and BCACS was curtailing animal abuse in the South Valley in a proactive manner. These preventive measures were not only applicable to companion animals, but also to include cattle, horses, goats, sheep, pigs, hogs, fowl and basically all other living creatures. In order for it to be effective and accepted by the residents, we needed the community's confidence and involvement in our new grassroots campaign. Only by going door-to-door, conversing one-on-one, could we be personally responsible for holding animal abusers accountable. BCACT was afforded the unique opportunity to prevent other crimes, this effecting a change in our community's attitudes regarding public safety. Our citizenry becomes better informed about animal care and animal cruelty laws; as a team the citizens and law enforcement officers can address possible solutions to current community problems. And through these stronger community relations, deterrence to other crimes in their neighborhood is increased.

TEAMWORK—"Working together, animal abuse can be more quickly identified, so we have a better chance of preventing it along with the associated crimes before they happen. By literally walking the neighborhoods of the community, BCACT will be building trust and confidence between citizens and law enforcement."

— Bernalillo County Sheriff Manuel Gonzales

Integrating the talents, experience and determination of both departments would create an awesome animal cruelty task force. Although this teamwork would bring together the expertise of both groups, it must also allow each division to retain their individuality to investigate and resolve their own cases. Because both groups then operated in mostly reactive modes, we recognized that this proposed team effort could only be effective in the valley if it became an example of proactive policing, often defined as the practice of deterring criminal activities by engaging the community to help us.

Matt realized that our twosome was incomplete, lacking a very important and necessary third party: a private, reliable and knowledgeable animal rescue organization whose members would be helpful during sweeps and would have the ability to shelter, provide necessary veterinarian care, train and re-home the animals we seize. Because we expected our sweeps to bring many animal-surrenders each day, Matt reminded me that BCACS's facilities were too limited to take care of those rescued. We had previously encountered the skills and humane dedication of Angela Stell, founder of NMDOG. Her intrinsic belief in rehabilitation of brutally abused dogs was legend. She happily accepted our invitation to become a member of our new task force, and little could we imagine the positive effect she would have on BCACT.

SCOPE OF TRAINING—"We want to see all 300 sheriff deputies with BCACT specific training and skills used in identifying and responding to animal abuse or neglect. These crimes could be an indication of the possibility of other violence occurring in that home."

– Bernalillo County Sheriff Manuel Gonzales

Enforcing our animal cruelty laws with our combined forces would definitely make a strong case for the abused animals. There was no doubt that the best way to accomplish this goal was unannounced neighborhood sweeps with a strong show of law enforcement presence, 'boots on the ground,' composed of deputies and officers from both the sheriff's office and animal services, both units trained and knowledgeable of the concerns, history and demographics of the neighborhood. Matt would need to contact other approved volunteer animal rescues when NMDOG was unable to respond.

BCACT sweeps would be randomly scheduled, concentrating on the county's highest service areas as defined by animal control calls to BCACS and NMDOG. For the safety of the sheriff deputies, animal care officers and the residents, team members would need to be in constant communication.

The lack of a wireless tele-communication system which would serve both units, BCACS and BCSO, certainly hampered their efforts in coordinating, investigating and cross-referencing possible crimes in the field. This lack of such an inter-agency communication system in our 21st century of advanced electronics appears to be archaic under CSI standards, but it is costly, thus not currently under consideration in this financially-strapped county.

Andi reminded me, *The concept of teamwork or cross-referencing within county departments was never a consideration by our county communications department…until now.*

Matt was insistent that during these sweeps, BCACT team members must also continually educate and communicate with residents. We needed their respect and their support. If the people don't know or understand the law, don't just explain it to them, also explain why. We do not want our residents to conceive of us as their problem, but to see us as a possible solution to their problem.

CONTENT OF TRAINING—"To be effective in fighting animal abuse in our county, we included this extensive training in our academy curriculum, and through BCACT's often-hailed accomplishments, Bernalillo County Sheriff's Department has been recognized as one of the most progressive and proactive law enforcement agencies in the world in addressing matters concerning animal cruelty."

– Bernalillo County Sheriff Manuel Gonzales

Knowledge, and instruction coupled with caution and experience would prepare our sheriff deputies and animal care officers for BCACT. In order to educate our residents, members of BCACT would have to be more knowledgeable. Therefore, training classes, in which both Matt and I would interact through team-teaching, would be a requirement for all deputies in field services and all animal care officers. Lectures would have to be coordinated, written, and scheduled.

My deputies and his animal care officers would also require cross-training so they were versed in city animal ordinances, applicable county codes and state and federal laws regarding seizure of property, domestic violence and animal fighting.

Recognizing animal abuse and being well versed in the city, county and state laws governing this crime would weigh heavy in the lectures. Interpreting the behavior of seemingly vicious dogs was of paramount importance, a skill which would have a positive impact on the present, unacceptable rate of lethal force executed against supposedly vicious or aggressive dogs by sheriff deputies in order to protect themselves.

Animal abuse arrests, investigation and prosecutions are now daily events that captures widespread media exposure. These are not rare crimes, occurring only at the hands of seriously deranged individuals; they happen every day, everywhere, at the hands of possibly future criminals. To be cognizant of the clues of those other crimes often associated with animal abuse, this task force would also need an understanding of the relationship and recognition signs of the many facets of the Deadly Link: child, elder, domestic and animal abuse. Animal abuse is often the red light signaling human violence within the household. Where one is present, look closely, there is usually more.

SCHEDULING OF TRAINING—*BCACT required and continuous eight-hour training sessions need to be accessible to all shifts.*

Because the training classes would be mandated for all animal care officers and sheriff's deputies involved in field service, Matt proposed that we should concentrate our information into one eight-hour session.

And so we did. We used inter-departmental memos to announce the training sessions, and present a detailed, written outline of the lecture subjects and materials, so that students could more easily follow and make notes, if necessary. This would also allow those students who were particularly interested, to research certain subjects and better acquaint themselves with a topic and provide them more credible information for asking pertinent questions.

To more easily fit into the tight schedules of my deputies and be less disruptive for his officers, Matt and I scheduled sessions only one day a week, two sessions per day. Each eight-hour session would duplicate the same information for each of the two shifts, the 7am-3pm and the 3pm-11pm Those sheriff deputies assigned to graveyard shift, 11pm-7am were forced to make arrangements in order to attend their eight-hour required class. Matt and I continued our exhausting, non-stop, 16 hours of instruction a day, once a week for four weeks in order to meet all the schedules. Specific-day class reservations were not necessary for students wishing to attend. The day of the week we chose to teach was Thursday, because the relief squad was available. Although Matt and I were both exhausted after such a grueling schedule, we were very pleased by their positive response and their well-thought-out questions and comments.

Because of the wealth and depth of required information imparted over a four week period to eight different groups, Matt and I agreed that no yearly refresher course should be required for these students.

CERTIFICATION OF TRAINING—*Continuing education credits are an incentive as well as a reward for this amount of concentrated class-time.*

Using the same outline as in the inter-departmental memo, as a certified instructor, I created a power point presentation and submitted it to the New Mexico Department of Public Safety (NMDPS) training academy to obtain State certification with continuing education credits. It took but a quick three weeks for them to check eligibility of the instructor, the training content and for us to receive positive feedback and accreditation by NMDPS.

BUDGET OF TRAINING—*The crux to our official approval was the lack of overtime and added expenses.*

Our sheriff, who was interested and supportive in our progress in creating an animal abuse team, firmly explained that the county budget for law enforcement was tight. There were no monies available to spend on any aspect of BCACT. Our joint venture would have to operate without any overtime expenses. This directive would not affect the hours of the BCACS officers, but it created a major obstacle for any deputies who were interested in joining BCACT. This edict of 'no overtime pay' would necessitate my adjusting their schedules so that they could still participate with the officers from Animal Care on neighborhood sweeps. No overtime pay would mean that volunteering to be a member of BCACT would be considered a secondary assignment.

It was a difficult responsibility to meet this challenge, but I was determined. We were so close. I knew that by utilizing BCSO's current three-shift, eight-hour watch pattern, our team members could request schedule changes ahead-of-time with the relief squad. BCSO Relief Squad works different commands to cover squad members when they are on their days-off. I could find no alternative. Our deputies, regardless of the area to which they were assigned, could choose to take part in sweeps during those days when our department had extra staffing, so switching their shifts meant utilizing BCSO Relief Squad. Using BCSO Relief Squad would not allow full team participation in randomly-scheduled BCACT sweeps. And scheduling and adjusting watches ahead-of-time could prove awkward, but it appeared to be our only option so that our animal abuse team could function, together, at no extra cost to the county taxpayers. Also, using the relief squad would not take away from deputies taking calls for service or from our proactive patrols for crime and traffic violations. Those were excellent selling points for the sheriff to present to the Bernalillo County Commission.

OPINIONS COUNT—*Utilizing the experience, insight and suggestions of the individuals that will make up BCACT is what will make it into a team.*

Before we submitted this well-worked, specific framework to Sheriff Manuel Gonzales for perusal and approval, our temporary written document of BCACT required input and complete acceptance by our officers and deputies. Over the next few months, we each shared with our units our proposed framework of a combined animal abuse task force. We actively solicited and noted their questions, experiences, opinions and ideas. Some interjected excellent *and progressive ideas and a few field deputies called to our attention possible pitfalls that would need to addressed and taken into consideration. Matt and I were very pleased. Their final assessment was unanimous: BCACT could make a difference, a big difference, a lasting difference.*

One field supervisor brought to our attention that this new team endeavor, an animal cruelty task force, would not be successful and make a real difference in our neighborhood unless we stripped ourselves naked...naked from our attitudes and our egos. This was baggage that could only hold back our unit, burdening our abilities to serve our community. Both groups had skills, knowledge and experience which needed to be shared, without any hang-ups, inter-agency rivalry or squabbles. Matt and I continually repeated that BCACT was an equal endeavor that could seriously curtail violence against animals in the valley... if we worked together. It was to be a joint commitment of both units, utilizing the knowledge and experience of animal service officers and the authority of the deputies of the sheriff's department, that could make a big difference...and it did.

We knuckled down on this project, and before we knew it, Matt and I had created a solid framework for BCACT: mission, teamwork without bias, animal know-how, officer safety, cross-reporting and communications, working schedules, training schedules, state, county and municipal laws, educational content and standards with required certified classes, and the all-important budget. It all came together so organically as things often do when the endgame is an unselfish act to give of oneself to save another.

Helen Keller's thoughts best described the strong bond of BCACT: optimism. **"Optimism is the faith that leads to achievement. Nothing can be done without hope and confidence."**

CHAPTER SIX

THE MOO FACTOR

"Until we extend our circle of compassion to all living things, humanity will not find peace."
– Albert Schweitzer

The rescuing of a suffocating, orphaned, bovine and a forgotten, kidnapped dog represented the why of BCACT, our new unit. The deciding event, the unexpected event that would bring about the ultimate formation of the animal abuse task force would occur only a few weeks later, August, 2012. The star participants were, surprisingly, a small, black and white calf and two observant, humane photographers, Sam Beam and Josh Brinkin, who were testing a recently purchased iPhone helmet in a desolate area of the South Valley. Curious about the hawks and vultures circling a nearby muddy watering hole, they drove closer to the site. Flies were thick around the lifeless body of a mother cow who lay silently in the mud, unable to help her orphaned calf, struggling, panicking and sinking in the quagmire, eyes, ears and mouth full of mud and sealed shut.

Without hesitation, these responsible men, heroes, worked diligently to free this calf from the mire, carefully carried him to their truck, rummaged through the contents of the truck bed and found a suitable container for drinking water. The young and muddy bovine was still shaking violently and experiencing difficulty in breathing as his muddy rescuers placed an emergency call to Bernalillo County Animal Care. Although the calf was able to drink some water, within a few minutes he went into shock. What a touching scene unfolded as these two grown men built a small fire over which they could heat their coats, then took turns wrapping them around the shivering calf. What relief, what joy as finally the calf's breathing became less labored and his shivering subsided due to the quick response of his saviors and their compassion in rendering first aid.

Clouds of dust on the county dirt road indicated the arrival of the welcomed Bernalillo Animal Care Services officers. After a cursory exam, a thank you and a handshake, the officers drove this frightened bull calf from the Pajarito Mesa to their veterinarian's office, where he spent a few days recovering from his trauma. However, because he was so young and without a mother to feed him, the deputies, not requiring any invitation, rolled up their sleeves and joined the gang, grabbing the warmed baby bottles with special milk and becoming active and eager participants at his feeding time. As they fed this weak calf, it dawned on a group of his eager adoptive parents that this orphan had no name. Ferdinand was the unanimous choice.

Matt's description of Ferdinand was best. "He was amazing! He was a lap cow. Because he was so small, I was able to carry him, a scene which was captured on my iPhone with this message to my wife, 'I found a cow. Can I keep it?'"

The news of these gratifying milking-and-mothering get-togethers quickly spread throughout both animal services and the sheriff's department. Ferdinand had no shortage of admirers and bottle-feeders, and, as more deputies and officers fed him, they began not only to bond but also to exchange information and ideas about other animal cruelty incidents in the South Valley. Realization! The proposed animal cruelty task force would combine their experience, talents and passion to protect all animals, domestic and farm, from abuse, neglect and violence in the South Valley. There should never be another Ferdinand left to be helplessly engulfed in the quicksands of indifference.

Once he able to ingest solid foods (grains of course), this popular little brown calf was quickly adopted by two retired law enforcement officers, Becky Koster and Robbin Burge and presently spends his days roaming on their 65 acre ranch south of Albuquerque. They are no longer surprised during winter months to hear Ferdinand occasionally clomp-clomp into the ranch house and plop his strong, handsome and sleek body next to the warm fireplace.

When a pleased Sam Beam heard of Ferdinand's new life, he visited his now 300 pound rescue, he was greeted as a friendly dog would. Sam was really surprised that Ferdinand remembered him and Josh so well. We were both amazed with the positive changes that this animal had made in the lives of some of the individuals involved.

Although our deputies have made many sweeps in the vicinity where Ferdinand and his mother were found in order to identify the owners and gain access to their land, existing state statutes did not allow us to investigate or charge this cattle company with any felonious action.

The positive media that came from the dual efforts of BCACS and BCSO in rescuing Ferdinand was splashed over a multitude of area newspapers and television stations, and because the media emphasized the importance of these two government agencies working as one, the praise for this innovative union went viral over the social media. County officials were now more strongly considering the value of this inter-agency county team we had proposed.

That pushed our BCACT acceptance by our Bernalillo County Sheriff even closer to acceptance. The final, necessary to 'seal the deal' event occurred a few weeks later when we three, Matt, Angela and I, made our first successful collaborative rescue of an abused animal.

While on a lunch break, driving south on Broadway Avenue, I tried concentrating on calming the many anxieties that had plagued my spring months. I was so lost in these emotions, that at first I didn't see the small lump littering the street, which, fortunately, cars were swerving to avoid. As I slowed and switched on my emergency lights, I could see this was an injured or dead animal. To avoid having other cars running over him, I stopped my unit directly in-front of the body, exited and murmured as I approached, "Please, please, don't be dead."

So that I didn't further frighten this injured animal, if it was still alive, I called softly to it, "Are you hurt, pretty one?" Very slowly, this exhausted dog lifted his head only slightly, then let it drop back onto the street. Her ears were engorged with ticks; her reddened eyes were swollen; the fur was mangy and matted. This pitiful emaciated body was shutting down.

"Not on my watch, little one," I whispered as I cautiously lifted her in my arms and further accessed her condition. She didn't appear to have the injuries associated with being hit by a car. I minced, imagining her pain as my exam revealed the gruesome condition of his back and neck. Devoid of fur, and glowing with sunburn, her neck was oozing from injuries consistent with being chained, and her skin was so severely stretched that it hung grotesquely. Our contracted veterinarian, after a thorough exam, shook his head and with sadness and explained that the extensive injuries of this dog indicated that he had been brutally used as a bait-dog for Pit Bull fighting, over a long and agonizing period of time. She would require extensive care. I needed help and contacted Matt. Before he arrived, I was reminded of the inability of BCACS, because of space restrictions, to accept this near-death pup. Fortuitously I remembered the name and called the one person who could help this dog: our new team member, whom I had never met.

Her reputation preceded her, "Angela Stell of NMDOG is always there for the animals." And, indeed, she was there...for this lucky dog.

Our recently rescued little dog's life as a bait-dog represents the greatest cruelty of the crime of dogfighting. Just as the name implies, innocent dogs (and puppies and cats and kittens), all sizes, all ages are used to enhance the ferocious training of the fighting dogs, teaching them to savagely attack, rip, tear and maim in the pit. These bait-dogs are usually stolen from yards, picked up from 'Free dog and cat' newspaper ads or giveaways in front of grocery stores or residences. Some can endure this violence and torture for years, but usually the longevity of bait-dogs is short as they suffer slow psychological and physical torture before their certain death, a death without mercy or mourning.

Our veterinarian did reveal that one positive discovery came from our emergency visit. This dog, sometime in her life, had an owner who had wanted and cared for her, because their scan of her neck revealed an lifesaving, identifying microchip, injected beneath the pet's skin near the shoulder blades. It carries a number giving the name and contact information of the owner. However, our elation was short-lived. Identified as a Pit Bull-Cattle Dog cross, this unfortunate pup had been stolen in an Albuquerque home invasion in 2008, four years ago. Unfortunately our records indicated that her owners had moved from New Mexico, so it took us some time and patience to locate them. Once we had that information, we all gathered in Matt's office to make the call; his officers and my deputies were all on pins and needles, anticipating the excitement, the tearful elation her owners would feel upon receiving the news that their kidnapped dog was found, alive, and receiving the extensive and competent veterinarian care necessary to save her life so she could soon be re-united with her real owners. Sadly, this phone call did not turn out at all as we thought it would.

Her owners were very saddened at the news of their pet being abused in such a horrific manner for all the years since her kidnapping, but wanted to explain their family's reaction to their pet's kidnapping. They confessed that they had not, at the time of the home invasion, truthfully shared the fate of their dog with their children. Understandably, the abduction of their dog by the perpetrators had devastated their children, and they had chosen not to subject their children to the actual fate of their dog. They agreed it would be cruel to prolonging their children's grief with the hope that their dog might be found. And they did not want their children to consider the possibility that their stolen dog was being abused by the perpetrators of the robbery of their home. Instead, they explained to their small children, that their family dog had been killed during the invasion. Both the husband and the wife expressed their gratitude for our rescue of their dog and the veterinary care he was receiving. Regretfully, the parents, prior owners of this once-loved, now damaged and abandoned pet, washed their hands of the current situation, and without volunteering any further help for the care of their once loved pet, they hoped that we could find a new and loving home for their pet and ended the call that had held so much promise. This entire conversation occurred without an audible catch in their voices or an emotional pause. How could people so easily dismiss their own loving and innocent creature, just like that...or maybe I cannot see clearly both sides of this sad story?

While we were pondering her fate, as she was in critical condition, at the vet's office, this seriously injured, totally exhausted dog lifted her head and placed it on my forehead. It was such a touching movement that I could barely catch my breath. It was as if she knew that we could pull together against our seemingly impossible difficulties. We could and did heal together.

I named her Moo Moo, the canine version of Ferdinand. And until Angela could find a permanent and kind-hearted family for Moo Moo, she resided at the home of a great foster-family, content to be safe, cared for and loved... again.

We had developed a special bond, so one evening each week, we both attended obedience training. Weekly Auntie Angela would bring her to the substation to visit with me and my deputies. Some behaviorists and veterinarians purport that because dogs are gifted with a universal sense (which humans do not have), they can often feel and interpret the negative and positive energy (emotions) of the other beings around them. Others attribute their ability to read humans to those emotional chemical changes, easily detected by the 220 million olfactory receptors of canines (humans have 5 million). Either would explain why Moo Moo was gifted in her ability to relieve the extreme discomfort of some of the victims who would walk in the doors of the sub-station, yet become the happy clown with children, calming their anxieties while waiting in a sheriff's office.

During that year Moo Moo underwent two surgeries. One was to repair the collapsed trachea due to chaining, and the second was to remove those tumors, which were a result of her constant exposure to the strong New Mexico sun. Within a year this remarkable lass recovered and adopted her fosters as her permanent parents. Finally the slightly fabulous Moo Moo is home.

Mark Twain's truism came to mind. "It is not the size of the dog in the fight, but the size of the fight of the dog."

To demonstrate that the size of our world is shrinking and that molecular energies can often communicate, the following unbelievable meeting really did occur. While waiting in line at Albuquerque International Sunport for a seat on a Southwest Airlines flight to California, April 2015, I was chatting (about dogs, of course) with the gentleman behind me. As he began explaining the sad tale of his rescued dog who was kidnapped in a home invasion in Albuquerque, I gasp, and questioned, "Moo Moo?"

He was so puzzled and taken back that his eyes opened in disbelief and mouth remained open as he slowly nodded in disbelief...two ships in a storm.

What a remarkably rewarding month! Our joint rescues of Ferdinand and Moo Moo quickened the formation of our animal cruelty task force, BCACT which officially became a reality as a government entity in late 2011.

March 2012, the BCSO, BCACS and NMDOG, together, as one unit, BCACT conducted their first boots-on-the-ground sweep. The unannounced presence of BCACT's uniformed deputies and officers, official vehicles with flashing lights, and small army of dedicated individuals and volunteers sent a message that was loud and clear: if you harm, neglect, violate, or refuse medical aid to any animal in your care, there will be consequences. News travels quickly and everyone enjoys a touching, feel-good story about a rescued abused or abandoned animal that is now living in a new loving home. Within hours of this first sweep, the compassionate actions of the newly formed BCACT, brought media raves in throughout area newspapers, radio and television stations. Its humane accomplishments peppered the social media; "innovative," "eye-opening," "a collective and shrewd decision reached decades too late," and "a simple but workable solution to effectively curtail animal abuse in our county."

Sweet success! BCACT had provided a small but much needed fix to New Mexico's embarrassing, calloused and indifferent approach to animal abuse and a boost in public relations for Bernalillo County, for New Mexico! Best of all...what a saving grace for the animals!

Matt and I had contended that if our units were allowed to cooperate, to work together, we would save more lives of the abused and abandoned in Bernalillo County. We were elated, not only with the success of the first sweep, but that we had been instrumental in forming a direly needed community-friendly, pro-active, inter-agency task force that could be used as a model for any communities interested in working together to make a serious dent in animal abuse in their community. I felt honored to work with him. His vast experience gave our newly created BCACT credibility and substance.

CHAPTER SEVEN

TRAINING:
STATE ANIMAL STATUTES

"It is law that determines when man has violated the rights of others. I am in favor of animal rights as well as human rights. That is the way of a whole human being."

– Abraham Lincoln, 16th U.S. President, author of
Emancipation Proclamation and Gettysburg Address

Andi's presentations covered primarily <u>New Mexico</u> laws, citing their strengths and weaknesses as well as their legal, social and safety implications. For a more inclusive picture, I have included this information for all states.

Our team-training sessions and classes began December 2011 for both agencies. Since then four training sessions have been conducted. Because Matt is no longer with BCACS, presenting the BCACT materials to our deputies has become my charge. As Humane Society of Detroit President, Matt and members of his Cruelty Investigation Department have initiated a similar BCACT program, adapted to the Detroit area, approved by the Michigan Commission on Law Enforcement Standards.

These are our team-presentations as originally outlined and planned, but, they are continually updated with current legal changes, disposition of cases and new and pertinent occurrences.

As law enforcement officials, it is our duty to enforce all laws, but as members of an animal cruelty task force, our responsibilities, when circumstances so dictate, increase to rescuing an injured animal, securing appropriate veterinarian care for it when required and working with our volunteer organization to rehabilitate and rehome the abused/injured animal.

A firm understanding of federal laws, state statutes and county and city codes and ordinances is necessary when executing citations, warrants and arrests and to provide the district attorney with a prosecutable case. Currently federal laws prohibit animal fighting and obscene "crush videos." In July, 2015 a federal anti-cruelty bill, the PACT Act—Prevent Animal Cruelty and Torture—was introduced that would empower the FBI and U.S. Attorneys to prosecute animal abuse cases that cross state lines, closing serious existing gaps in federal law. It was referred to committee.

This session will cover the laws regarding state animal cruelty crimes. Most carry punishments that are not sufficiently stringent to deter a reoccurrence, even for the more vicious cases of animal abuse. The usual plea-bargaining for these crimes is evidence that animal welfare is not regarded with the seriousness that its established link between animal, child and family abuse should demand. Given the lame excuse that the judicial dockets are crowded, most extreme animal felony convictions are pled down to misdemeanors, so a felony charge that is not convicted as a felony becomes untraceable, and recidivism flourishes.

New Mexico statutes are ranked by Animal Legal Defense Fund (ALDF) in the bottom five. These statutes, not recently updated, specify that only after the third convicted offense of extreme animal cruelty does the offense become a felony. The state does not require mandatory forfeiture of animals upon conviction and the courts, and does not restrict ownership of animals after an animal cruelty conviction. Animals are not included, therefore not protected, in the state's protection orders concerning domestic violence cases, but New Mexico's 2015 legislature did authorize $300,000 to cover costs of temporary housing pets of victims of domestic violence.

According to up-to-date figures by New York's Animal Alliance, 71% of domestic violence victims report that their abuser also targeted their pet. The inclusion of pets and the care of in domestic violence protection orders are written in state statutes of Arizona, Arkansas, California, Illinois, Louisiana, Massachusetts, Minnesota, North Carolina, Tennessee, Vermont, and Wisconsin. Specifics of these codes can be viewed at "Pets in Protection Orders by State" on National Link Coalition website. Seven states statutes define acts of animal abuse which are intended to intimidate or coerce a spouse/partner as an act of domestic violence. In these states: Arizona, Colorado, Indiana, Maine, Nebraska, Nevada, Ohio and Tennessee prosecutors have choices and can charge crimes involving animal abuse or domestic violence. Alaska legislators introduced a pet protection bill with an unusual twist, allowing the courts to decide who gets to keep the animals when people divorce, with consideration of what would be best for the animal.

Illinois adds extra penalties when animal cruelty is committed in the presence of a child, and the poster for <u>New York's</u> Alliance for Animals proclaims with its bold headline, "An estimated 1 million animals are abused or killed each year in connection with domestic violence."

Insurance companies in <u>Sweden</u> follow a different dictate for animal abuse. After her dog had been beaten to death by her boyfriend, the owner filed a claim with her pet insurance company for her veterinary bills. The insurance company paid about $5,000 to the animal clinic. But once the insurance company learned that the dog had been abused by a family member, the owner was ordered to forfeit their insurance payment, which was eventually paid by the boyfriend once he was convicted of beating his girlfriend. If the pet had been beaten by a stranger, the veterinary expenses would have been covered by the insurance company.

Some legal decisions about animal abuse charges are made difficult because the verbiage of the statute or ordinance allows for them to be misconstrued. To assure that violence against animals crimes are well presented by the prosecution, it will be your knowledge of these laws that will help you to recognize and differentiate the crimes of animal abuse or neglect (a misdemeanor) from extreme animal cruelty (a felony).

- *Federal laws are passed for the safety of all United States citizens. They are the building blocks for county and municipal regulations.*

- *State statutes incorporate the federal laws and add their own to establish a framework which apply to all state residents. State laws cannot violate federal laws. <u>New Mexico</u>, along with several other states categorize infractions only according to animal cruelty-misdemeanor and extreme animal cruelty-felon, which can be cross-referenced with intentional or malicious cruelty.*

- *County codes usually only represent the unincorporated areas of the county and are not the law for incorporated villages, towns and cities within the county.*

- *Municipal ordinances incorporate and cannot violate federal and state laws, on which they build their own additional restrictions. They usually, but are not required to honor county ordinances.*

- *Pueblos and reservations have their own distinct set of tribal laws. High incidences of poverty, unemployment, abuse, addictions, governmental policies of neglect, rural locations and varying jurisdictional disagreements over law enforcement occupy greater priority than animal welfare and control.*

"Native American children experience double the rate of abuse and neglect of white children. American Indian women experience the nation's highest rates of domestic violence and sexual assault," explained Diane Webster, president and founder of the Native American Humane Society. She also revealed that the resources to control animal populations or there are not funds available to provide basic care including inoculations of pets. However, through education, consultations, hotlines and community involvement, she intends to establish zero-tolerance policies for animal abuse on tribal lands.

Recently the FBI classified animal cruelty as a Group A Felony defined by these categories: simple or gross neglect, intentional torture or abuse, animal sexual abuse, organized abuse to include Cockfighting and Dogfighting. For legal ease, ALDF, Allie Phillipe and Randall Lockwood of The National District Attorneys' Association further refined the difference in animal cruelty crimes by adding four additional categories in addition to those of the FBI.

1. Simple Neglect (FBI) includes the failure to provide necessities (food, water, shelter) and basic or emergency veterinary services. Such abuse is usually attributed to the elderly, infirm, indigent or uneducated, and is felt to be most successfully handled with education and assistance from local resources.

Unusual stipulations under the animal cruelty category Simple Neglect include six state statutes. Animal cruelty in New Jersey is deemed to be a "Disorderly Person's Offense" carrying a fine of $250-$2,500 and/or six months. Maine stipulates that giving an animal an alcoholic beverage constitutes animal cruelty. The decision of a 2009 Oregon court was that an individual accused of starving 20 horses and goats on his own property could only be charged for one punishable animal cruelty offense, because animals are considered as "property." His 90 days in jail was suspended. An appeals courts disagreed, ruling that animals can be "victims," and thus changing the perpetrator's charges to 20 counts of animal abuse, which required re-sentencing.

2. Abandonment, the most common form of animal abuse, is rarely prosecuted. This cruelty is usually attributed to economic situations, changing of address or when owners no longer want the responsibility of taking care of a pet.

Statutes regarding this offense are confusing, vague and weak. Some states have realized the importance of designating, as a separate category with separate penalties, the animal cruelty category of Abandonment. Ohio, Oklahoma, Rhode Island, South Carolina and Florida regard it as a felony; Montana cites specific abandonment on railroad tracks as well as roadways; New Jersey fines those convicted $500, but, if on or near a roadway, the fine is increased to $1,000. Virginia terms abandonment as highway littering with a fine from $250 to $2,500 and/or 12 months. Both the fine and the time will be suspended if convicted agrees to help with removing litter from Virginia state highways.

3. Severe Neglect (FBI) is regarded as the intentional act of not providing necessary shelter, care or sustenance. Often this crime is associated with puppy mills, backyard breeders, hobby breeders, hoarding, animals left in hot vehicles. Internet puppy mills were incorporated into this federal section in 2013.

Reckless conduct animal codes recognize the extreme suffering of animals left to tragic fates, which include leaving an unattended animal in a hot car. These laws are enforced in numerous localities as well as Bernalillo County and Albuquerque. Even though New Mexico lacks such a humane law, 19 states specifically prohibit leaving an unattended animal in confined or parked vehicle, endangering the animal's life. Lora Dunn of ALDF issued a reminder to all communities in all states stressing that it only takes moments for the temperature inside a parked car to rise to levels that are dangerous for a helpless animal trapped inside.

In 2016, a new Illinois law took effect making it a misdemeanor to leave pets outside during extreme weather.

4. Intentional torture, abuse or harm (FBI) makes up those cases in which the violence involved in knowingly harming an animal and presents the greatest threat and causes the greatest concern to the community because of the fear that the perpetrator involved will extend the violence into the neighborhood.

Covering a wide assortment of cruelty crimes, these laws have been helpful in the successful prosecution of many more violent crimes against animals. After the 2014 successful passing of South Dakota's new intentional cruelty as a Class 6 felony, all 50 states, plus District of Columbia, boasted of such felony statutes. However, not all South Dakota legislators were pleased with their joining those states concerned about animal abuse, especially one state representative, who was especially negative in her assessment of her state's legislative vote. "If we're going to go along with the felony and endanger our ranching industry in this state, then there should be no objection to taking the word 'humane society' out of anywhere in the bill."

But even though states now designate intentional cruelty as felony, judgements for such violent acts are not necessarily examples of retributive justice. They are examples of a judicial system, hamstrung by archaic laws with little time to devote to animal cruelty. Overworked prosecutors who do value the life of animals are not familiar with animal cruelty statutes and are seeking a quick trial, usually pled down to a misdemeanor.

A Tennessee puppy, ribs continually kicked until broken, mouth wired shut, hung by wire from a tree, finally succumbed to the multiple stabbing wounds. Her assailants were sentenced to 2 years of probation and 200 hours of community service.

An angry Burbank, South Dakota man beat his neighbor's dog to death with a hammer. The court-set punishment for his intentionally cruel behavior was a single year of probation and fines totaling approximately $2,500.

A smart Texas jury failed to buy into the incredulous story of Bradley that his Chihuahua, Buddy reached through the gate on the kennel and turned on the stove burner before jumping into the pot filled with water. Bradley was sentenced to 15 months in prison. Buddy's critical condition (burns over 100% of his small body) caused him to be euthanized.

In New York, animal cruelty cases do not allow courts to have access to prior convictions of such, thus granting a free pass to repeat offenders.

In Roswell, New Mexico, August 2012 occurred one of the most brutal and disturbing dog beatings reported in New Mexico's history. He pleaded "no contest" to burning a dog with chemicals and severely beating another dog with a bat (the dog had to be humanely euthanized). He was sentenced to 18 months in jail, but this time was reduced to 90 days.

Bernalillo County Undersheriff Rudy Mora brought to my attention a recent crime of animal violence against one of their own, Rex, a BCSO specially trained canine. "Animal abuse sometimes occurs in our own ranks, because BCSO employs K-9s specifically trained to assist deputies in their duties and are sometimes utilized in unstable situations. In late April 2016, Rex, our six-year-old Belgian Malinois, a patrol and explosives sniffing dog, was working alongside one of our deputies who was summoned with his partner to an early morning domestic violence call in the South valley. One of the two brothers who had become violent and threatening further escalated the situation by wielding a knife and a baseball bat. When the brother tried to escape the deputies, Rex accompanied the deputy into this dangerous situation to help take the brother into custody. Rex was there to protect the deputy from harm's way. The brother became so enraged that he directed his anger toward Rex, stabbing him several times, then beating upon his bleeding body with the bat.

"After emergency surgery, a brave and heroic Rex recovered from his wounds. The brother faces felony criminal charges including those of extreme animal cruelty in state district court. This specific situation will put to test the intent and strength of our animal cruelty laws. Hopefully it will not be pled down. Rex is a very important, well loved and respected member of our BCSO team.

"The Belgian Malinois is an alert, high energy, herding breed, recognized by AKC in 1959. Because of his high sensitivity and loyalty coupled with his easy trainability and extreme intelligence, this exceptional canine is often chosen for police and military efforts as well as search and rescue."

In 2015, Oregon's new law designating animal neglect as a felony (passed with support of ALDF and Oregon Humane Society) was credited with their convictions of several accused perpetrators of animal cruelty. The state's newly created, successful, one-of-a-kind in America, crimes-against-animals prosecutor was a position created and funded through the cooperation of ALDF, Oregon District Attorneys' Association and Benton County District Attorneys' Office.

5. Organized Criminal Enterprises (FBI) promote and sustain the animal fighting, which flourishes underground and is included in state racketeering act.

6. Bestiality (FBI) involves sexual contact with animals. Cross Video Production and Distribution are regarded as a sub-genre of the sadomasochist world.

Jenny Edwards of the Chandler Ohio Edwards law enforcement research center wrote a letter supporting Ohio's Bestiality Bill in 2015. Her information was shocking. "The instances of animal sex abuse are growing; One Internet site for zoophiles has more than 10,000 followers online at any given time. Bestiality, particularly when experienced as a child, has been shown to be the single largest risk factor and strongest predictor of increased risk for committing child sexual abuse. This is a crime that has far-reaching implications."

Testifying at the Ohio legislative committee hearing was Jeremy Hoffman, a detective at the Fairfax County, Virginia Police Department. "With more states joining in passing laws prohibiting sexual abuse of animals, zoophiles will seek places where they can engage in this conduct without repercussion. I am most certain that the people of Ohio do not want their state to become the preferred place for animal sex offenders to live." This bill waits in the Criminal Justice Committee.

Sexual assault of an animal, which can differ than bestiality, is a felony in 20 states, <u>Arizona</u> being the lone Southwestern state. <u>South Carolina</u> refers to it as "buggery." <u>New Jersey</u> became the 38th state to ban animal sexual abuse. In 23 states (not <u>New Mexico</u>, <u>Arizona</u>, <u>California</u>, <u>Colorado</u> or <u>Texas</u>) an individual convicted of bestiality must register for bestiality. However, bestiality is included in the definition of child pornography/obscenity and most states (including the five Southwestern states mentioned above) require registration for the production, promotion, distribution and possession of such media or participation in live shows.

Jessica's Law, which was modeled in 44 states (the only Southwestern state not was <u>Colorado</u>) was successfully applied in <u>California</u> against a defendant who strangled and sexually abused an eight-month old Chihuahua. The first conviction for animal pornography, production and distribution under the "Crush Video" Federal Law was a 24-year-old Houston woman, ordered to serve 33 months in prison, of which she was credited with time (42 months) served. She will not serve additional time after her completion of a ten-year sentence on related state charges.

Filming of Bestiality is illegal in <u>Alaska</u>. Oregon's 2015 bill creates a new misdemeanor crime of encouraging sexual assault of an animal, defined as possessing or controlling a visual recording of a person engaged in sexual conduct with an animal. Until recently sexual contact with animals (bestiality) was included in state laws of crimes against nature. But strangely states have decriminalized these laws, forcing states to re-enact new bestiality laws even though opponents contend that their behavior constitutes a "lifestyle choice." Prosecutions for this crime are still rare as they present unusually obtained evidence and unique challenges. There exists no federal law prohibiting this degenerate action.

7. Ritualistic Abuse involves the gang/occult/religious torture and mutilation of an animal, which is displayed to invoke public horror. Because form of abuse is receiving more publicity and thus more emotional concern within our communities, it is a recent inclusion in several state statutes. These disturbing crimes often require law enforcement personnel to be more knowledgeable about those gang and occult practices within their commands and for the possible escalation of this depraved violence.

8. "Crush Video" Federal Law, refers to any photograph, motion-picture film, video or digital recording, or electronic image that is obscene or depicts actual conduct in which one or more living non-human mammals, birds, reptiles, or amphibians is intentionally tortured, crushed, burned, drowned, suffocated, impaled, killed or otherwise subjected to serious bodily injury.

9. Animal Abuse for Entertainment addresses current abhorrent entertainment practices as well as many phases of our constantly changing electronic world. Today's surge of social media and smart phones that can capture photos of crimes as they occur. Because this has increased the awareness of all people (not just animal lovers) as to the plight of animal abuse, several cities have instituted smart phone applications that specifically allow the reporting of crimes against animals with the inclusion of photographs, videos and GPS data to help locate the incident.

However, animals need legal protection when these electronic forms of social media are used to record and distribute staged animal abuse. In Illinois it is illegal to photograph or record, using any media device, or cruelty to an animal as well as to sell, create, promote, buy, or process such.

Florida makes it illegal to exhibit any deformed, mutilated or disfigured animal for compensation. Connecticut outlaws baiting, harassing or worrying any animal for purpose of making it perform for amusement, diversion or exhibition.

10. The Federal Dog and Cat Fur Protection Act prohibits dog and cat fur trade. Alabama and Florida specifically prohibit the skinning, buying, selling or marketing of pelts or hides of domesticated animals. However, there are no penalties for abusing animals on fur and leather farms in China, the origin for more than half of the finished cat fur and dog leather clothes sold in America. PETA's (People for the Ethical Treatment of Animals) webpage has interesting but graphic articles about how dog leather is gathered and prepared, and they warn consumers that products made from dog leather, cat and bunny furs are deliberately mislabeled, then exported throughout the world and sold to unsuspecting customers. The intentional mislabeling of these items by dishonest inhumane manufacturers of furniture, home and personal accessories and clothing is to thwart this existing federal act. So if you buy fur or leather, remember…there is really no way to tell whose skin you're really in.

Not all acts of animal cruelty are addressed in these ten categories. Some are included in agricultural, fish and game, animal sports such as racing, service dogs, exotic pets, or personal property.

Alaska's **16.05** Fish and Game Code reads:

> "Any dog that habitually annoys any wild deer, reindeer, sheep, cattle, horse or other animal, bird, either domestic or wild—may be lawfully killed when it is found at large."

Alabama **1-13A-11-16** states:

> "Animals which participate in greyhound racing, may not be put to death by any means other than lethal injection and cannot be removed from the state for the purpose of being destroyed." Seven states still run active Greyhound tracks despite a first-ever, devastating report (released by ASPCA and GREY2K USA) revealing the enormous number of recorded deaths and injuries involved in the dog racing industry. Those seven are **Alabama, Arizona, Arkansas, Florida, Iowa, Texas** and **West Virginia.**

Alabama veils a threat among its animal cruelty exclusions, "It is legal to shoot a dog or cat for urinating or defecating on property."

Nevada stands with few states whose legislators have failed to enact statutes regulating exotic animals as pets, but one county, Clark, has passed such an ordinance.

One important animal law in 16 states, which is not classified under cruelty, makes it a criminal offense to fraudulently represent a dog as a service animal.

A disturbing 2016 incident in New Mexico had law enforcement officials pondering about, "Was this a crime of animal cruelty or not?" Having received a report of two men viciously cutting off the tail of a dog at a busy city intersection, they responded. The "dog" was a coyote, a road kill. The animal had not been mutilated while living, and although the officers found the actions to be "gross," ALDF reports that many states such as Montana have legalized "salvaging" roadkill, and allow the dissection of the wildlife carcass for consumption. The same principle applies to a 2016 teacher-sanctioned game of jump-rope over a cat's intestines in Texas.

Other laws which determine the treatment or disposition of animals such as safe-haven, pound seizure and ag-gag are not categorized under the previous categories of "animal cruelty."

Safe-haven laws, seldom included in the animal codes of most states or communities, establish a minimum time that an abandoned or owner-surrendered pet must be kept by the municipal or private shelter, allowing adoption, before another dispositions are considered. This is an important humane issue, and one of the most difficult and emotional, facing all municipal and private shelters in all states. (This is not covered in <u>New Mexico</u> statutes but in HEART, (Humane and Ethical Animal Rules and Treatment), see Appendix.

<u>Colorado</u> is among those progressive states which recognize the importance of creating a humane minimum holding period that shelters must hold found pets, while allowing pets to be adopted. <u>Oklahoma</u> provides that only unlicensed dogs, after being impounded for 25 days and licensed dogs, after an impound period of 30 days, can be delivered to research facilities.

<u>Utah</u> has a holding limit of only five days for stray animals before final disposition of animal. Utah's animal protection laws are rated by ALDF and HSUS among the worst five in the United States.

Pound Seizure addresses the provisions to sell or release impounded animals from a shelter to research, testing or educational facilities, and is included in the exceptions/exclusions of most state animal cruelty statutes. Usually this is located at the end of previously addressed statutes.

Many of the state pound seizure laws which were passed in the 1940s and 1950s still exist today. They either still allow for pound animals to be sold to research facilities or avoid the moral dilemma and elect to hold individual counties and municipalities to be responsible for inclusion or exclusion of pound seizure. The undaunted efforts of determined animal activists in some states have resulted in the repealing or amending of some of these inhumane pieces of legislation. The ALDF Model Law for Pound Seizure can be referenced on the website of Animal Legal Resource Center.

The National Association for Biomedical Research, one of the largest lobbying groups representing those who sell animals and torture them for research, is also associated with Policy Directions, Inc., the supplier of animals to Merck Pharmaceuticals of <u>New Jersey</u>, Covance Research Facilities worldwide, and Charles River Laboratories of <u>Massachusetts</u>, the world's largest breeder of animals used in experiments. Animal testing facilities using multiple caged animals exist in every state, but are more concentrated on the east coast and in California.

An active campaign led by Physicians Committee for Responsible Medicine to stop the use of live animal labs in medical schools resulted in ceasing those experiments in more than 90% of the schools. Vanderbilt University School of Medicine in <u>Tennessee</u> did not follow suit; their medical students still are instructed to make incisions into the chest cavities of live animals to practice emergency procedures.

PETA interceded on the part of the thousands of <u>Utah</u> shelter dogs and cats who had been sold to the University of Utah (a state requirement), intentionally made ill, then used in laboratory experiments. In 2015 both the school and the state ended its purchase of animals from shelters.

Tobacco companies continue to turn a blind eye to the suffering their product causes and under violent conditions by utilizing animals in their ongoing experiments. During combat training, live animals continue to suffer unnecessary tortures.

Colorado's pound seizure **35-42.15-101, II** stipulations are lengthy and specific.

> **"Pounds and shelters shall not participate in the practice known as 'red tagging', which, for the purposes of this section, means the isolation, without opportunity for adoption, of healthy, amiable dogs and cats for research animal buyers. No dog or cat shall be designated as a candidate for medical or any other kind of experimentation unless such dog or cat has been made available for adoption during the two-week period it is cared for by the pound or shelter for 'experimentation,' which includes any research, or testing, or the use of an animal for the training of students or medical personnel."**

Ag-Gag laws pertain to allowing animal cruelty, but are not written in the section dealing with animal cruelty. Termed as anti-whistle blower laws, this legislation criminalizes the whistle blowing of animal cruelty practices in research laboratories, farms and ranches. The purpose of these ag-gag bills is not to expose, but to prevent the exposure of unnecessarily cruel practices at these facilities. Animal activists were relieved both times these laws were defeated in the New Mexico Roundhouse, 2013 and 2015. And in a legal milestone, Idaho ruled that the state's Ag-Gag law violated the First and Fourteenth Amendments to the U.S. Constitution.

Documentation of intentional cruel, malicious and torturous practices on farms, ranches and research facilities have led to the removal of Sparboe Farms of Minnesota as an egg supplier for McDonald's, Target, Sam's Club. Their videos have resulted in the largest meat recall in U.S. history. Excessive cruelty was exposed in a North Carolina ButterBall facility as well as in Winchester Dairy Farm in Dexter, New Mexico (supplier of Leprino cheese to Pizza Hut, Papa John's, and Dominos). These brave whistle-blowers capture violations so egregious that USDA can actually close the offending facilities. Influenced by the well-funded Center for Consumer Freedom, whose goal it is to thwart these type of agricultural investigations, a few states, Idaho, Iowa, Kansas, Missouri, Montana, North Dakota and Utah, have passed this appalling ag-gag legislation.

Some states are lauded for their innovative, positive approaches to pursuing animal cruelty. In *Guidebook on Safer Communities, Safer Families and Being an Effective Voice for Animal Victims*, The District Attorneys' Association of America offers excellent and strong considerations for state, county and local attorneys prosecuting animal abuse cases.

Animal law is also expanding. There exists an international emergence of animal law conferences, publications in animal-focused law reviews and textbooks, animal law courses at prestigious law schools. Schools are now hiring full-time professors specializing in the area of animal law.

New Mexico's newly-established Albuquerque Metro animal court, PAW, (Pre-adjudication Animal Welfare Program) was recently established by two University of New Mexico law students and patterned after the court established in 2012 in Tucson, Arizona, the first of its kind in the country. This court does not hear violations of leash and license laws, but concentrates their hearings on animal neglect and cruelty. Rather than incarceration of the offenders, it provides the tools which will help these violent offenders to stop re-offending through intensive treatment and supervision by an elite unit of legal and therapeutic providers. The decisions of this new court will be further facilitated in the towns of Bernalillo and Santa Fe, who recently purchased Taser lapel cameras for its animal control officers.

Prior to 1968, felony penalties existed in only four states. Recognizing the gravity of this situation, 19 states (not New Mexico) have enacted felony penalties for any act of animal cruelty which will enable prosecutors to better prosecute those charged of such. In the last decade, only one Southwestern state, Nebraska, showed the foresight to upgrade their animal cruelty laws to first offense felony.

Although all state statutes concerning animal cruelty differ, those written without professional and legal guidance, from animal legal organizations such as ALDF, are usually much more difficult to successfully prosecute because both the verbiage and sentencing are open to many interpretations. Statutes in some states are unusual enough to mention, such as those few states that are seriously protective of their state's tourism, hunting or recreational industries.

All interested state and local law enforcement agencies receive the complimentary services of ALDF, HSUS, PETA, and ASPCA (American Society for the Prevention of Cruelty to Animals)—all broad-based national non-profits. Timely alerts and legal updates are made available to both state residents and law enforcement agencies as to upcoming or completed animal humane legislative actions. They provide projected implications of any failed/passed law and analyze the votes of each state legislator on each animal cruelty bill throughout each specific legislative session. Instrumental in lobbying and designing animal cruelty statutes, these animal rights associations possess the knowledge and skills to work closely with and support those legislators. They represent the strongest and most positive force animals possess in state and local legislatures.

To provide professional and strong animal cruelty, ALDF Model Animal Protection Laws are available online. Their detailed, professional content and classifications can serve as a base with which you can compare with your community's animal protection laws. They address specifics lacking in most state statutes and include definitions of terms, general prohibitions, defenses, and pre- and post-conviction provisions. They also offer a convenient template with which your local government can create its own animal cruelty laws.

State statutes concerning animal cruelty differ widely and are not always efficient or effective. Some are not even animal-friendly. Some are definitely lacking in the respect of life category. Some fail to require strong penalties for felony crimes. So states can continually examine and upgrade their existing statutes, HSUS and ALDF annually study and rank the animal cruelty statutes of all states.

NATIONAL RATINGS OF ANIMAL CRUELTY STATUTES

ALDF and HSUS are recognized as being instrumental in bringing about stronger laws and offering their animal cruelty-specific legal assistance to prosecutors. Because of their history and their database of sentences in animal abuse cases throughout America, they are the go-to experts for district attorneys seeking the strongest possible penalties in their animal cruelty cases.

Their yearly and independent rating of the effectiveness of animal cruelty statutes in all 50 states and D.C. uses 72 points of reference. These evaluations provide an excellent indication of a state's improvement in the last 12 months and which specific animal cruelty issues the state should address. Sometimes these ratings and suggestions can make the deciding difference. It is an important step for all city and state animal departments and governing agencies to reference the yearly HSUS/ALDF ratings for your state online, along with suggested improvements. The humane treatment of the animals in your state is dependent upon these agencies.

But, year after year, <u>Alabama</u>, <u>Alaska</u>, <u>Idaho</u>, <u>Kentucky</u>, <u>Mississippi</u>, <u>Missouri</u>, <u>North Carolina</u>, <u>North Dakota</u>, <u>South Carolina</u>, <u>South Dakota</u>, <u>Utah</u> and <u>Wyoming</u> continue as bottom feeders, content to remain in the worst 10-13 spots. And the animal spotlight continues to shine on the humane accomplishments of <u>Arizona</u>, <u>Illinois</u>, <u>California</u>, <u>Colorado</u>, <u>Maine</u>, <u>Massachusetts</u>, <u>New Jersey</u>, <u>New York</u>, <u>Oregon</u>, <u>Virginia</u> and <u>Washington.</u>

Despite APNM's attempts to work with our state legislators to strengthen <u>New Mexico</u> anti-cruelty laws, they were ranked in 2010-2014 by ALDF as among the worst five (48th of 50) in our nation. HSUS ranked us 27th. Both cited the following as major areas needing improvement in the state.

- Inadequate felony penalties for neglect; none for abandonment and sexual assault

- Weak, confusing, inadequate definitions of classifications

- No increase in penalties when abuse is committed in presence of a minor

- Sub-standard requirements of basic care for our companion animals

- Felony provisions available only for cruelty and fighting against select animals

- No mental health evaluations for offenders

- No statutory authority to allow protective orders to include animals

- Inadequate cost mitigation and recovery provisions for impounded animals

- No required cross-reporting between social and law enforcement agencies

- No database tracking convicted offenders

- No provisions for veterinarians or other select non-animal-related agencies/professionals to report suspected animal abuse

- Inadequate animal fighting provisions

IMPLICATIONS OF PRESENT STATUTES ON HEALTH AND SAFETY IN A STATE

"When humans harm an animal, it is a powerful, not-to-be-ignored indicator that human victims are possibly being abused as well. It is a proven predictor of future violence. If crimes of animal cruelty are taken seriously by our legislators, they can enact the necessary laws so that law enforcement officials can make early interventions."

– Bernalillo County Sheriff Manuel Gonzales

BERNALILLO
COUNTY
ANIMAL CRUELTY
TASK FORCE

CHAPTER EIGHT

TRAINING: COUNTY AND CITY ORDINANCES AND CODES

"The custom of tormenting and killing animals will, by degrees, harden their hearts even toward man."

– John Locke, English physician,
Enlightenment philosopher

County animal codes build on state and federal laws. They, along with city ordinances, cannot contradict state and federal laws. They do not supersede ordinances of villages and communities located within the county. County codes are usually applicable only to the unincorporated areas of the county, those without incorporated municipalities.

Village, town and city animal ordinances cannot negate federal or state statutes, but, instead, must build upon them, shaping and improving to better meet the particular needs of their citizens. They are usually longer, more specific, and more involved, example the HEART (see Appendix).

There are unusual occasions when many of these law enforcement agencies cooperate to arrest a perpetrator. Example this case on Facebook. To demonstrate the diminutiveness of their dog, an Albuquerque, New Mexico apartment complex couple posted, December, 2013, on Facebook a photo of their live white Chihuahua puppy, Baby, enclosed in a clear plastic freezer baggie. In no time their deviate antic caught the eye of a Good Samaritan and both mother and son were arrested by our deputies for extreme animal cruelty, a felony charge.

Legal entities were not cooperative but adversarial after a 2015 Facebook posting by a licensed Texas veterinarian who used her bow and arrow to shoot a cat, then posted with accompanying photo lauding, "My first bow kill, lol. The only good feral tomcat is one with an arrow through it's (sic) head. Vet of the year award...gladly accepted."

There followed an outcry when the state veterinarian board only suspended her license. But when the Austin County District Attorney's office closed the case, claiming no proof that the cat was killed in a cruel manner or even that the Facebook killing occurred in Texas, ALDF actively pursued this injustice. Their fast action resulted in the October revoking of her license to practice veterinary medicine. In retaliation, the DA's office is reviewing the revocation.

A former Birmingham, <u>Alabama</u> attorney pled guilty to slitting the throat of his family dog, a American Staffordshire Terrier, texting a photo of this to his then wife, and leaving her a voice mail stating, "Your day is coming, girl." His sentence, after a five month probe by police and a thorough investigation by a Florida animal forensics lab, was a suspended sentence, probation and one day in jail for a later no-contact order charge.

In 2015 a Springfield, <u>Missouri</u> man, who admitted breaking into the apartment of a woman who had spurned his advances and stealing, then killing her puppy by tossing it 46 feet out of a third-floor window was sentenced to probation. The concerned mother of the woman, testified in court, "Your community should be very concerned if he is walking the streets."

Bernalillo Care Animal Care officers are experts in the legalities involved when seizing an animal or writing a citation, but lack the arrest power of my deputies. We depend on each other when we cite or arrest suspected offenders, so that our evidence will stand up in court. As we report individual animal cruelty violations, it is important that the prosecutor and judge are made aware of those factors which will help to determine the degree of threat of the abuser.

- *Vulnerability of animal, as to size, age and level of aggressiveness*
- *Number of animals involved*
- *Number of abusive instances within a specific time frame*
- *Severity of injury inflicted*
- *Multiple wounds on same animal*
- *Abuse inflicted while animal restrained or unrestrained*
- *Premeditation of abuse*
- *Abuse involving one or more individuals*
- *Weapons used in abuse*

- *Cruelty included torture or mutilation*

- *Past history of abuse of animals or humans*

- *Perpetrator documented abuse*

- *Cruelty included satanic-type rituals*

- *Past history of interaction between animal-owner and perpetrator*

- *Duration of abuse*

Peace officers can apply to courts to obtain warrants to seize animals, including livestock, whom they suspect of being abused, according to the <u>New Mexico</u> Livestock Code. During the seizure, official documentation including written and video, will be made of the animal, its living conditions and surroundings.

As Andi's information unfolded concerning the specifics of the animal cruelty laws of Bernalillo County and surrounding city and villages, I pondered a way to present, in a different light, some of the animal cruelty codes from around the country that are actually harmful to the pets they should be protecting. And as I interviewed, examined, questioned, read and re-read both excellent and shameful ordinances, codes and laws of various towns, cities and counties, nationwide, a savvy Colorado animal shelter director cautioned me, that when comparing and researching animal care codes, sometimes the proof of the pudding lies within the internal, unpublished, administrative regulations.

Joila! Her tip changed my focus from those that are to those that should-not-be, and I had no further to look than my own city of Albuquerque. One "do-not-expose-my-identity" volunteer for one of our larger, best known rescue group revealed (at great length) her displeasure with one particular internal AAWD administrative policy. She was adamant that the citizens of Albuquerque were being taken advantage of. She explained that, without posting any fee, rescue groups can come into both shelters to pick and choose the animals which will best fit the requests of their adoptive clientele, which includes entire litters of puppies. Not only did AAWD oblige the rescue groups by making sure that these adoptable pets had veterinary exam and inoculations, they also underwent required neutering, micro-chipping, teeth cleaning and any necessary surgery. When necessary, they have been groomed. The rescue groups incurred no expenses. This assures this homeless pet will be re-homed by these rescue groups, who have strong vetting procedures and make numerous house calls.

She noted that it was not surprising that the animals chosen by the rescue groups were the cream of the crop, leaving the old, large, black, shy, disabled or Pit Bull Terriers. Because they are easier to adopt, rescues usually take the smaller, fluffy, friendly, pure-bred, designer-dogs. This leaves AAWD's perspective pet adopters with their choice of left-overs, the favorite among those tender of heart; most are easy to love and need a loving home.

My queries around AAWD facilities had struck a gold mine of relatively unknown-to-the-general-public information. One employee voiced displeasure over the owner-surrender/stray internal policy that designates a stray, when picked up by a stranger, to become an owner-surrender if kept by the rescuer for more than 24 hours, which totally misrepresented the animal's true status in city records.

Another, a veteran employee, was concerned of another internal policy in which AAWD imposed a limit on animal intake in both of their facilities, which sometimes is crowded with pets from other communities. This often forces AAWD to turn away Albuquerque's own owner-surrenders, who might have fretted over this difficult decision and finally chose to give up the animal, doing the right thing for the pet because they are no longer able to take care of them. This policy continually creates very emotional encounters when the pet-surrendering owner is told that his name will be placed on a waiting list to be contacted when kennel space is deemed available. And, this in-house administrative dictate has resulted in unwanted innocent animals being abandoned on our streets, a hazardous and life-threatening situation for both the pet and our citizens.

AAWD allows recidivism of animal abuse to continue with its in-house policy not to prosecute those who relinquish their pets, suspected victims of animal cruelty. Although the damaged pet is saved (usually), the owner is free to adopt from any other adoption agency, because our city, county and state have no animal cruelty database of convicted felons. The city does place the owner's name on an exclusive AAWD list which only bars them from adopting a pet from a city facility for a certain period of time.

This in house policy resulted in a January, 2014 wiggly, wrinkly addition to our household. Because my husband and I often take-in animals that are considered unadoptable, we received a call for help from a capable and long-time AAWD employee, who asked us to consider adopting a small but vicious 18-month-old Pug, a recent owner-surrender and the tortured victim of animal cruelty. The admission form stated that the dog was stabbed and sprayed with Clorox, a probable case of animal cruelty.

Did AAWD save one innocent by allowing other innocents to be abused, by the same family? Are they protecting an innocent but allowing a cycle of abuse? Perhaps it is the necessary, humane trade-off, because it is imperative that our shelters, without probing inquiries, accept these abused pets and provide for them the protection of a safe haven. With owner-surrenders, there are never witnesses to the abuse or to the identity of the abuser.

As Andi discussed the HEART ordinance, it brought forth answers to how two government agencies coordinating their efforts in BCACT can work with two opposing animal codes.

Albuquerque HEART ordinance can override county codes. I will discuss this city ordinance in depth (excerpts written below are important for your knowledge of proper animal code enforcement) because this strong ordinance, written in concise language, is the one that is valid when dogs and cats are picked up in Bernalillo County and delivered, by contractual agreement, to the Albuquerque Animal Welfare Department (AAWD). When a stray animal is picked-up by my deputies, and if it lacks a collar with ID or rabies tags, my deputies usually have no micro-chip scanners to ascertain the identity of the owner even though, as of 2013, microchipping is required by Bernalillo County Animal Ordinance. This stray or lost pet is then, through contractual agreement, delivered to AAWD because of lack of holding kennels at BCACS's small and limited facility. Once in this AAWD shelter, the HEART ordinance (see Appendix) becomes effective. It offers excellent, far-reaching protection to animals, and could easily be adjusted, then adopted by any community earnestly concerned about animal welfare.

The HEART ordinance, requires a pet be wearing identification, chipped, spayed/neutered, state licensed against rabies and registered with city tags. The costs of these services to bring the dog into compliance with HEART are extremely inexpensive, less than $50, charged to an owner when the animal is reclaimed. If the pet's owner had shown the responsibility to microchip the pet, the owner could be contacted through the number registered to the micro-chip. Obviously, if the no-collar, no-tag pet has not been micro-chipped, the possibility of locating its owner is unlikely, and, after a specified time, the animal is usually placed for adoption or euthanized.

A gossipy subject of employees of both shelters involved a Titled, Grand Champion Pit Bull Terrier, micro-chipped, intact and licensed to breed, but lacking the City's required intact permit. It was picked up running loose with no collar or identification by BCACS officers (who usually have no access to microchip scanners). Once this dog was brought to AAWD, the chip was read and the owner was contacted and notified that this confirmation (breeding) champion would have to be, according to HEART ordinance, neutered and the owner would be responsible for the very reasonable veterinarian charges for such. Can you imagine the heartbreak of the owner as well as the frenzy, the fire and the fury that followed? And, with proper communication, scanners and some make-sense, dual ordinances, this sad story would not have been. It could have also been avoided by a phone call from a concerned AAWD employee to the owner, alerting him of his violation of the intact license, and allowing the owner to rush to the AAWD office to purchase the required intact license.

The importance of micro-chipping to be required by all ordinances and access of their personnel to the scanners cannot be underrated. A 2012 accident on a dark county road resulted in a dog being struck by a car. He was bleeding profusely and badly maimed. Thankfully this was observed by an AAWD employee, who rushed to the aid of the injured dog, who had no collar, no tags, no identification. On the chance that this dog might have been microchipped, the city employee thought to do a quick scan and contacted the owner. Rather than take the dog to the intake of AAWD where the dog would likely perish, the employee transported the critically wounded dog to the dog's veterinarian, where the injuries were immediately treated. The recovering dog's grateful owner felt fortunate that his microchipped dog had been found by someone possessing a scanner. That near-death happening should have been another compelling reason why, for as long as county animals were to be held to city codes, there should be coordination between our county and city. No doubt our BCACT duties would be made easier by such cooperation.

But microchip information, like all personal stats, needs to be updated. A California-bred, large and handsome, male, white German Shepherd, Snowball, was sold in 2013 to an Albuquerque resident who never updated the breeder's microchip information to his own. When the dog was brought into AAWD as a stray, the chip information led them to the breeder, who had current contact information for the owner. The breeder paid all reclaim and boarding fees, then made the arrangements for Snowball to be driven back to <u>California</u> (he was too large to be accepted by airlines) by an individual (round-trip expenses paid including meals, car rental, gasoline and boarding).

The zero-tolerance, no-chain law of Bernalillo County (stronger than any in the Southwest) is definitely making a positive difference in the care of the dogs and the attitudes of their owners. Every day this ordinance earns its worth by unchaining many of the county's previously permanently chained and neglected dogs, and, at the same time, teaching the owners about alternatives to chaining. Because of the concentrated efforts of PETA, a few communities have followed the lead and enacted no-chain laws as strong as those of Bernalillo County. Others have made attempts to address some of the crueler aspects of an animal being permanently affixed to a chain. Their fixes offer only temporary relief for the chained animal and include stipulating limitations of time and the length of chain. Zero-tolerance, no-chain laws as strong as that of Bernalillo County should be a humane must in all states, all counties and all communities.

Lack of such was exampled by the 2012 discovery of a severely malnourished, dehydrated, gray with black Sheepdog-cross in Los Lunas, a small community south of Albuquerque which has no laws concerning tethering. This emaciated, 46 pound dog was dragging a rusted, cruel and heavy 25 pound chain, which had been wrapped around his neck long enough to rub-off not just the skin and fur underneath but also some tissue. After the dog was tranquilized, the chain was cut off by the fire department using their special rescue equipment; the wound was cauterized and sewn. Once this three-year-old canine recovered, gained weight and was rehabilitated, Almost Home New Mexico Rescue was successful in relocating him into a new and loving home. To assist in locating the calloused perpetrator, a steadfast APNM offered a sizeable award.

Former Albuquerque mayor and animal lover, Martin Chavez, felt that the only option to lower the frightening rate of euthanasia in our city shelters was to lower the number of animals coming through the doors of the shelters. His idea was to mount a live exit program through the creation and strong enforcement of an animal city ordinance that actually protects the largest number of animals possible, not the selfish whims of their owners or individual situations.

For Albuquerque the 2006 HEART ordinance labored over and authored by Councilor Sally Mayer could provide a safeguard for all City animals, not just those residing in our shelters, but our city budget is too strained to cover the costs of additional shelter and employees as well as the necessary serious enforcement. Still some of the contents of her admirable endeavor have changed the lives of our companion animals, thus reflecting a seemingly more humane and enlightened City.

At Council hearings, not all animal owners were pleased with the strict provisions of the ordinance as some argued with this naïve belief, "What will most help our companion animals to better fare is public education about animal issues rather than legislating required care."

The fallacy of this opinion was scoffed at by a former Albuquerque

Police officer, who pointed out that our city, county and state have been educating people for years not to drink and drive, but we still have one of the highest DWI statistics in the nation. He reasoned that we still need serious laws against drunk driving, just as we need strong laws to protect our pets. At the end of his presentation to the Council, he paused briefly, then concluded with an appropriate quote from Charles de Montesquieu. "There is no nation so powerful, as the one that obeys its laws not from principals of fear or reason, but from passion."

As the director of the education program for Animal Humane Association of New Mexico (AHANM) and Watermelon Mountain Ranch No-Kill Shelter, I visited, along with my staff of volunteers, thousands of classrooms in more than 40 communities yearly, armed with excellent educational resources and training from the world renowned Helen Woodward Animal Center in <u>California</u>. We were saddened and perplexed when, ten years later, the animal impound and euthanasia rate in most of those communities, both urban and rural, remained alarmingly high. The only New Mexico town where we taught that showed significantly lower statistics was Albuquerque, due in part to the HEART ordinance. We learned. Education was not the best answer to curb animal cruelty, but it was a necessary tool to understanding the real answer: city, state and federal laws and codes.

Those educating experiences brought us in total agreement with the assessment of ALDF's Zero Tolerance for Cruelty program, which partners with law enforcement and prosecutors nationwide. Their mission, "to protect the lives and advance the interests of animals through the legal system" requires their focus on what ALDF considers to be their main obstacle to success: the lack of adequate laws. Their quarterly newsletter explains, "That's why we're redirecting the energies of our member attorneys toward fundamentally changing how the law views and treats animals. Curbing animal cruelty requires that all states and their communities within must strive for stronger enforcement, stronger legislation."

Andi voiced her frustration about the lack of protection some of the animal cruelty laws provide. *Some animal cruelty occurrences are unusual and not adequately addressed in our statutes, laws, codes and ordinances. These cases reveal but a few of thousands of examples of aggravated pet abuse that occur on a yearly basis, and they example New Mexico's current lack of concise, broad and strong laws written, enforced and prosecuted for the ultimate protection of our animals from abuse. These episodes did not have to be.*

Dognapping was a seldom reported crime until recently. This crime can be sticky because domestic animals are designated as 'personal property' in most states including New Mexico, but laws exclude domestic animals from their lost property. In nearby Moriarty and Edgewood, between 2010 and 2012, more than 60 dogs were reported as kidnapped. These animal thefts were confusing and heartbreaking to the families returning from work to find their home/yard empty of their treasured pet. When arrested, all were surprised at the identity of the perpetrator, a 59-year-old animal activist, well-known for her kindness in helping the local animals. For many years, she alerted animal control officers as to neighborhood dogs who were left without shelter (and sometimes food and water) in inclement weather, animals who were untagged and wandering around the neighborhoods.

And when arrested, the suspect threw two Pit Bull Terriers from her moving car; neither were seriously injured. After thorough investigation, authorities realized that she had felt that these animals were being neglected. Most were continually tethered in the yards without shelter or were just wandering around the neighborhoods. She stole them because she cared about their well-being, and took them to nearby shelters claiming they were strays.

Her fellow-animal activists mirrored her accusations about the inactions of animal control officials in those small towns and felt that she was being set up in a county where animal abuse runs rampant and was openly ignored.

Our office, in 2014 and 2015 was plagued with a wave of calls reporting dognapping. Dogs were disappearing from secure yards, cars and shops. Such complaints also flooded the animal care facilities of Valencia, Sandoval, Torrance and Santa Fe Counties. Authorities surmised that they were taken to be used as fighting or bait dogs, both facing torturous fates. Although sizeable rewards for information have been offered by APNM and Albuquerque Mayor Berry, few dogs have been returned. A Pug, brutally injured by puncture marks and by a deep slice across his neck to remove the microchip, was found after missing for 4 months. He was slow to recover from his injuries and the trauma. Help came too late for the January-stolen Miniature Schnauzer, who was discovered, mauled to death. The penalty for dognapping ranges from a misdemeanor to felony larceny depending on the value of the dog, which is legally considered as personal property. If the house (not the yard) was broken into to when stealing the dog, the charge is felony burglary.

A 2014 series of animal thefts from six city and county shelters puzzled officials. When the unknown perpetrator released one of the stolen dogs whose condition warranted an immediate visit to a veterinarian, it was decided to charge the culprit, when apprehended, not only with the kidnapping and breaking and entering, but also with extreme animal cruelty, fourth-degree

*felony charge, for sodomy, as the National Crimes Against Children and Sexu-
ally Violent Registration Act does not explicitly rule out such offenses against
animals. Although the dog recovered in a foster home, and was welcomed into
a new family, our state, county and municipal laws had failed him.*

*The tortuous effects of chaining are not addressed either in our state
statutes, but we are relieved that our new Bernalillo County zero-tolerance
no-chain code will free hundreds of our tethered animals…but what of those
still waiting, suffering in other New Mexico counties and municipalities?*

*I am impressed with the success of cash awards, which have been helpful
in snaring the abusers. APNM and their generous monetary rewards for solid
information on animal cruelty happenings offers law enforcement the ability to obtain true witnesses and informants into the often clandestine world of
animal cruelty. Money can be a very strong motivator for some.*

*An example of the power of APNM's reward program occurred through
a tip, allowing authorities to identify and charge the scum in 2012 who
poured paint into the eyes of a kitten and left him, instead of at an Albuquerque animal shelter, in a dumpster, clinging to his dead sibling. Because
of the generosity of an anonymous donor, this kitty Tuffy received the necessary care from an animal ophthalmologist before being adopted into an
adoring home.*

*Another case which brought a quick result after APNM offered a reward
occurred in 2010 on the Isleta Pueblo in Bernalillo County where a dog, later
named Brownie, wandered onto the property of Pickle Heights Library, Brownie had a metal chain collar deeply embedded in his bloody neck. Attached to
this chain collar, Brownie was dragging a heavy chain. APNM's reward offer
brought two separate tipsters identifying Brownie's owner. Animal cruelty
charges were brought against this cruel individual, who pled guilty and surrendered Brownie. After proper veterinarian care and rehabilitation, he was
adopted into a devoted home.*

*Speaking for all members of Bernalillo County Sheriff's Office and Berna-
lillo County Animal Care officers, "Hats off to APNM."*

New Mexico is not among the states enacting tougher humane laws with
teeth, improving them with provisions that trigger felony prosecution automatically with the first offense, instead of a later offense. The result of these
provisions is a greater number of prosecutions and convictions. While most
episodes of animal cruelty go unreported, the fact that animal abuse now
occupies the media spotlight has made it more difficult for law enforcement
and courts to plea down the offense or look the other way.

Animal cruelty has so many facets, so many categories, so many laws (whether effective or not) that it would not be possible to elaborate on all of these in this publication. Research has shown that some animal cruelty statutes and ordinances which are most misunderstood, least enforced, or most difficult to enforce include those pertaining to hoarding, chaining, animal fighting, backyard breeding, dangerous dogs and breed specific legislation, Those specifically are addressed in following chapters.

IMPLICATIONS OF ANIMAL CRUELTY ON THE HEALTH AND SAFETY OF COMMUNITIES

"Effective law enforcement response and strict judicial handling of animal abuse crimes is an important element of community-oriented policing. Many see animals as innocent victims, making their victimization more disturbing than human-to-human crimes in which parties could be conceived as sharing some responsibility for the action. Community reaction to animal abuse is strong and emotional. Cruelty to animals is a destabilizing force to municipalities."

– Bernalillo County Sheriff Manuel Gonzales

BERNALILLO
COUNTY
ANIMAL CRUELTY
TASK FORCE

CHAPTER NINE
TRAINING: UNCHAINED

"Chaining removes all owner responsibility from owning a dog. A dog's gift to humanity, his loving nature, is stifled and not allowed to grow and glow. Instead the dog is reduced to his most basic animal functions: protecting its turf, performing bodily functions and eating...sometimes."

– Unknown

Matt Pepper of BCACS was firm in his conviction, "No animal should live its life at the end of a chain. Compassion for those forced to live like this is what drove our ordinance change."

November, 2012 brought great cause for celebration with the announcement by Matt Pepper of BCACS concerning the county's new zero-tolerance no-chain, no-tether animal code.

Cheers and tears of joy came from animal lovers throughout Bernalillo County. Area animal activists, animal control officers, municipal and private animal shelter workers were elated that their efforts of many years had born fruit. Notorious for their no-nonsense belief in a no-chain policy for all dogs, these committed individuals had cared enough for the forgotten, chained animals to spend their efforts and time to relentlessly pursue a no-chain policy. During their many years of many meetings with officials from every arm of government: judges, law enforcement officers, employees and volunteers of community animal shelters and rescues, these dedicated citizens concentrated mainly on the South Valley where most reported chaining violations occur. Because the new BCACS director, Matt Pepper, was also deeply committed to this humane cause, the new ordinance was enacted. Our BCACT has already rescued and removed hundreds of dogs from chains and been instrumental, through education, in keeping that dog in the same home using humane alternatives such as fencing.

Because the effective date of this new code was not for nine months, ample time existed for officers from BCACS to saturate county residents and dog owners with their educational presentations. As they visited community, senior and youth centers, clubs, schools, and almost any event they could wrangle an invitation to, the officers gave detailed explanations of why chaining presents a multitude of dangers for neighbors and their pets as well as affecting health care costs.

"Chained dogs are typically not socialized properly and often not provided high quality care. The result is dogs that are behaviorally unsound and that is what creates a more significant public safety risk than those dogs which are provided a positive environment. A chained dog is made aggressive by chaining and is, therefore, more dangerous, more likely to bite, and more likely to attack when loose from his chain. And it is possible that the victim will require emergency medical care."

His BCACS team continued. "Even with a mobile tether on a swivel, the tether could become entangled on objects within the dog's range of movement. Sometimes dogs are able to break loose and present a menace if they are aggressive. Alternates to chaining such as fencing or dog runs are less dangerous, more humane, and assure an aggressive dog cannot attack anyone outside that designated location." *They presented their audiences with copies of the applicable new county codes and Albuquerque's HEART ordinance in regard to tethering.*

BERNALILLO COUNTY ANIMAL CARE SERVICES CODE 6-43:

A person owning an animal or having custody, care or control of animal shall keep the animal on his or her premises within a secure enclosed pen or in an area with a fence or wall of sufficient height surrounding the perimeter of the property. It shall be unlawful to tether a companion animal as a form of confinement.

HEART ORDINANCE, CITY OF ALBUQUERQUE 9-2-4-2.
THOSE ACTIVITIES WHICH CONSTITUTE ANIMAL CRUELTY:

(G) Chaining an animal to a stationary post, pole, or other immovable object by means of any instrumentally or other extension device including, but not limited to, a chain, tether, coil or rope and leaving such animal unattended for more than one hour in a 24-hour period.

9-2-2-2

- When not accompanied by a person, chaining is prohibited as a means of outdoor confinement for more than one hour during any 24-hour period.

- A trolley system consisting of a cable strung between two fixed points, with a dog on a short lead attached, can be used for up to nine hours in a 24-hour period if a city permit is obtained.

- When chaining is used:
  - It shall weigh no more than an eighth of the animal's weight.
  - It must be affixed to the animal by use of a non-abrasive, well-fitted harness.
  - It must be at least 12 feet long and fastened so that the animal can sit, walk and lie down, using natural motions.
  - It must be unobstructed by objects that may cause the chain or the animal to become entangled.
  - It must have a swivel on both ends.
  - The chained animal shall be surrounded by a barrier sufficient to protect the animal from at-large animals and to prevent children from coming into contact with the chained animal.

CHAINING: FROM THE VIEWPOINT OF THE LAWMAKERS

Animal activists and animal control personnel in New Mexico have, over the past decades, continuously raised the red flag about the needless cruel practice by too many dog owners who persistently chain or tether their dogs for long periods of time. These objections were not just in reference to heavy or short chains, or chains that fit too tightly around the dog's neck, but to any tethering device at all. These pleas fell on deaf ears until 2007 when the legislature ruled to consider these concerns serious enough to request a study by the New Mexico Department of Public Safety (NMDPS) addressing the public safety and humane implications of continually chaining a dog. The core of those findings are discussed below.

Public safety implications stated that chaining increases aggressive behavior in the majority of dogs so that when confronted with a perceived threat, most dogs respond according to their fight-or-flight instinct. A chained dog, unable to take flight, often feels forced to fight and will attack any unfamiliar animal or person who wanders into their territory.

The study's caution was reiterated by HSUS. "A chained dog realizes one thing: he cannot get away, so his only recourse may be to growl, bark, lunge, or bite in self-defense.

When the tethered dog finally does get loose, it is apt to chase and attack any moving object in its path, be it an innocent child, adult or another animal."

A clear dictate from the American Veterinarian Medical Association and American Society of Plastic Surgeons was also included in this NMDPS research. "Confine your dog in a fenced yard or dog run when it is not in the house. Never tether or chain your dog because it can contribute to its aggressive behavior."

Animal Law Resource Center studies animal statutes and codes throughout our states and offers model laws in many animal cruelty categories. One which is germane to chaining is their "Act to Prevent Dogs From Running at Large," which offers legal solutions to dogs running loose, a potentially dangerous situation.

When I contacted National Canine Research Council (NCRC) for permission to use a quote from one of their board members regarding the dangers of chaining of dogs, I was totally unprepared for their reply that the NCRC no longer takes any stand on chaining. They examine each case of dog chaining on a strictly individual basis.

Humane implications in this study revealed that "chaining of dogs also results in overall aggressive behavior due to lack of socialization with humans and other animals, stimulation, proper exercise, limited space, shelter from the elements, proper placed and amounts of food and water, unsanitary conditions and timely checks on the animal's health issues. These tethered animals are forced to eat, sleep, lie, urinate and defecate in their limited, small, disgustingly filthy allotted space. In addition, their solitary confinement on a chain causes them to become helpless victims: vulnerable to attacks from other animals and cruelty from people. The chain often becomes entangled on surrounding stationery objects such as trees, bushes, posts, or, if provided, a shelter structure. It is common occurrence for the tethered animal to hang himself when attempting to jump at or over a nearby object."

Seven years after this study was commissioned by the legislature, New Mexico statutes still do not include a no-chain law. Such legislation, although limited, has been passed in more progressive states such as California, Nevada, and Connecticut and Texas, which address the actual length of time that an animal is chained. The Southwestern states of Arizona, Colorado, New Mexico, Oklahoma and Utah have no laws addressing tethering. Recently other states proposed statutes regarding tethering, but because most were vague or poorly written, they are confusing and easy to misinterpret.

Websites of both APNM and PETA listed studies and comparisons of existing and proposed tethering ordinances (both strong and weak) of more than a hundred communities and states. APNM concluded that only 6 of those 103 towns, including the Albuquerque's HEART ordinance, and 10 of our 33 counties, including Bernalillo County, have sufficient detail and clout in their tethering code to protect the dog and the public.

When queried, Tijeras, New Mexico, responded that their village ordinance listed a provision to address chaining. It existed in one hidden code, **32-D2.** "A chain must be at least 8 feet long."

PETA noted that few American towns address tethering at all and if they do, they impose time limitations specified as, "a reasonable amount of time," or "no longer than is necessary for the person to complete a temporary task," or "during the major part of the day." Some allow tethering if it "does not endanger the health of the dog," or "unreasonably limits the movements of the dog," or "as long as the dog can travel five feet from his shelter." One states that "the chain cannot be too heavy."

So representing much of America as the poster child for their no-chain, zero-tolerance policy is our Bernalillo County. Because of its effectiveness in addressing both the public safety and humane aspects of no-chaining, it negates most possible conflicts with residents that carries the potential threat of liability. "Hats Off" to a recently enacted (2015) ban of chaining of dogs in Silver City, New Mexico.

CHAINING: FROM THE VIEWPOINT OF ANIMAL WELFARE/RESCUE GROUPS

Because a no-chain/no-tether policy is at the very heart of the policies of NMDOG, Angela and her volunteers jumped right in to further help the efforts of BCACS. Adopting as their fencing motto, "Unchain BernCo," NMDOG sent out pleas via the internet for donations of fencing supplies from which they skillfully constructed fences and dog houses for approved and interested dog owners in the county. Three years have not produced a week in which NMDOG volunteers are not sawing wood, cutting chain link, stapling, digging, and doing so with a smile for the dog whose life their fence will drastically change for the better.

NMDOG's website also lists Angela as an informed speaker for any community wishing to convince their officials to enact a similar no-chain/no-tether animal code. This produced Facebook pages "Unchain Santa Fe" and "Chain-Free Las Cruces and Dona Ana County." These proved to be very successful in coordinating community efforts to end the cruel chaining of animals."

In an attempt to provide alternatives to the chaining of dogs, near-by Placitas Animal Rescue, located in adjacent Sandoval County, hosted a gathering to construct 50 dog houses, which were distributed to needy homes within the locale. PETA, the largest animal rights organization in the world, has published a guide, *Legal Shelter for Your Dog*, with recommendations to better care for those pets who spend most of their time outside, many with sub-standard housing. An added bonus of this free pamphlet are simply-worded directions to build a dog house/shelter.

Many of the dogs rescued by municipal and private shelters must be retrained before they are adoptable. And the majority of those suffer from being previously chained. For both the rescuers and the dogs, it is a long, hard road, filled with disappointment, before they are trained and tested to be released, safe for adoption.

This should be ample reason for citizens to call upon their commissioners, councilors, mayors and legislators to propose upgrades in our tethering laws (with tough penalties) which will result in the increased safety of the public and the humane treatment of pets. Strong laws and serious enforcement, along with an educational campaign, are the keys for those changes, and they are in the hands of the community leaders, answerable to you and to me.

CHAINING: FROM THE VIEWPOINT OF THE DOG

MY WORLD
Written by Heather Leughmeyer

Twelve years ago this heavy chain
Became the world I knew
Rapidly the dust replaced
The space where grass once grew
At first I cried from loneliness
I haven't cried in years
I gave that up to hopelessness
They never see my tears.

When winter comes I dream of spring
As I shiver through the night
My water freezes into ice
While my world turns into white
When summer comes I long for fall
The sun is unforgiving
As my water quickly disappears
So does my thirst for living.

This circle of dirt beneath my feet
Has seen a million paces
As I have watched pass by me
At least a thousand faces
All of them too busy
To stop and be a friend
I'd pull and tug and wag my tail
The chain would always end.

Twelve years ago this rusty chain
Became the world I know
A world of isolation
A world where grass won't grow
A world of bitter coldness
A world of searing heat
A world where no one comforts you
When your heart beats its last beat.

CHAPTER TEN

TRAINING: "DANGEROUS DOGS"

> "Behaviorally, dogs are not a product of breed—while clearly there are some differences—but rather a product of their owner and their environment."
>
> – Matt Pepper, President,
> CEO Michigan Animal Humane Society

"Dangerous Dogs" present an unknown but frightening situation. Always keep in mind that BCACT's priority and main responsibility is to secure the safety of its citizens.

There exists a multitude of misunderstanding of this term "Dangerous Dog." To ease your understanding, I am using my own classification of two categories of "Dangerous Dogs," each pertaining to different circumstances, different laws and different crimes.

Most individuals, be you a citizen, a member of a law enforcement team or even a burglar, hold the opinion that dogs are a definite deterrent to crime. The dogs do not need to be big, aggressive or dangerous. They only need to be vocal, sending an alarm that all is not right for homeowners or neighbors to become alert, possibly concerned enough to call the home or the police…something might be amiss. Vocal dogs who are not particularly dangerous can bring that unwanted attention that burglars stray away from when exercising their breaking and entering skills. These household dogs are not "Dangerous Dogs."

But there are residents and businesses who choose to protect their property with seriously dangerous, aggressive guard dogs, registered and licensed, safely restrained according to the law. Emphasizing the safety of the community, city codes for these dogs address many regulations (fencing, signage and permits) for their owners. Because our citizens are protected by these enforced codes, these guard dogs are statistically not the ones legally categorized as "Dangerous Dogs," so they represent my category one.

My second category of "Dangerous Dogs" speaks to those that pose a potential risk to the public safety of our citizens and their pets. They are the dogs about which "Dangerous Dog" ordinances and news articles are written. These canines are those usually owned by irresponsible, possibly cruel or neglectful, home owners who have often self-trained (versus professionally trained) their canine to be dangerously aggressive. Many of these animals have been so criminally neglected so that, in turn, their behavior has turned aggressive. They present a lurking threat to neighbors, immediate family members and any animals residing/visiting in the immediate vicinity.

In a position statement, ASPCA discusses the term "Dangerous Dogs" from the perspective of public safety as well as the dog owner. "In order for dogs to live harmoniously with people and with other companion animals, it is critical to hold guardians responsible for the proper supervision of their dogs and for any actions on their part that either create or encourage aggressive behavior. At the same time laws that target "'Dangerous Dogs" must be mindful of the rights of pet guardians and afford them due process."

Laws in most states, counties and communities (including New Mexico) make inadequate and uneducated attempts at addressing "Dangerous Dogs" or at protecting their citizens from their sudden, vicious behavior, often lethal. It's not illegal to own a "Dangerous Dog" in most cities, but laws require the owners to keep their dogs leashed while off their property, keep a minimum in liability insurance, erect required warning signage and permit unscheduled inspections of the property by the city.

Occurring weekly and nationally are gory and heart-breaking injuries and deaths of humans and household pets who, while being walked by owners, are attacked by vicious dogs in their own area neighborhoods. Ivan Gurrola, a first grader in Floyd, New Mexico, was honored by the mayor for his "bravery while facing a dangerous animal." By placing himself between an approaching angry dog and his four-year-old sister, Ivan's badly bitten leg required 17 staples and his sister was spared injury.

Supervision of these dogs is a must, inside and outside. Owners of aggressive/dangerous dogs should understand the proven risks they pose to children in the home, as the residence is one of the leading locations for grave attacks by aggressive "family" dogs on children.

Massachusetts Assistant District Attorney, Tracey Cusick, shared one of his strongest jury instructions concerning "Dangerous Dogs." "It is a well-known fact that dogs may be trained to attack people."

These frightening attacks on humans and pets, serious public safety issues for all communities, always result in a surge of editorials and blogs pleading for stronger "Dangerous Dog" ordinances, and stronger penalties for aggressive dogs off-leash, a definite danger to the public at large as well as to wandering or abandoned pets. Sometimes this front-page attention has brought forth the expected promises by government agencies to right these wrongful injuries and deaths and better secure our neighborhoods for pets and citizens alike. But if the concerned citizens do not keep this issue in the public eye, the fervor will most likely quiet down. Time will pass, other "urgencies" will capture headlines and their attempts of these concerned citizens to rectify the existing soft laws surrounding "Dangerous Dogs" will once again be met with government indifference or bureaucratic bungling.

Little punitive action is usually taken even though most existing communities have legally-mandated protective measures in their existing city ordinance which allow animal control officers to seize a dog who presents an immediate danger, or issue a search warrant if there is cause to believe that the dog poses danger to public safety. And usually no new or revised codes to make our communities safer from these aggressive dogs are proposed and signed into law by city commissioners or councilors. It has been demonstrated that downplaying the needs of their constituents by the purposeful inaction of their city officials has sometimes led to a concerned, angry and mob-minded citizenry.

Sometimes charges are filed against the owners of dogs who maul or kill neighborhood dogs, and the case, instead of offering a glimmer of retribution for the owner of the injured or deceased pet, becomes a travesty of justice. The offending animal's owner is charged with violation of the leash laws, no permanent seizure, no fines, no jail time, no mandated behavioral training, and usually a suspended sentence, a sure indication of the court's assessment of the value of the lost life of the mangled pet. Example the 2015 Albuquerque, New Mexico occurrence, (in the Mayor's neighborhood) in which an aggressive Rottweiler, loose (not for the first time), viciously attacked and skinned a leashed 11 pound, white Terrier, Angel. Her teary owner, devastated and in shock, kept repeating, "All I did was go for a walk in the neighborhood." The hearing resulted in no fine or jail time for the careless owners of a proven "Dangerous Dog."

Various town councils have proposed remedies which include mandatory seizing of all dogs whose behavior has resulted in the wounding or killing of a person or another animal. The offending dog would become city property until a hearing officer decides that dog's fate: it could be returned to the owner with restrictions, turned over to rescue groups for behavioral rehabilitation, or be euthanized. Other suggestions include requiring a larger amount of liability insurance for the owner of a deemed "Dangerous Dog."

But there are some communities in which "Dangerous Dogs" are recognized by law enforcement and animal control officers as a serious threat and are dealt with firmly. In another New Mexico community, Belen, a long distance runner was attacked in October, 2015 by a pack of five dogs. The animals were immediately seized by the Police Chief and their owner was charged with having vicious animals, having animals that were responsible for the biting of a person, improper restraint of vicious animals, allowing vicious animals to run at large, possessing animals without rabies vaccinations or city licenses.

Because most communities with "Dangerous Dog" codes incorrectly employ this nebulously defined term, without the reference points of standardized behavioral tests for the dogs in question, they encounter unfortunate and risky situations for both the dogs and the humans as well as poorly prosecuted court cases. These results are easily preventable through consultations with ALDF, who offers professional aid in writing or editing "Dangerous Dog" codes, resulting in legal protection for both, with proper documentation and without the usual inconsistencies.

"Dangerous Dog" is widely misused and misunderstood by law enforcement and animal control officers, the court and citizens alike. This is because the term "Dangerous Dog" does not recognize that most dogs react to an abusive situation, past or present. There exist many situations in which aggressive behavior is justified, such as when a dog is protecting itself or its litter, its owner, the owner's property. It is also possible that, because of past abuse, the dog has reason to fear that abusive individual. The skills of an animal behaviorist would enhance any animal care staff who had the funding.

Many of the millions of dogs euthanized in America's shelters today because of supposed aggressive behavioral problems are given a bad rap, an incorrect and unfair diagnosis of their behavior. That behavior can usually be attributed not just to the abuse of the pet but also to the irresponsible behavior, lack of supervision and training of their owners as stated by ASPCA. Usually the owners' lack of accountability cannot be documented, and the victim, the other witness, cannot speak for itself.

While I discussed with Sheriff Gonzales and his deputies their concept of an accurate picture of "Dangerous Dog," Undersheriff Rudy Mora, nationally recognized for his contribution to working dogs by the California

Narcotics Canine Association, emphasized the importance of reminding canine owners. "Often dogs react to stressful situations as animals, not as human's cuddly pets. It is that reaction that often causes their behavior to be labeled as aggressive whereas, if the owner would have taken preventive measures, with this possible threat in mind, the dangerous situation would probably have not occurred."

The charge of all individuals of authority in municipal and private shelters is to protect the public from a "Dangerous Dog" and the dog from further cruelty. These administrators must demonstrate the courage and skills to recognize when an impounded dog poses a danger in the community…to the families who adopt him and those with whom he will have contact, not to mention the kennel workers whose responsibilities are to care for the dog…before adoption. Although the decision to euthanize a potentially "Dangerous Dog" is a tough one, it is the right one, the one which ultimately affords the least danger to society and to the dog in question.

An easy, low-cost, preventive approach was offered during this discussion by Undersheriff Greg Rees. "Every dog in a shelter has a history, usually unknown, violent or neglectful. Shelters have an opportunity to be proactive and educational for their prospective dog owners. The down-time at an animal shelter (waiting for adoption papers to process and be approved) could be used to alert pet owners to possible dangerous situations. Many of these which are accepted as part of their family's everyday life are perceived differently by their pet. Using a video educational format, the video screen in the waiting room would continually replay safety precautions for dog owners. These should include cautions about food aggression, possession aggression, lightning and thunder reactions, and interactions between other family pets, tone of voice, establishing your owner dominance without fear, harsh or angry words or actions. The necessity of ongoing, reinforced training all dogs will be stressed."

It is taken for granted that these dogs present yet another hazard, that facing the vulnerable workers and employees of shelters where these dogs are impounded. But it would never enter the minds of most citizens that the shelter administrators would be responsible for the release of "Dangerous Dogs" to the general public as adoptees…adoptees into the unsuspecting homes humming with the sounds and activities of children, other pets, families.

For most of 2015, investigative reports about such unthought-of occurrences at AAWD headlined the *Albuquerque Journal*. They exposed the public safety implications of AAWD's recently changed internal policy which allowed the adoptions of the shelter's proven "Dangerous Dogs," without notifying the new owners/volunteer organizations of their documented histories of biting children, attacking AAWD workers or maiming, sometimes killing other dogs.

What a shocker when two AAWD complainants, a staff behaviorist and an animal program administrator, filed a formal complaint against AAWD, March 2015 to the Inspector General! They cited 215 shelter dogs who failed the shelter's SAFER canine behavioral test and were not recommended for adoption by the staff behaviorist.

According to a director mandate, all were to be offered for adoption, including those with documented aggressive histories. Eight cases were documented in which the director demanded that the breed of the dog be changed to make the dog more adoptable and that its SAFER test results and negative behavioral evaluations also be withheld from the public. More than 100 of these dogs were allowed to be adopted without adequate, if any, warning to their new owners and an additional 32 were given to unaware rescue groups. Eighty-seven of these dogs who did not pass the SAFER test were released back to their owners by AAWD, regardless of their impact on public safety. Histories of these 87 revealed that some had previously attacked, bitten or killed other animals, members of their human families or kennel workers; one reported permanent damage, losing part of a finger.

The filed complaint quotes the director stating, "AAWD should not be concerned if a dog in our shelter has a history of killing, especially if the victim was a small dog. We should become concerned only if the animal has killed large dogs."

Past AAWD internal policies required that the future of those dogs who receive a negative test result from SAFER depended on an additional assessment from the staff behaviorist. It was this behaviorist who was instrumental in bringing this serious situation to light and was later forced to resign. With great emotion, she explained her conviction. It was her conscience and concern for the safety of her already injured and stressed co-workers, as well as the families of adopters of these dangerous canines that caused her to act. She considered her decision a no-brainer, because it should be the moral obligation at AAWD to offer safe companions for adoption to the public.

Also fired was the kennel supervisor in charge of euthanasia who had also refused to cooperate in the director's dictate to release these potentially "Dangerous Dogs" on an unaware public. Her assessment was mirrored by the appalling findings of three separate city and private teams investigating these situations at AAWD which implicated the director in severe, purposeful negligence.

Several follow-up investigative reports by the *Albuquerque Journal* reveal that this risky situation had been occurring on a regular basis since her 2009 appointment as the current director. In his complaint, animal program analyst, Jim Ludwig, presented a grim picture, as carried in the *Albuquerque Journal.* "Our responsibility is not just to the animals staring us in the face as they stand in our cages. We have a responsibility to the animals and children who are out of sight and out of mind…who might pay the price if we unleash the dogs we should euthanize for public safety reasons."

An unidentified kennel worker suggested, "These unethical and unsafe administrative decisions were reflective of our director's continually-mentioned, obsessive goal to have AAWD considered a no-kill shelter. Our monthly intake and euthanasia figures printed in the *Journal* paint a rosy picture for our shelter animals, but behind the scenes, nothing could be further from the truth."

However, many state animal lovers dismissed these accusations, current policies and unsafe actions. They credit AAWD's current director for bringing this shelter out of the Dark Ages, saving thousands of lives of area pets (euthanasia rate has been decreased by 35%), and promoting innovative, humane and progressive ideas in the adoption of those sheltered pets.

The ASPCA-approved SAFER behavior test is administered by many shelters across the nation to determine aggressive, unfriendly, unsocial or dangerous behavior in their intake animals. It also can provide indications of dominance, submission, fear or food aggression. The test examines stability, confidence, shyness, friendliness, protectiveness, prey instincts, play drive, self-defense instincts and ability to distinguish between threatening and non-threatening situations. Part of temperament can be hereditary, but influenced by the environment and the owner's training or lack of.

There are other behavioral tests for shelter dogs; nothing is standardized, and it would be foolish to credit the results of such testing to be the "end-all." Behavioral training by professionals has proven to shape a dog's attitude and response towards people, children, other dogs, things and places. All living beings are imperfect, so there is no perfect canine to fit the needs of all households, evidence the incredulous excuses that people concoct when surrendering their household pet for adoption. Even with the input of a licensed behaviorist, any behavioral exam can only offer a partial assessment of a dog's temperament. This places the grave responsibility of making a final disposition of a "Dangerous Dog" on sometimes shaky ground.

Due to political motivation and public perception, several states, including Texas, have been experiencing a deluge of "Dangerous Dog" ordinances in their cities. Some even defy federal law, state statutes, health and safety codes already established to define and set procedures, hearing requirements, and disposition options for the court.

Further muddling the waters, these "Dangerous Dog" ordinances differ in their definitions and approaches throughout towns and states, leaving most open to a wide range of individual interpretation. Many municipal codes (such as those in Clovis and Ruidoso, New Mexico) boast with powerful, but widely interpretative and dangerous statements about the disposition of such dogs. All lack a professional description of "vicious/dangerous," and are void of credible standardized behavioral tests or any professional input of a behaviorist.

Presently animal law practitioners must rely on these poorly written provisions in state statutes and city ordinances. To ensure greater public safety and give fair behavioral assessments of each dog in question, city ordinances can solicit the help of ALDF to re-define their "Dangerous Dog" code, making it safer, stronger, more balanced, easier to enforce and less confusing for both our courts and our dog owners.

CHAPTER ELEVEN

TRAINING: BREED-SPECIFIC TRUTHS

"I have a dream that one day I will not be judged by my appearance but by the content of my character."

– Martin Luther King,
adapted by Wisconsin Voters for Companion Animals

Eyebrows rose and mouths dropped when I obliterated the myth that all Pit Bull Terrier type dogs are violent. The Journal of American Veterinary Medical Association revealed that their studies found no evidence that one kind of dog is more likely to injure a human than others.

Our Matt Pepper was firm in his professional assessment, "The behavior of most dogs, any breed, are usually indicative of the treatment and training they receive from their owners as well as their living conditions (i.e. chained outside, no shelter, water, food or needed vet care."

We need to follow his advice during our boots-on-the-ground, South Valley sweeps as we will encounter mainly Pit Bull Terrier crosses. It is important for your safety and that of the dog that you are well acquainted with the actual facts pertaining to this much maligned, abused breed.

Today's pit bull is a descendant of the original English bull-baiting dog, bred to bite and hold large animals around the head. It is easy to recognize by its compact, muscular build and powerful jaw. Most of the Pit Bull type dogs we encounter in our community are the result of random breeding and are considered to be the result of cross-breeding with or between one of these purebreds: the American Staffordshire Terrier, Pit Bull Terrier, American Bulldog or English Bulldog. All have histories of being bred for fierce combat with other animals. A characteristic behavioral trait of this breed is that, once its intense aggression has been triggered, it persists.

Because 'baiting' large animals was outlawed in the 1800s, owners began fighting their own any-breed dogs against each other for fun. They discovered that by crossing these larger and slower Pit Bull dogs with the smaller and faster Terriers, a more agile fighting dog resulted. Today those specifically selected dogs, bred to fight, could have the tendency to fight with other breeds. "Could" does not imply that they are unpredictable in behavior or that they cannot be trusted around other animals. "Could" most always depends on their relationship with their owner.

Any dog of any breed can be menacing when intentionally or unintentionally raised to be aggressive. Sometimes their aggression is not a learned behavior but the result of a neglectful situation...or both. Unfortunately, Pit Bull breeds often find themselves in disgusting, abusive and highly neglectful conditions in many communities and are at greater risk for developing aggressive behavioral patterns. These dogs are continually put to violent uses (dogfighting, guard dogs) and are intentionally exposed to violent situations by their owners, who must be held legally and morally responsible and take the blame for the behavior of their dogs. High-risk dogs such as Pit Bull Terriers are considered to be part of the high-risk life style chosen by their owners, most of who have considerable more criminal convictions than owners of low-risk dogs.

A big shift in serious negative sentiment toward Pit Bull Terrier-types began in the 1980s. In the beginning, it didn't seem to be the breed itself that had communities in fear, but people were questioning the aggressive manner in which their owners (most of questionable character) were choosing to train and abuse these dogs. Dogfighting, by then illegal in most states (not New Mexico), was making a comeback and Pit Bull Terrier-types were the fighter of choice. Training them as aggressive guard dogs also became common practice among an unsavory element including drug dealers and gang members.

With more and more originally non-combative dogs being trained by their criminal owners to be dangerous, there followed an increasing number of gruesome dog attacks reported by the press and social media.

2014 brought three tragic incidents to one New Mexico community, Roswell. Three Pit Bull Terriers escaped from their Doggy Saviors No-Kill Shelter and attempted to maul a nine-year-old boy. A few months later a Pit Bull Terrier-cross killed a small family dog while the small nine-year-old girl held onto the leash at a soccer game. The mayor's knee-jerk reaction (which was the third tragedy) was his temporarily banning all adoptions from the local animal shelter by all in-state rescue organizations.

A 1985, Tijeras, New Mexico mauling of a nine-year-old girl by her grandfather's four Pit Bull Terriers brought forth a moving search, 30 years later in 2015, by the victim, Laura, wanting to thank her nurse Angie, who tenderly and compassionately cared for a critically injured, nine-year-old child, who bravely endured the pain of 30 surgeries. This loving nurse taught her small, insecure and frightened patient to look beyond her deformities and scars to see her shinning inner beauty and courage. The 2015 personal interest story of *Albuquerque Journal* columnist, Joline Gutierrez Kruger brought about a surprise reunion between these two strongly connected souls in the Seattle area. The two women (victim and her caregiver) had lived but an hour and a half apart for the past 18 years.

It was due to this horrific incident that Tijeras enacted the toughest Pit Bull ban of the country, allowing animal control officers to seize and destroy them on sight without compensation to the owner. But because this ordinance violated the state law, "Extreme animal cruelty, a felony, to animals exists when a person kills an animal without lawful justification," it was rewritten as only a ban on breed-specific Pit Bull Terriers or crosses of such.

Such attacks by family dogs are usually met by a frenzy of community activity. Instead of demanding meaningful sentences and larger fines for the purposefully irresponsible owners of these vicious animals, many states and communities rushed (as early as 1986) to enact BSL (breed specific legislation) banning the ownership of Pit Bull Terrier type dogs. Currently 19 states either prohibit municipalities from regulating or outlawing certain dogs based on breed alone; some require proof of a dog's supposed dangerous qualities beyond mere breed.

Considered as ineffective legislation and a waste of public resources by professionals in the dog industry, humane associations throughout America also described these bans as ineffective and dangerous because they create a false illusion of the public safety.

During one such Ohio council hearing for the enactment of BSL, a wise councilman voiced his "Nay" vote along with his astute observation that dogs are not the issue. "Owners are."

The American Kennel Club also urged the law to instead target the dog owners and warned of the further dangers of BSL. By branding the breed with an unfair and biased stigma of dangerous has resulted in an overload of this breed in our nation's shelters and kennels, with only a small percent (approximately 20%) being adopted. That means the greatest percentage of this breed, once incarcerated, are euthanized.

In the Southwest you are speaking of one-third of all dogs in municipal or county shelters. Slowly, national attitudes are changing as evidenced by the recent study of Dr. Weiss of ASPCA documented an increase in Pit

Bull types being adopted, fewer left in shelters and fewer euthanized. However these dogs are still the most common dog-type found in shelters, and the most often euthanized.

And yet 292 military bases and 763 U.S. cities in 40 different states have BSL laws. Council Bluffs, Iowa and Denver, (even though Colorado has anti-BSL laws) implemented BSL ordinances in 1989. By banning the dog, it stands to reason that they also inadvertently banned the dog owners, because both have since reported a significant drop in serious Pit Bull-type dog bites.

Another result of this outcry by an uninformed public for BSL is an over-load of Pit Bull Terriers and similar breeds in city shelters. Also victims of aggressive dogs, though seldom considered, are those who work in municipal or private shelters as employees or volunteers. Animal welfare organizations as well as volunteer and municipal shelters usually have little or no knowledge as to the backgrounds or prior abuse of their rescued animals: treatment, training or lack of, or conditions in which the pet lived or endured. All of these affect an animal's behavior.

An example of such a dog's sudden mercurial and violent behavior was an unprovoked attack which occurred on the 90-acre grounds of Fur and Feather Animal Assistance, the largest New Mexico no-kill animal shelter, located in Pie Town. In 2014, while feeding an unadoptable Pit Bull Terrier rescue, the owner was ferociously attacked. His life was saved by a walkie-talkie 911 call to his wife, who while pulling his body from the raging dog, also sustained permanent injuries.

There exists no single universally accepted and utilized database for the reporting of fatal or non-fatal dog bites. Although Wikipedia, DogsBite and the National Canine Research Council (NCRC) reports include incomplete and sometimes conflicting documentation, their statistics give the reader the most defining picture of dog bites in America

Approximately 78.2 million dogs are pets in American homes, and the NCRC has recorded an average of 4.5 million dog bites per year with 80.4% (four out of five) causing no injury or being an injury too slight for medical treatment. Only 0.01% were serious injuries, requiring hospitalization.

Their 2010-2014 analyses for reported human fatalities from dog bites present an eye-opening conclusion. Although the majority of the violent dogs involved in this five year period of all reported deaths were Pit Bull-types (representing but 5% of all the dogs in our nation), their relationship was described as family pets. They were labeled as such because they belonged-to or lived with not only the mother, father and child, but sometimes with grandparents, sons, daughters, step-fathers, step-mothers, live-in girlfriends and live-in boyfriends.

These so designated family pets injured a family member in 69% of previously reported animal-abusive households; in comparison, this figure in non-abusive households was a mere 6%. This documentation points directly to the lack of parental supervision during these deadly attacks: 74 (86%) of the 86 children who were victims during this five year period were only ages two days to five years. For these 86 attacks, I located an appalling small number of criminal charges (11) of child neglect or abuse or in those cases even though it was proven that the majority of the deaths occurred when the child was unsupervised. Because of the sheer size and power of these guard dogs trained by their owners, they should never be left unsupervised with children or other pets. Some have a neighborhood history of attacking other area animals, possibly indicative of a tragedy waiting to happen.

Diane Jessup a retired Washington animal control employee, tried to soften these violent encounters when she explained that when an animal shows aggression to another animal, it is not always indicative that they're dangerous to a person. Hunting dogs and Greyhounds often attack and kill rabbits as well as other small animals. Although a dog can be devastatingly aggressive to other dogs if he's allowed to be, that same dog isn't necessarily going to be aggressive to humans.

Andi posed the question. *Is the Pit Bull Terrier to be yet another animal to be included in the long list of those man has destroyed? Or could it be possible that, through intense education of the owners of Pit Bull Terriers, our city, county, state and national legislators, as well as our law enforcement and animal control officers, we can save this maligned breed?*

Cesar Millan showed caution. "This would be an admirable quest, but it would require considerable education, training and effort to restore this breed, Pit Bull Terriers, to its rightful place as a faithful and trusted family dog. It would require tough legislation with serious law enforcement and stiff penalties for owners who perpetrate violence in their dogs. That is a tall order, but I feel we can help."

ASPCA Rescue Central, PittiLoveRescue, ItsThePits, and a multitude of others, who can be accessed online, are scurrying to educate the public to place the blame for this violence on their irresponsible, violent owners, thus keeping this breed afloat.

Another successful rehabilitation and placement organization for rescued Pit Bull types is Animal Farm Foundation (AFF) in Dulchess County, New York, which provides Assistance Dog training for their shelter-rescued

Pit Bull type dogs and donates these service dogs to veterans needing help recovering from the stresses of violent encounters. These once thrown-away now rescued and rehabilitated dogs have been given a second chance and have been trained to easily and quickly meet their owner's crisis by climbing on-top and awakening their restlessly sleeping owners from a frightening flashback, calming them when crowds trigger a panic attack or stabilizing their owners when vertigo or poor mobility might cause a fall. A former marine, suffering from experiences in Afghanistan, received an AFF dog, and marveled how it changed his life so that he could attend college, shop in area malls and begin to allow the public back into his once-solitary life.

Pits for Patriots, provides Comfort Training for their rescued Pit Bulls and donates them to veterans and first responders: police and firemen, who easily identify and bond with the Pit Bulls because they, too have suffered the severe traumatic experiences.

Without missing a beat, the website of DogsBite countered the above press release by Associated Press by releasing their opinion that there exist at least 100 other more suitable breeds with more reliable behavior than Pit Bull types to perform service tasks for the disabled.

Although Pit Bull Terrier types compromise most of the dogs rescued or surrendered during BCACT's unannounced visits to area neighborhoods, 80% of these rescues have been successfully rehabilitated and adopted into new and responsible homes. Our community through AAWD has been supportive in efforts to end the cycle of public misconception, homelessness and euthanasia negatively affecting <u>New Mexico's</u> Pitties. Their free one-hour training classes (four different agendas) for Pit Bulls and their families were very successful and received with enthusiasm by the dog owners.

I consider this maligned and intentionally tortured breed to be victims, and I am asking you to include them in your circle of compassion. It is our duty as members of BCACT to keep safe all members of a family, including pets of any type or breed. To put all of this into perspective I offer some additional information that I discovered. In the United States, approximately: 2,000 children are killed every year by their parents, through abuse and neglect (A child is 800 times more likely to be killed by their adult caretaker than by a dog).

Stay alert. Stay safe and remember that all dogs, not only those of a particular breed, can, suddenly, without warning, turn violent.

CHAPTER TWELVE
TRAINING: ANIMAL FIGHTING

"Dogs used in dogfighting are the victims of the crime as well as individuals, not the instruments of the crime."
— Dr. Randall Lockwood, Sr. VP, ASPCA
Forensic Sciences and Anti-Cruelty Projects

If today's society were to be judged by the humaneness of our people and those laws they have enacted, our prevalence of animal fighting would be a disgrace. Although illegal as of 2013 in state and federal governments, these obstacles contribute to this stigma.

- *Current animal fighting laws, penalties and enforcement tools are weak, ineffectual, inconsistent, ambiguous and confusing.*

- *State statutes not only differ; some contradict, and others actually contribute to the crime. Possession of animals for fighting may be legal or only a misdemeanor offense.*

- *Clandestine locations in the difficult-to-find, rural localities of America are chosen for these fight-to-the-death matches.*

- *Often more lucrative than drug trafficking, animal fighting is a business fueled by greed.*

- *The "interstate or foreign commerce" requirement allows federal court jurisdiction over an activity otherwise regulated by the state.*

The Federal Animal Fighting Prohibition Enforcement Act of 2007 dictates felony penalty statutes for the interstate commerce, (importing, exporting, selling, buying, delivering, receiving or transporting) as well as the possession, training of fighting dogs, fighting cocks and paraphernalia.

A maximum federal penalty of five years in jail and a $250,000 fine can be imposed for each offense. In 2014 an amendment was added prohibiting the attendance at animal fights and adding an additional penalty if minors are brought to such events.

In New Mexico a conviction of dogfighting is a fourth degree felony, while cockfighting is a petty misdemeanor. In shame and disgust of dogfighting practices, the Baltimore, Maryland Mayor's proposal to prohibit the possession of dogfighting equipment was approved unanimously by the City Council. This vote followed the indictments of 22 individuals involved in dogfighting fighting operations in 18 locations in Maryland and West Virginia, in which 225 dogs were seized and at least 20 weapons. Also confiscated was animal fighting paraphernalia and dog breeding stands which are referred to by dogfighters as "rape stands." Several of those arrested had ties to dogfighting in New York and North Carolina.

"Kentucky's shiner," according to Debbie Wimsatt, of Lost and Found Pets in Kentucky, "is an embarrassment for the United States." She spares no words. "Not only is our state known as 'the best place to be an animal abuser,' but our legislators refuse to pass any bill related to animal abuse. Even with continually introduced **HB 154** which seeks to prohibit the possession of four-legged animals for the purpose of fighting (Kentucky is the only state without this statute), the lobbying game commences with objections from the special interest groups including The Kentucky Houndsmen, League of Kentucky Sportsmen and others in the hunting community."

Both HSUS and ALDF rate Kentucky's anti-cruelty laws as the "worst" in the United States.

DOGFIGHTING—*Dogfighting has been a curse on humanity for decades, and its participants need to be attacked with aggressive laws and enforcement.*

Two specially bred and trained dogs (usually Pit Bull Terrier crosses) fight, often for as long as two hours, with uninhibited viciousness, and usually to the death, in a pit located in a rural area, for the purpose of amusement but primarily for gambling (sometimes the stakes can be as high as hundreds of thousands of dollars). Most organized dogfighting rings have a minimum of 30 people involved. They exist because of the participation of many individuals — breeders, trainers, property owners, organizers, spectators and gamblers to name a few. There are several types of dogfighting organizations: street level, hobbyist and professional. These names represent the seriousness of their involvement.

While state laws provide a way to prosecute the individuals who are most directly involved with an animal fighting venture, stopping a single animal fighting operation is not as effective as shutting down its entire support network. In addition to offering charges related to spectatorship and the presence of minors, federal law provides a way to prosecute the individuals who support animal fighting ventures by supplying animals, equipment or money across state lines or to foreign countries.

In his 2007 speech to Congress, U.S. Senator Robert Byrd of <u>West Virginia</u>, a recipient of HSUS and PETA People of the Year awards presented a precise description of dogfighting. "Dogfighting is a brutal, sadistic event motivated by barbarism of the worst sort and cruelty of the worst, worst, worst sadistic kind. One is left wondering, who are the real animals... the creatures inside the ring, or the creatures outside the ring...May God help those poor souls who'd be so cruel. I am confident that the hottest places in hell are reserved for the souls of sick and brutal people who hold God's creatures in such brutal and cruel contempt. Barbaric!"

The spectators at this grisly carnival are usually actively involved in money laundering, racketeering, use and distribution of drugs, possession and sale of stolen goods, concealed weapons, and other types of criminal activity including prostitution and murder. Activities of both the spectators and the dog owners could be likened to leeches as they feed off one another.

These were not always, by nature, particularly volatile and vicious-natured canines, but dogs who, through intentional abuse, neglect and cruelty have been taught to behave in an aggressive manner, by their owner, for the money, the unspeakable bloodbath, the excitement of the kill and the self-importance it gives the owner. Wins in that bloodied ring can be a source of considerable income for spectators and owners, although the dogs involved in these cruel bloodbaths usually die of their many, severe injuries: broken bones, loss of blood, dehydration, exhaustion and other life threatening injuries. For the losing dogs who do not die in the ring, their few remaining hours are gruesome as they are usually drowned or bludgeoned to death, in the ring, as a sacrifice to appease the crowd. Few might be kept to serve as bait-dogs, fodder with which to teach the Pit Bull Terriers to tear, maim and maul the opposing dog.

For the surviving winning dogs, their training and care ranges from systematic to haphazard, indifferent to cruel. Most are neglected and abused by the owners, whose ignorant creed reasons that the more hunger pain, punishment and beatings that a dog endures, the more ferocious a fighter he will become. These dogs are chained, heavy and short, often wrapped around weights or tires filled with cement. A Pit Bull was found wandering the streets of the South Valley, March 2015, with 60 pound chains wrapped around his neck, either for training or punishment? However, a few sophisticated dog-fighting rings do exist with treadmills, weights and a separate room designated for the breeding female.

Dogfighting owners are not known to be well-read, so they do not realize or possibly they are so calloused that they do not care about the negative impact that the dog's sparse diet, usually without nutrition, has on their performance. But these canines are pumped up with vitamins, stimulants and narcotics. Most attempts at conditioning are uneducated guesses or voodoo-like concoctions prepared by their owners and involve the use of drugs, both legal and illegal. Anabolic steroids are administered to enhance muscle mass and to increase aggressiveness. Narcotics can increase aggression as well as mask the pain of those gaping injuries sustained during a fight, which seldom receive veterinary care but might be stapled shut, at best.

Owners often crop the tails and ears of their dogs for two reasons: to limit the body area exposed during the fight and to make it more difficult for the opposing dog to "read," through the movement of the tail or ears, the reaction or intention of their dog. Before a match their teeth are filed to sharp points as to inflict greater damage and often their skin and fur is sprayed with a poisonous substance to weaken their opponent.

Flourishing from San Francisco to <u>New York City,</u> these gruesome matches occur all over America, from an organized event in a dirty, well-hidden, sometimes elaborate arena in rural locations to an unorganized street-level temporary ring in urban sites: dingy and dark alleys, basements, parks, vacant lots, abandoned buildings, warehouses and playgrounds. Because it is conducted in clandestine circumstances, the average public is unaware. Our unincorporated areas of Bernalillo County are definitely active sites.

Indications of a dogfighting ring residing or operating within a neighborhood can include a greater-than-usual number of "Lost Pet" signs tacked to utility poles, street signs, fences, gates, windows, doors, cars and businesses. This is because these "Lost Pets," including rabbits and other small mammals, are needed as live bait to train, condition and foster aggression and confidence in these fighting dogs. "Free Pets" advertised online and in newspapers are another source for bait-dogs. The longevity of these innocents is short, but they endure slow psychological and physical torture before their certain last breath. Their suffering, often viewed as entertainment, is great and without mercy or mourning.

Bloodied, beaten, mauled and mutilated bodies of six bait-dogs were recently tossed into <u>New Mexico's</u> Conejo County Solid Waste Center during *the period of one week. All showed signs of severe choking, mauling and neglect; four had one of their rear legs chopped off; two were still clinging to life. The one survivor, an American Pit Bull, Eddie, was covered with severe puncture wounds and scars. Although he weighed in at a slight 37 pounds, his healthy appetite helped him to reach a healthy 82 pounds while undergoing rehabilitation at a nearby dog sanctuary. APNM offered a $10,000 reward.*

In 2013 occurred the second largest dogfighting raid in U.S. history in which 367 dogs were rescued from multi-state dogfighting properties in Alabama, Mississippi, Texas and Georgia. Most of these animals had spent their lives malnourished, abused and neglected, living in atrocious conditions that the U.S. Attorney Beck called "extraordinary cruelty." He continued, "The number of dogs seized and the amount of money involved in this case shows how extensive this underworld of dogfighting is. These defendants were betting between $5,000 and $200,000 on one dogfight."

Working with the FBI and the Attorney General of the United States, these dogs were seized and placed in the custody of more than 55 local and national humane societies.

Sentences for the eight men convicted of animal fighting in this raid ranged from six months to eight years, the longest dogfighting term ever given in a federal dogfighting case. Participants in this high-stakes dogfighting ring were also ordered to pay two million dollars in restitution to ASPCA and HSUS for expenses incurred while treating and housing these dogs seized in this federal raid. As Judge Keith Watkins ended his sentencing, he voiced his opinion that federal sentencing guidelines for dogfighting are wholly inadequate to address the seriousness of such a crime in which these defendants had injured or killed an estimated 420 to 640 dogs in the course of their dogfighting operation.

Tim Rickey, Vice President of ASPCA Field Investigations and Response, when testifying at the trail, stated, "This is a landmark case for the animal welfare community. We hope this case serves as a precedent for future dogfighting cases and sends a message to dogfighters everywhere that this crime will be prosecuted to the fullest extent of the law."

The reaction of Wayne Pacelle, president and CEO of HSUS, was one of elation. "This series of raids reminds every dogfighter that they are not beyond the law and their day of reckoning will come. We are committed to eradicating dogfighting in every dark corner where it festers."

For years Texas law enforcement officers had been disturbed about a dogfighting subculture that had strongly entrenched itself in East Texas country sides. Wagers of weekly matches topped $40,000 and their star dogs were trained to rip off the genitals of other dogs. Violence, hip-hop, drugs and Mexican cartels ruled these moveable bloody pits. It was into this prize-fighting scenario that law enforcement agencies were able to infiltrate and, after 17 months, bring down this secret society of criminals possessing long records along with a few other surprising participants: a high school English teacher.

After the Michael Vick case occupied center stage in 2007, the Texas legislature acted quickly to change the penalty of dogfighting from a misdemeanor to a state jail felony, making the penalty worth bringing down this East Texas dogfighting ring in November 2008, charging 55 people and seizing 187 Pit Bull Terrier type dogs which agents located outside in muddy yards, chained to axles sunken in the ground. Due to their severe aggressive behavior, most were euthanized. The attending veterinarian for Harris County was exceptionally saddened. "It was heart-wrenching and not the dogs' fault. That lies with the cruel people who have taken and exploited this breed."

Texas District Attorney Bill Gleason made a suggestion so firm that it was almost an order, stating that it was the moral responsibility of state and federal lawmakers to put dogfighting in the same category as drug raids for the forfeitures and seizures of property. This new designation for dogfighting would increase the danger of being convicted and decrease the bounties (asset forfeiture) of the perpetrators.

Lack of conformity in dogfighting laws and penalties differs from state to state, inviting confusion and lax enforcement. In most states possession of dogs for the purpose of fighting is a felony offense. But many state legislators are finally realizing that because spectators are a necessary ingredient for the success of animal fighting, laws should also deem their attendance as be a felony, thus deterring some of the illicit revenue generated. There has long been an outcry from the many child welfare agencies that taking a child to these obscene matches must be a designated as a more serious felony crime.

State laws throughout America still do not require a minimum mandatory jail time for animal fighting and the punishments imposed for dogfighting and animal cruelty are largely at the discretion of our judges. The judicial system is hamstrung by archaic laws and give little importance for laws involving animal cruelty.

In Florida, where dogfighting arrests are a common occurrence, felony abuse of a cow or horse carries a mandatory prison sentence, but not for a dog. Arizona and California statutes require veterinarians to alert local law enforcement concerning any dog injuries or deaths they think were inflicted in a dog fight.

In 2013, a Las Cruces, <u>New Mexico</u> jury found a woman guilty of nine felonies concerning dogfighting and extreme cruelty. She was additionally convicted of 23 misdemeanors, most for animal cruelty. Even though her behavior during the hearing was openly aggressive and angry, the state district judge remarked he noted a positive change in her behavior and sentenced her to five years of probation, then deferred her punishment.

<u>Wisconsin</u> statutes require that dogs alleged to be a part of dogfighting are seized and held for evidence for a period of time from weeks to months until the court case is completed. Because this time period can be lengthy, it can decrease the likelihood of the impounded dog being rehabilitated and adopted. This statute was recently changed so that the owner of this canine must pay the reasonable costs for housing and care during the trial, thus giving the defendant reason not to bog down the trial.

<u>Delaware</u> enacted similar legislation. Their past statute required that all dogs seized from animal fighting were dangerous and must be euthanized. Their new more humane **SB245** requires that these dogs be evaluated for possible rehabilitation and adoption.

Animal fighting, like big-business, has diversified. Now quite a few states including <u>Mississippi</u>, <u>Florida</u>, <u>Louisiana</u>, <u>North Carolina</u>, <u>South Carolina</u> and <u>Alabama</u> have been forced to write new laws to include the new contenders in the bloody animal fighting ring: Pit Bull Terriers VS feral or domestic hogs (whose tusks have been broken off with a steel pipe, hammer or bolt cutters), termed "hot dog rodeos," "hog catching," or "hog baying" or "dog-on-cat fighting."

For strength and conformity, ALDF has drafted a recommended amendment to state laws that would enable prosecutors to charge dogfighters under the respective state's Racketeer Influenced and Corrupt Organization Act, commonly referred to as RICO. This statute was originally written to fight organized criminal efforts such as gambling and drug dealing. When applied to state animal fighting statutes, it would provide prosecutors with an additional and stronger charge for animal fighting. Thirty-two states statutes already include RICO provisions to which this amendment could be applied, the newest state being <u>New Jersey</u> which includes the offense, "leader of a dogfighting network." ALDF amendment listing dogfighting as a RICO predicate offense were signed into law in 2008 in <u>Oregon</u>, <u>Utah</u> and <u>Virginia</u>.

When, as a member of BCACT, you encounter scenes of possible *dogfighting, it is your responsibility to immediately secure the scene and document, photograph and seize, among other items of relevance, the evidence listed below. Photographic and video-graphic evidence are compelling evidence and will help seal a conviction. All animals involved as live evidence should be taken for a thorough exam to the agency's contracted veterinarian. While <u>New Mexico</u> law requires the preservation of evidence, it does not require prolonging the lives of those critically injured and suffering animals considered as live evidence.*

DOGFIGHTING*—*Incriminating evidence to identify, document, photograph and seize:*

- *Signs of fighting: scars, mutilated faces, ripped tissue around eyes, ears and legs*

- *Training or conditioning devices for the dogs, such as treadmills, catmills and fighting pits*

- *Logging chains*

- *Hanging devices to strengthen and condition dogs*

- *Hanging devices to hang animals used for bull-baiting*

- *Veterinarian supplies, drugs and vitamins used to treat dogs or to enhance their performance*

- *Evidence of mutilated animals (usually kept in small holes or kennels) used as bull-bait for training dogs to fight, maim and kill*

- *Carcasses of animals killed during fights or training*

- *Newspaper classified ads run by breeders*

- *Although a Pit Bull Terrier is registered with American Dog Breeders Association (ADBA) it alone does not indicate it is a fighting dog.*

- *Arenas or fighting pits*

COCKFIGHTING — "Cockfighting was illegal in Oklahoma until 1963, when a judge ruled that chickens are not animals and therefore unprotected by anticruelty laws."

– U.S. News & World Report, 1999 December

Cockfights are savage and organized matches, usually to the death, between two roosters, whose natural spurs are fitted with sharp instruments up to 3½ inches, specially designed to slash, maim, cripple, disfigure and maul. The mangled, dead loser is usually discarded in the trash, and the winner may or may not recover from his deadly injuries.

Cockfighting is not about culture; it is about cruelty. It has not been linked to any specific cultural or ethnic tradition. <u>Massachusetts</u> was the first state to ban this crude, violent activity in 1836. Forty-three states followed suit by banning it before World War I. It is now illegal in all states and a felony in 40.

Because of the often-mentioned wives' tale that cockfighting is part of the Hispanic culture in <u>New Mexico</u> and is protected by the Treaty of Guadalupe Hildalgo, a poll of New Mexico Hispanics was conducted in 2001, and the results revealed that 76% of the state Hispanics favored a ban on cockfighting.

<u>New Mexico</u> became the 49th state to make cockfighting illegal but the law has no teeth and its penalties which are virtually ineffectual. A first offense is a petty misdemeanor. Yet in news conferences our state boasts that it has devoted vast resources to ending the sport. The same weak ordinances exist in surrounding town and counties.

The cockfighting law in <u>Louisiana</u> was upgraded in 2010, designating it as a crime to knowingly attend a cockfight. An elated Julia Breaux, Louisiana state director for The HSUS, stated that although Louisiana may have been the last state to ban cockfighting (in 2008), it now has one of the best animal fighting laws in the region. She was sure that her state would never again be a refuge for those who engage in these cruel spectacles where roosters are forced to fight to the death.

Most state prosecutors and courts are hamstrung by limp laws. Cockfighting has no importance on their dockets. No state laws require even minimum mandatory jail time, so although arrests and convictions can be disruptive to today's cock-fighting entrepreneur, his business continues to flourish.

Several states' toothless cockfighting penalties allow those actively involved in animal fighting to continue to challenge state and federal laws, reaching from their bottomless pits of gambling and drug money, and muddying the waters in the courts in such issues as violations of civil rights and illegal searches and seizures. Under the umbrella of the New Mexico Gamefowl Association, a nonprofit cockfighting advocacy group, game-fighters file appeals claiming tribal, religious and cultural sovereignty; currently these have yet to win exemptions from the ban.

It is understood that taking down a cockfighting ring requires considerable manpower and resources. Investigating these savage fighting activities is often frustrating, time-consuming, and sometimes fruitless. These blood-letting activities, usually shroud in secrecy, might involve working with law enforcement officials from nearby counties or cities. Because these fights often involve criminals with big money, investigators also have to deal with their informants, bribing, and the criminal's own dossiers and information on law enforcement officials. But, the common cockfighters who bring their rooster to fights, hoping for a considerable cut of the purse, usually leave the pit empty handed: no money, no live rooster.

Many arenas/pits (some hold over 400 spectators) are located on well-hidden and sprawling rural sites. Lookouts are stationed atop dusty mesas, and audio speakers, which in the past blared mariachi music, now carry feeds from police scanners. Our South Valley, because of our vast unoccupied spaces, is notorious for hosting these barbaric clandestine matches. Arenas are often situated near our Rio Grande drainage ditches, which offer perfect cover for quick escapes.

Cheering spectators are offered tamales, burritos and sodas while drugs and alcoholic beverages are usually sold from campers or pick-up truck concession stands. Other attractions flourish: illegal gambling, sale of drugs, weapons and other stolen merchandise. Personal crimes of violence are common occurrences.

Owners and promoters consider these blood-letting, repulsive affairs to be not only entertainment for adults and children alike, but instrumental in desensitizing children to violence and brutality, a necessary attribute for animal fighting. Those spectators with seats close to the ring are subject to flying masses of bloody tissue, feathers and bone fragments from the injured animals.

Underground publications advertising fighting animals and their records and fighting related paraphernalia are available on special Internet sites as well as through foreign publications which circulate throughout America. Although fight locations are sometimes advertised in local newspaper want ads by using codes, the Internet is the more frequently used vehicle for setting up and reporting on matches.

With only one misdemeanor conviction thus far, New Mexico attracts cockfighters from four of our five neighboring states, where cockfighting is considered to be a felony. A 2009 cockfighting raid in Bernalillo County landed 37 roosters in the AAWD shelter, where employees' time was taken from the shelter animals to instead constructing 37 wood and wire cages so that the impounded fowl could be used as evidence. A frustrated BCACS officer mentioned that waiting for that raid to come to trial cost BCACS thousands of dollars for the

AAWD daily impound fee and for the cages. A 2016 raid in which 56 fighting roosters were seized from an inter-city Albuquerque residence resulted in only six misdemeanor counts, including a single petty misdemeanor for cruelty to animals.

One Albuquerque Police officer, infuriated and outspoken about the toothless cockfighting laws in this state, snapped. "We don't often thoroughly investigate misdemeanors on other crimes. We sometimes scoff at these investigations. My unit just wasted $10,000 on a recent misdemeanor. I'd rather use that for a D.U.I. checkpoint and take 20 people off the road in the three hours and save lives over chickens. I feel good when we save chickens, but whoop-de-do, a misdemeanor? Cockfighting is blatant and intentional extreme cruelty to animals, and just as other kinds of intentional extreme cruelty to animals, it should be punishable as a fourth degree felony."

Their attitudes, disheartening but understanding, reflect the hurdles law enforcement officers face all across America, because a misdemeanor mirrors the importance that legislators attached to that crime.

Federal law represents itself as a way to prosecute individuals who support animal fighting ventures by supplying animals, equipment or money across state lines or to foreign countries. But even our federal legislators turned a deaf ear to an international appeal from the United Nations. This international organization emphasized that the spread of the deadly avian flu can be attributed to the exceptionally risky, international factor of cockfighting birds, and pled for the United States to enact greater enforcement and harsher penalties for cockfighting.

More than any other business, cockfighting involves the illegal, unregulated, often hidden, transport of birds across borders, resulting in the rapid spread of avian flu. Especially prone are those cockfighters who use their mouths to clear away the blood and mucus from a dying rooster's throat to buy a few extra seconds of combat from their gamebird. By their touch, it is spread to other roosters, who when fighting spread it to their opponent, and on and on goes the deadly cycle of avian flu, a highly pathogenic virus responsible for the deaths of hundreds of millions of birds around the world.

Andi was firm in her approach. *"By enforcing the cockfighting laws, we will certainly uncover a wealth of the unrelated crimes, occurring on grounds, concurrently with the fighting. Below is a list of incriminating evidence."*

COCKFIGHTING*—*Incriminating evidence to identify, document, photograph and seize:*

- *All fighting cocks*
- *Fighting paraphernalia including gaffs or sharp instruments designed to be attached in place of the natural spur of the fowl.*
- *Sharpening stones and instruments, leather wraps, sparing muffs*
- *Veterinarian and medicinal supplies, drugs, vitamins and supplements used to enhance performance*
- *Cages/kennels for transporting*
- *Evidence of gambling, cockfighting literature*

I'll close this session with an eye-opening observation by Julie A. Canter, Assistant District Attorney, Sullivan County, Tennessee. "I can say that every animal fighting prosecution that I have personally handled has begun as an investigation into a crime against a child."

IMPLICATIONS OF ANIMAL FIGHTING ON THE SAFETY OF THE COMMUNITY

"Animal fighting is part of organized criminal enterprise, attracting criminals engaged in use and distribution of drugs, money laundering, possession and sale of stolen merchandise, concealed weapons, soliciting sex and racketeering. Exposure to these type of serious crimes is dangerous as their violence can easily spread and involve as well as affect the surrounding neighborhoods of the community."

– Bernalillo County Sheriff Manuel Gonzales

---

* As recommended by Investigating Animal Cruelty in New Mexico, A Field Guide for Law Enforcement Officers, NMDPS, APNM, HSUS

CHAPTER THIRTEEN

TRAINING:
ANIMAL HOARDING

"A good Samaritan shares for the well-being of animal.
Hoarding is not sharing."

– Unknown

ASPCA reported that there are 2,000 known cases investigated each year. HSUS documents that hoarders claim 250,000 lives of innocent animals yearly, and that 80% of these animal hoarders have accumulated on their premises an unbelievably large number of pitiful companion animals in various stages of disease and death.

The intentions of an animal hoarder are not cruel but are so unfocused and confused that, due to their uncontrollable need to acquire these animals, it is difficult to label their torturous act as either a cut-and-dried case of animal cruelty or unintentional neglect. It was first recognized in 1999 as a disease which so consumes the mind of the hoarder that it brings excruciating suffering to those very rescued animals whose critical deterioration is due to his/her total lack of even the most basic care for them.

The Hoarding of Animals Research Consortium (HARC) at Tufts University emphasizes that this disorder is not considered to be a compulsive behavioral disorder. Their research contends that these abusive actions are satisfying a human need to pathologically collect and control an excessive amount of animals, any animals, although the number of animals is not the factor in establishing hoarding; it is the care…or more specifically, the lack of care. HARC specifies that this human need is far greater than the needs of the animals, who receive not even minimum standards of sanitation, nutrition, shelter, veterinary care.

The National Center for the Prosecution of Animal Abuse of the National District Attorneys' Association categories hoarding into three behavioral patterns.

1. The <u>overwhelmed caregiver</u> owns pets which, because they were not sterilized, have produced too many offspring for the individual to properly care for.

2. The <u>rescue hoarder</u> resides in an area where there are a great many throw-aways or strays needing assistance. Even as the number of animals increase beyond the ability of the hoarder to meet their basic needs, the hoarder refuses help in placing them in new homes or in caring for them.

3. The <u>exploitive hoarder</u> is considered to be the hardest to work with or help. Their assortment of animals, most of which are undernourished, ill or diseased, serve their own personal needs and often are the bait to solicit money from the public by misrepresenting the quality of care they are providing.

Demographics by HARC profile a typical animal hoarder as middle-aged to older, female, retired or unemployed, and living alone in a single-family home. An alarming finding (with serious health implications) is that many of their residences are discovered to be without plumbing and/or electricity.

A 2013 study created by the <u>Delaware</u> Interdisciplinary Task Force, which systematically tracked animal and non-animal hoarding cases. It discovered locations varying from trailer parks to mansions, demonstrating that the crime of animal hoarding does not recognize the borders of affluence. Confusion reigns. Not only is the hoarder misunderstood as well as his crime of hoarding, but so are state and local animal cruelty laws specifically regarding hoarding. If in existence at all, such codes are poorly written, ambiguous and have no substance, which could be attributed to two factors:

1. Our government officials and our citizens are misinformed, indifferent or unaware of the deplorable, lethal conditions, not to mention the overwhelming public health issues, of animal hoarding. Most state senators and representatives admitted that they had not been educated about the horrific consequences of animal hoarding and the unbelievably large numbers of companion animals effected by the actions of one hoarder. Could this professed ignorance really exist, among both groups, in spite of popular television reality shows and news features.

Both 'Confessions: Animal Hoarding' and multi-media news

exposés have been instrumental in heightening public aware-ness of the disturbing existence of hoarding. One particular New Mexico case, aired on the A&E "Hoarders," highlight-ed a repulsive collection of 75 living and dead cats occupying the unbelievably squalid home of an elderly Lordsburg wom-an. The director of the same television show later requested assistance from a team of New Mexico animal abuse investiga-tors involving a hoarding case in southern Illinois where more than 600 pounds of bird feces had to be removed from one res-idence, on camera.

2. All of these entities and individuals alike mistakenly take for granted that animal hoarding is encompassed in the ani-mal cruelty sections of their state or municipal codes where standard requirements of substance and veterinary care, unin-tentional, misdemeanor offenses are addressed.

    The simply stated animal cruelty codes of most states and communities cannot possibly cover the many torturous infrac-tions of animal hoarding. And even when made aware of the appalling results (short and long term) of hoarding, a paltry few government officials are willing to devote the necessary resources to halt the repulsive crime.

    Actually, because hoarding is one of the greatest causes of animal suffering (causing more injuries, deaths than the inten-tionally felony cruelty laws address), its seriousness should result in municipalities and states re-labeling it as a separate offense and re-defining it in stronger worded ordinances and statutes.

All professional animal humane associations highly recommend that an animal hoarding code should also carry a penalty for each animal involved. To help prevent recidivism, the convicted hoarder should be prohibited from future ownership of any animals through a software program (dis-cussed in Chapter 17) required to be used by all private and public animal shelters and rescues. And such software would offer the least expensive and most thorough means to stop recidivism.

Currently there exists no conformity in state hoarding laws. Many have and are seeking professional services, including ALDF, HSUS and ASPCA, in revising, updating and tightening their laws, enforcement and sentencing.

Under the direction of ASPCA, <u>Illinois</u> **SB626** Companion Hoarding Bill (2001) and <u>Hawaii</u> **SB3203** (2008) have created a legally clear definition of a "companion animal hoarder."

Only <u>Illinois's</u> Humane Care for Animals Act earmarks specific prohibitions and carries felony consequences, mandates counseling for those convicted and restricts future animal ownership.

<u>Hawaii</u> enacted the only penal code that actually prohibits animal hoarding, its specific wording allows prosecutors to charge animal hoarding with multiple counts, covering separately each and every animal hoarded, but it is still labeled as a misdemeanor crime.

<u>New Jersey's</u> Animal Hoarding Statute was designated as a Model Law, and can be accessed online at Animal Law Resource Center.

<u>Montana</u> and <u>Vermont</u> were unable to successfully pass such specific animal cruelty legislation due to the concern of constituents that such laws would infringe on the rights to pet ownership…the right to abuse.

<u>Delaware's</u> severe hoarding situation was discussed by Kevin Usilton of SPCA-First State Animal Shelter (FSAS) Director, who detailed the unacceptable manor in which hoarders are viewed by the justice system. He estimated that his state has 45,000 citizens who exhibit hoarding behavior, resulting in monthly complaints to his office. However only a fourth of those prosecuted cases reach a judge, who usually charges them with animal cruelty misdemeanors, even though half of those animals, mostly cats, rescued from hoarders are euthanized because of chronic respiratory problems, Feline Leukemia Virus or lack of socialization (with people).

Lenient charges and sentences in animal hoarding cases in other states fail to reflect the excruciating and prolonged pain, suffering and neglect of their hoarded animals. Their misdemeanor charges are but a token to rid the judicial docket of even the most extreme examples of animal cruelty.

In their defense, many courts find their hands tied because of the lack of inter-agency communication, for most government agencies do not require inter-agency computer databases (such as DoNotAdopt) nor do they utilize cross-reporting between private, municipal, social and law enforcement agencies. Sadly, this black-out of the knowledge necessary to fight animal cruelty crimes exists between the courts, law enforcement and social agencies in most states.

Yet there were some municipalities, because of their lack of defining laws, who put forth great effort in actually dodging animal hoarding cases. Example the saga of the infamous and colorful Ms. Vikki Kittles, whose decades of animal abuse spanned five states, causing continuing embarrassment among their law enforcement and judicial communities, and resulting in the taunting, angry media referring to them with the handle, "Keystone Cops." Only the progressive state of Oregon reacted by re-writing their animal abuse statutes.

After several outrageous encounters and charges with law enforcement officers representing different Florida counties, Vikki fled the state in 1985, before her trial, leaving her 73-year-old mother with 40 dogs, cats and horses, all housed within the residence.

Two years later Florida authorities chased her again when she was discovered with another 40 dogs and cats, living in a shed, trailer and her car. Awaiting trial, she spent but a few months in jail, but the judge did not sentence her to additional time, fines or community service.

Her hoarding, cruelty and dishonesty continued through the 1980s in Mississippi and Colorado, until she swindled $15,000 from some Washington investors to purchase a school bus for travel to Oregon, where she and her orange school bus, which was carrying 115 malnourished, diseased and wounded dogs traveled blissfully without so much as a ticket. Most authorities turned their heads, but those law enforcement officials who finally did confront her about her crowded dog-mobile chose not to charge her, and instead gave her money for enough gasoline to exit their town.

Amazingly, this pattern continued for several years until, in 1993 she was found-out and charged in Oregon. Extradition from Washington took a lengthy three months. She convinced a judge to bar veterinary care of her canines, convincing him that she had her own special treatments. Ms. Kittles' erratic behavior turned her $150,000 trial (even with ALDF free legal research in support of the prosecution's case), into a five-week circus of discord, deceit, disrespect, manipulation and impropriety. She was eventually convicted on 42 counts of animal neglect in the first degree.

After serving eight months in jail, she was given unsupervised probation and moved on to Wyoming where she with 80 dogs and 40 cats inhabited a trailer. Oregon did not pursue her extradition and she took up 1997 residence in a house trailer in Sweetwater County, Wyoming, but she failed to seek permission from the owner. When authorities responded to the land-owner's complaint, they found, not Vikki, but the 74 dogs she had left behind.

The following day, a Carbon County, Wyoming deputy arrested her for driving with obstructed windows (5 dogs, 40 cats and a rabbit). Although ALDF offered the Carbon County prosecutor free legal services and background information to help with the case, the prosecutor dropped charges saying he would just as soon let her "sound-off somewhere else."

That "somewhere else" would still be in <u>Wyoming</u>, back in Sweetwater County, 11 months later, in which during her eight months of proceedings for an assortment of animal abuse charges, the judge ordered her to travel, without sheriff escort, to the State Hospital for a mental evaluation. She was a no-show and her case was finally dismissed in 2000.

Still enjoying the laxity of animal abuse laws of <u>Wyoming</u>, she convinced a property owner in Laramie County to allow her to live there with her 48 cats in July. When her trailer with sick kitties was impounded, she began living out of her car. Her six horses, which were kept on someone's property, were confiscated by the sheriff's office. The cost to the county for the boarding and veterinary care for her 48 cats was $20,000.

Through 2003, legalities became entangled with each new eviction, impounding and seizure of malnourished and diseased animals. Two of these cases finally made their way to circuit court in Laramie County in 2003. A jury found her guilty of misdemeanor breach of peace, failure to vaccinate, livestock at large and lack of automobile insurance. The judge sentenced her to 15 days in jail (suspended) and a fine of $250.

The Kittles saga continued into 2006 with more of the same hoarding and abuse antics in <u>Colorado.</u>

While this costly 21-month case (1993-1995) in <u>Oregon</u> was proceeding, it exposed a must-fix blind spot in the Oregon animal cruelty statute: the animal victims were, during the course of the lengthy court proceedings, continuing to suffer and die at the whim of their abuser. ALDF was determined to do what they could to help by strengthening Oregon state animal protection laws, producing the Kittles Bill, <u>Oregon</u> **HB 3377**. This legislation elevated aggravated animal abuse from a misdemeanor to a felony and allowed shelters to provide veterinary care to impounded animals and to move them from temporary shelters to foster homes. In spite of political motivations to kill the bill, ALDF and Oregon animal activists were adamant in their support of **HB3377,** which became effective in 1995, after she had been charged and sentenced.

In conjunction with the Kittles Bill, <u>Oregon</u> passed a second germane bill, **SB 653,** both humane and financially oriented, which would allow courts to order forfeiture of abused animals prior to the disposition of a criminal case.

Between 1996 and 1997, her animal cruelty escapades covered three counties. The only legal "fix" proposed, took place the following year, at the local level, in Rawlings, where new and updated animal codes were enacted, making such future adoptions and hoardings illegal.

Actions of hoarders, as exampled by those of Vikki, are repetitive and unpredictable. AHANM received a winter visit from a pickup covered with mud and snow, the bed of which was loaded with two crates, each crammed with six Chihuahuas. After checking the contact information of the individual who found the strays, the adoptions director asked APNM and BCACS for help in investigating.

It took two weeks to locate, legally seize and unload from the remote and rural New Mexico residence housing 33 additional Chihuahuas stuffed wall to wall. A hole in the wall served as a doggie door. This property was located in the mountains in terrain so rugged and muddy that county, city and AHANM four-wheel drive vehicles required multiple attempts. The property owner claimed six of these dogs from the AAWD shelter, and denied ownership of the remaining 27, who were sheltered by and put up for adoption by AHANM.

The hoarder/owner was not charged. Attorneys for the county explained that even if the woman were to be charged and prosecuted with multiple counts of misdemeanor animal abuse, this case would just add to an already strained court system and would probably result in little more than a fine, because the owner surrendered the animals. No one anticipated that there would actually be any public concern that New Mexico courts should not have the power to require that hoarders be denied future ownership of any pets.

Misha Goodman, BCACS Director, in news releases, explained the future requirements of the owner and of the BCACS. "The six dogs that the woman kept will be spayed, neutered and microchipped, and BCACS will continue to check the property before and after their release, sometimes even unannounced. Without assistance or very direct supervision for hoarding behavior, recidivism is just rampant. Past cases have taught us that long-term positive outcomes in hoarding cases is poor without additional intervention from various mental health and public support agencies. When hoarded animals are simply removed from the hoarder, they will just get more of them."

Her assessment was mirrored by two New Mexico cases, each sharing the same defendant. April 2011 brought the Rio Rancho police to the home owned by Rio Rancho veterinarian Deborah Clopton (licensed since 1991), where they discovered dead, sick, injured and starving dogs and cats abandoned in the residence. After her 2013 move to Edgewood, law enforcement officers would visit the rented home of this veterinarian (license revoked in March, 2013) and discover a house of horrors.

Forty-eight dogs, mostly indoor, were living in heinous neglect, with accumulations of old and new canine waste materials found throughout each room. The dogs themselves were evaluated by Santa Fe County and Dona Ana County Sheriff's officers to be in fair to poor condition. Due to their poor health, only three needed to be euthanized. Clopton was charged with 48 counts of animal cruelty, four other counts of veterinary drug abuse. She was ordered to pay Santa Fe Animal Shelter and Humane Society $20 a day for the care of the "Edgewood 48," those seized dogs plus puppies resulting from impending births. The overall bill from HSUS was more than $27,000. She was unable to pay even $6,000 on this running tab, and lost custody of all of the animals to HSUS. Can you imagine the strain the intake of these 48 frightened, abused dogs put on the HSUS and their ability to accept dogs relinquished by their owners or found by control officers or compassionate citizens?

In 2007, after answering numerous complaints from neighbors, Rio Rancho police arrested and charged mother and daughter homeowners (both housekeepers by profession) with animal cruelty. Fourteen cats were found living in unsanitary conditions, their feces and urine caked to every available space: counters, floors, furniture, and mattresses. Because the 13-year-old daughter/granddaughter was also living there, the two women were charged with child abuse as well as animal cruelty. Their punishment was only probation and an ultimatum that they could never own any pets except the two left behind.

Two years later the same family was evicted from a nearby Paradise Hills home, so overridden with cat liquid and solid waste that these materials clogged the air vents. Their explanation was reported, "We just love animals."

These above cases demonstrate the extremely high rate of recidivism of animal hoarding which might never have been if laws in <u>Colorado, Florida, Mississippi, Nevada, New Mexico, Washington</u> and <u>West Virginia</u> laws required DoNotAdopt databases to be shared within appropriate agencies. Obviously they also demonstrate the need for stronger legislation in our cities, counties and states which would directly address the crime of animal hoarding and require psychological treatment and prevent their future ownership of companion animals.

And, to add further confusion to the animal hoarding issue, there exist animal shelters who represent themselves to be "no-kill," but have become hoarders instead of rescuers. A 2009 visit by <u>Nevada</u> authorities to the site of FLOCK, For The Love of Cats And Kittens, a 501(c)(3), revealed a collection of 700 felines, emaciated, dying, ill and injured. A 2015 investigation of Innocent Hearts Animal No-Kill Rescue in Mountain View, Arkansas, resulted in custody by ASPCA and their partners of more than 100 unsterilized, neglected dogs ranging from 2 days to 10 years old.

In September 2013, Sheriff Deputies in Chaparral, New Mexico received a call about a domestic violence disturbance at Mission Desert Hills Sanctuary for Dogs, another legally registered no-kill facility. What they found was disturbing: 208 dogs on the premises with no food, no water. Some had reverted to their feral instincts and were killing and eating each other for food. The rooms were saturated with dried and fresh animal wastes. Dead dogs were literally stacked in the garbage receptacles. One hundred emaciated and sickly dogs were taken to Otero County Animal Shelter and other animal shelters for medical care, and hopefully, after recovery, adoption. Fifty were left in the home. Fifty-eight, due to their health, were euthanized. And to their surprise, deputies also discovered a 70-year-old woman, who had been beaten and held captive by the homeowner Felix, who was arrested and charged with battery and false imprisonment.

County veterinarians who examined these imprisoned dogs reported that several had 'severe internal injuries' indicating that they had been sexually assaulted by a human or an instrument. For many months following, several animal rescue groups involved in housing those animals kept abreast of this case closely, as rumors ran rampant that no charges had yet been made and the case would be dismissed.

The owners of Chaparral's Howl-A-Day Inn (a kennel where many of the Mission Dessert Hills dogs were being boarded) joined in a concentrated effort with these other rescue groups, all determined in their continued insistence that Felix be charged with animal abuse. "We did not want this horrific case of abuse to be swept under the rug."

Three months later, finally, Felix from Mission Desert Hills Sanctuary was charged with 156 counts of animal abuse.

Andi explained. *Animal hoarding in* New Mexico *is governed by our city and county, have ordinances dealing with animal cruelty and requirements of multiple companion animals at a single site. Multiple Companion Animal Site Permits, are tools to help us to keep an eye on possible sites of animal hoarding, puppy mills and backyard breeding. Although most individuals involved in these crimes do not bother to get the permit, much less comply, permits are required by both Bernalillo County and City of Albuquerque.*

Be prepared. Law enforcement officers who have been called to the home of an animal hoarder by the complaints of concerned or angry neighbors or friends have expressed many of the same graphic adjectives to describe the mind of the hoarder as pitiful, confused, complex and disturbed. The deputies describe their experiences as assaulting, frightening, overwhelming and sickening. The hoarder's accumulation of animals, diseased, dying or decaying exist in inconceivably disgusting, unsanitary and squalid living conditions that defy the imagination.

One of NMDOG's requested rescues in another county represents an extreme example of the consequences of hoarding. Volunteers encountered neglect conditions so extreme that the 20 dogs were unable to walk; they could only crawl. These loving volunteers taught these hoarded canines the basic principles of enjoying a healthy and happy canine life: barking, playing, wagging their tails, coming inside the home, making human contact and eating their food from individual dishes. Some even had to learn to stand. All had skin infections, loss of hair and festering wounds, were emaciated and lacked socialization, with other animals or people. Most were quiet, frightened and all had to learn to try to trust humans...again. Although dogs are extolled for their forgiving nature, it is not synonymous with forgetting. That is their safeguard.

It cannot be overlooked that one cause for hoarding cases to be indefinitely postponed or to fall between the judicial cracks of state and local government agencies is the poor manner in which evidence is gathered and presented. Animal control officers, their veterinarians and our deputies should coordinate their effort in raiding a possible site of hoarding and cover them in a veil of secrecy. Have ready the required information to issue a warrant, gather the below evidence, and making sure you have ample supply of collars, tags, animal carriers, identification kits, animal surrender forms and veterinarian exam forms for each animal. Below are the guidelines.

HOARDING*—*Incriminating evidence to identify, document, photograph and seize:*

- *The property, inside and outside, including all adjacent buildings, floors, ceilings, walls, furniture, plumbing, trash, electrical outlets and appliances*

- *Water and food bowls of animals hoarded*

- *Check air vents and plumbing for further evidence of clogging by animal matter*

- *Live animals as well as carcasses, who were victims of hoarding*

- *Veterinary records*

- *Veterinary medications*

- *All food bills*

- *Crates, cushions, rugs, pads, beds to preserve excrements and squalor*

- *All other items which have been urinated or defecated upon*

- *Signs of rodents and insects*

Sometimes, even though the evidence is gathered, documented, and photographed in the above manner, courts still, not recognizing the implications of animal hoarding, will not convict or will plea down. Let me example a current case of NMDOG, called independently to help in San Miguel County raid, where their volunteers took custody of 29 of the many dogs suffering in unspeakable, sickening conditions. Even though the evidence was legally obtained, well documented and ready for legal action, the county officials did not take animal hoarding very seriously, a disappointment for all involved.

But we as members of BCACT will keep trying, because we, BCACT will make a difference.

IMPLICATIONS AND IMPACT OF ANIMAL HOARDING ON PUBLIC HEALTH, ZONING, AND CODE ENFORCEMENT

This frightening and dangerous behavior of animal hoarding not only takes a toll on the innocent animals who are victims, but also present, by the filth, squalor and disease resulting and their attraction of rodents and insects, a danger to the health, safety and properties of those residing within the neighborhood area. Although hoarders are not likely to be involved in inter-personal crimes, those that live in homes with other dependent family members, such as children or elders, are exposing them to serious health situations. Successful results usually involve long-term monitoring by social service agencies, mandated by the courts.

---

*As recommended by <u>Investigating Animal Cruelty in New Mexico, A Field Guide for Law Enforcement Officers,</u> NMDPS, APNM, HSUS

CHAPTER FOURTEEN

TRAINING: BACKYARD BREEDERS AND PUPPY MILLS

"Don't breed or buy while animals in shelters die."

– Colorado license plate

Andi warned, *Deputies and officers responding to calls of puppy mills experience many of the same depressing, deplorable and disgusting scenes that they encountered with situations of animal hoarding. But instead of roaming freely, these emaciated animals are packed tightly in unsanitary conditions, fur matted with excrement, lice and ticks. They are often unable to walk due to lack of grooming or exercise. Dogs are usually found with open sores; they lack water and food bowls, adequate shelter.*

As with hoarding laws, state, county and city district attorneys apply existing animal cruelty laws to the guilty perpetrators of these inhumane situations because they lack specific, applicable codes, ordinances and statutes. Because of concentrated efforts of lobbyists, our lawmakers are usually fairly well versed in the many, heartbreaking problems presented by backyard breeding and puppy mills. Thus they cannot cry "ignorance" to their indifferent actions.

Each year while city and state residents continue to wait for caring legislators to pass the necessary bill to stop backyard breeding and require timely and thorough health inspections of puppy mills, two events have been occurring simultaneously: 2.7 million unchosen, healthy pets are being put to death by euthanasia yearly across America...senseless killing...while, at the same time, yearly, millions of new pups flood the market, the result of both backyard breeding and puppy mills. There are between 4,000 and 5,000 puppy mills in the United States, each holding 75-150 actively breeding dogs. They sell their commodity, puppies, to pet stores and individuals, through Internet and newspaper ads, burdening the ever increasing pet population which is currently overwhelming our private and public animal shelters.

Cute puppies, indeed, (but then all puppies are cute) are welcomed into homes of anyone who will pay the puppy mill/backyard breeder discounted price. Perspective owners are not vetted for their ability to provide, financially and responsibly, for their new pet nor are they given a background check for a previous conviction of animal abuse. And because the pet has come from the horrific conditions associated with puppy mills and backyard breeding: neglect, abuse, unsanitary living conditions, disease, lack of socialization, unethical and illegal breeding practices, it may carry into its new and unsuspecting home, along with their eagerness to play and their wagging tail, many health and genetic problems that will produce future emotional consequences and financial burdens for the unsuspecting adoptive family. These irresponsible, uncaring and negligent breeders also produce emotionally damaged pups, the product of their unsafe, unlicensed and unhealthy environment.

With the added, more convenient, less expensive and less personally invasive options offered by purchasing pets through newspaper and internet ads, prospective dog owners need to be especially cautious. A pet should never be purchased, sight unseen, without physical interaction. Better Business Bureaus usually offer a wealth of information about the history of the breeder's business including health inspections, consumer complaints and how they were resolved. It is vital that a buyer meets the breeder, peruses the breeding facility and receives health certification and guarantee for the pet. It is of utmost importance that pet owners desiring a purebred dog conduct the research necessary to determine which are the ethical breeders.

Our deputies are also seeing an increase in puppies smuggled in from Mexico and being sold for cheap prices. These puppies are usually very sick with Parvovirus and other incurable diseases due to lack of proper nutrition and care. Buying a pure-bred Siberian Husky on a street corner for $100 should send up red flags that the dog might not be not healthy and the seller might not be legitimate.

Community shelters have assumed the role in educating possible pet owners making the public more aware of the safety involved in dealing with licensed, legitimate breeders who try to place their healthy dogs in competent homes. Research your perspective breeder using his USDA license number. Responsible breeders are easy to identify by the services they offer:

- Guided tours of their facility to check-out the care not only of the puppies but of all dogs on the property

- Invitations for you to play with dogs whom you are considering as a choice.

- Volunteer references of others who have purchased from them

- Offer to take back a dog/puppy regardless of the reason, and refund the fee

- Expert knowledge in the breed's health, temperament, behavior, genetic history

- Puppy age at least 6-8 weeks old

- Does not offer puppies year-round, yet may offer waiting list for interested parties

- History as a USDA breeder

- Discussion concerning family lifestyle and requirements which best meet the needs of this breed

- Breeding, health, inoculation and veterinary records

- Health records of the pet's sire and bitch which might offer insight into possible future genetic concerns

Some of these irresponsible breeders can truthfully tout that the dog comes with American Kennel Club (AKC) papers. According to Source Watch website, it is not difficult to register a dog: simply complete the required paperwork and pay the designated fee. Although AKC, Continental Kennel Club (CKC) and American Pet Registry, Inc. (APRI) are admired for setting the standards for breeds, their organizations are sustained by fees breeders pay to register puppies. AKC and others, according to HSUS, list no health standards for breeding other than a minimum age of eight months. Registration only documents that the dog's parents were registered as a recognized breed. Certified paperwork does not guarantee a dog's health, temperament, or breed specifications, but it does usually guarantee that the selling price for the papered dog is greater. More than a dozen of the HSUS assisted puppy mill rescues in North Carolina were of AKC linked pups. In 2012 an AKC inspected "champion" ranked breeder of Malamutes was charged with 91 counts of animal cruelty. Twenty-five years of his 30 year prison sentence were suspended. Because of its lack of criteria in inspections and because AKC has repeatedly aligned itself against more than 150 laws introduced to harness or stop puppy mill abuse, HSUS in 2014 awarded AKC "The Worst In Show."

Termed "The Cattle Dog Catastrophe," a 2014 Mississippi team of Pearl River County Sheriff deputies conducted a raid on an AKC inspected and approved Australian Cattle Dog breeding facility. Sixty diseased dogs covered in open sores with broken teeth and missing ears were found in sheds with temperatures exceeding 100 degrees. Their crates were imbedded in two inches of excrement. Owners were charged with 249 charges of animal cruelty/neglect, but in <u>Mississippi</u>, animal cruelty charges are limited to two per person.

Regardless of public warnings and laws, backyard breeding business is still booming. The demand for designer and purebred dogs is increasing. Individuals who prefer no valid paperwork or history probing involved turn to the internet or newspaper ads of backyard breeders and puppy mills. Both produce puppies strictly for their cash value. They are a business. Dogs are forced to breed, as often as possible for their whole lives until they are physically incapable. A female dog is kept pregnant or nursing during their entire lives at the mill. Some, in their short life, never leave their filthy 24" x 48" wire mesh kennel. They usually live in crowded, squalid conditions, often without required inoculations or veterinary care. But some puppy mill dogs also exist in tractor trailer cabs, tool sheds, lean-tos, horse trailers; some have been found hanging in cages from the ceiling or tethered to trees. Once they are unable to carry and care for a litter, they are taken to a shelter, let loose to roam the streets, or disposed of. They are non-productive inventory that requires cash outflow, merchandise to be sold before it requires more food and care, and especially, before it grows…less attractive to the perspective buyers. Breeders and pet stores are able to reach maximum profits by not spending the money necessary to provide basic animal care for their pets.

Animal rescue groups who are aware of puppy mills operating in their towns are often tempted to tromp right in, swoop up the abused animals and save these physically and psychologically injured animals from further harm. But only law enforcement officers can legally serve the necessary warrant, enter the property and make the determination whether or not animals can be seized by examining the evidence and violations of animal cruelty or neglect. They usually contact larger humane associations for professional assistance in the handling and transporting of the injured and abused animals. Then volunteers can be requested to help in tending to these victims.

One such successful case and one of the most significant puppy mill busts in Jefferson County, <u>Arkansas</u> history was in February, 2014. More than 120 dogs, but 183 animals total, were rescued with the help of volunteers from RedRover Responders with Humane Society of the United States. Owners were charged with aggravated animal cruelty.

Manpower from ASPCA was requested on a 2015 raid on a puppy mill in Needham, <u>Alabama</u>, where 130 Chihuahuas, Yorkshire Terriers and Pomeranians were treated for hyperthermia, dehydration and diseases of both the eyes and mouth. Besides being charged with animal cruelty, the owners were also charged with possession of illegal drugs, with purpose to sell, and money laundering.

Puppy mills and hoarders are usually hidden from public scrutiny, so it was quite a shock when a volunteer at Cedar Creek, <u>Texas</u>, answered the phone one August morning in 2013 to hear this request. "I need help to feed my 400 puppies who are not selling well." After obtaining the obligatory search warrant, the Humane Society of Texas and county sheriff deputies arrived. Waiting for them were 600 dogs, underfed, sick with infections, crowded into repulsive conditions. Their 72-year-old owner-breeder denied the unhealthy conditions in which they were surviving. "These dogs have been in my life, sleeping in my bed, for more than 50 years. They are my family. We love each other."

After a record number of complaints about a puppy mill in <u>Arkansas</u>, HSUS in <u>Washington, D.C.</u> and Jefferson County Sheriff conducted a raid. They were so appalled at the condition of these 183 sick animals, 121 of which were dogs, that they were sure that some of the charges would be upgraded to aggravated animal cruelty, a felony. Humane Society executives pointed an accusing finger at <u>Arkansas</u> legislators accusing that theirs was one of the most problematic puppy mill states because it has no laws to protect these innocent animals.

The total lack of a comprehensive federal law and the lack of state law and enforcement are the culprits in the continued existence of the thousands of heart-breaking puppy mills dotting America, along with no strong and enforceable sterilization laws. Strong assistance will not come from the Federal Animal Welfare Act, which regulates animals in science and research, not animal cruelty; their standards are far from what most people would consider healthy or humane.

As of 2013 "Internet Puppy Mills" was incorporated into this federal act and now requires USDA inspections in these locations. Also for the first time, it allows federal inspections to go behind previously closed kennel doors.

A confusing kernel of information: Just because a breeder adheres to USDA standards does not mean it is not a puppy mill. This is due to the laxity of USDA standards for even the most basic care.

According to Source Watch, it is easy for puppy mill to obtain their required USDA license for sales to pet stores. USDA is so overwhelmed with responsibilities, they lack sufficient trained personnel to enforce their very basic requirements. Some of their harried inspectors have issued licenses to facilities which their written reports reveal have untended-to cases of mange, disease as well as uncared-for emaciated animals and even rotting carcasses on the grounds. Their inspectors number a mere 100; these few are responsible for inspecting and monitoring 10,000 facilities: animals bred and sold by dealers, animals in entertainment, zoo animals and laboratory animals.

A closer examination of USDA reveals that their standards are minimal. They do not limit the number of animals confined to cages for their entire lives; they do not address environment, socialization, exercise, nutrition or the size of the space in which pets are kenneled.

Although more prevalent in some states, puppy mills/backyard breeders are not indigenous to one geographical region, existing in backyards in both urban and rural locations throughout America. And because these breeders operate nationally, their litters live, on display, in more than 1,500 pet stores throughout the states. Those not sold to pet stores are advertised in local newspapers; some (usually the unchosen, stolen or sick) are available, for free or for a discount, from boxes in front of stores, from the back of pickup trucks or on street corners.

Unsuspecting Hollywood stars boasted and purred that their pets were special and near-perfect because they were purchased from a local pet store whose discerning owner carefully chose these specific dogs and cats from small, licensed, caring and breed-recognized hobby AKC breeders. Curious, HSUS decided to investigate this claim; they discovered the sources were local puppy mills where more than 100 dogs were surviving in stressful, filthy conditions. With the required warrant, authorities seized these vulnerable animals and placed in healthy shelters.

The obvious conclusion of this example is that pets purchased from any pet store will support, directly or indirectly, the puppy mill problem, a large contributor to the yearly euthanizing of millions of unchosen healthy companion pets. An estimated number exceeding 500,000 puppies are sold, yearly, by pet stores in the U.S. The Model Law for Pet Shops/Pet Dealers can be referenced on the website for the Animal Legal Resource Center.

Even though 26 states have addressed some aspects of commercial breeding in their statutes, these laws are riddled with inconsistencies and do not address all of the mandatory considerations: sanitation, exercise,

humane or veterinarian care, shelter, ventilation, food and water requirements, inspections, licensing and a governing agency.

If states and communities cannot agree on definitions of important terms such as "breeder," "dealer" and "kennels," one can only cringe
when imagining the many other more complicated legal loopholes and
inconsistencies.

Arizona, California, Texas and Colorado are the Southwestern states
which have chosen to address puppy mills, passing loosely written and confusing statutes concerning licensing and inspections. In 2011 Texas passed
HB1451, which requires licenses, inspections as well as criteria for housing, health and veterinarian care for all companion animal breeders with 11
or more intact females and selling more than 20 puppies or kittens a year.
Breeding and intact licenses are obligatory.

As of 2015, New Jersey's Pet Purchase Protection Act, **SB1870**, prohibits
stores from sourcing dogs and cats from breeders who fail to meet the basic
care standards prescribed by federal and state law. This New Jersey act also
dictates that pet stores post, on the animal's kennel, all medical information about each pet including age, breeder, breeder's USDA license number
and breeder's contact information. It also allows customers access to USDA
inspection reports for all breeders.

New Jersey Sen. Holzapfel, one of the sponsors of this legislation, was
pleased that this measure which protects the purchaser from buying sick pets
for their families is now law. It requires a pet store to disclose the history at
the point of sale, allowing consumers the opportunity to research the breeder
and then to make an informed decision on where to make their pet purchase.

This New Jersey legislation was chosen by Animal Legal Resource Center to serve as a model for other states to enact humane statutes which
would seriously impact the puppy mill–pet store connection. New laws
should further regulate the unethical backyard breeders and puppy mills
that plague our animal shelters by forcing them to operate as licensed, mon-
itored businesses.

Indiana's 2009 statute stipulated such safeguards but failed to provide
power for law enforcement or animal care officers to seize dogs found in
these abusive circumstances.

Virginia was forced in 2008 to enact strong statutes regarding puppy
mills and commercial breeding after HSUS discovered in 2007 more hundreds of puppy mills existing in trailers, basements and suburban backyards
in the state. During that period of time, over 900 dog breeders were selling commercially, most of whom were unlicensed, unmonitored with no

oversight by any state or federal agency. Virginia's current law, VA **3.2-6507-6517,** is considered to be a model for controlling and lessening the animal cruelty involved in backyard breeding, puppy mills and commercial breeding. Its legislatures were far-sighted enough to make provisions to funnel appropriate funds to the specific department responsible for state-required inspections, but failed to lower maximum number of breeding dogs. Virginia's statute does not become effective until breeder has more than 30 breeding females.

Missouri has passed several unusual, innovative and humane laws regarding puppy mills and backyard breeders. Missouri's Animal Care Facility Program **2 CSR-30-9,010-2 CSR-30-0, 030** regulates breeders, dealers, boarders, shelters and pet stores so that they meet state standards regarding feed, water, shelter, veterinary care, building maintenance, socialization, identification and record keeping. Legislation passed in 2016 requires dog breeders to provide more space for the animals and prohibits the use of wire-strand flooring in dog kennels.

Missouri's Operation Bark Alert provides a successful manner for the public to go to their online link to report substandard breeding or living facilities in both puppy farms and pet stores. Their staff of 16 is responsible for investigation. Another successful part of this act is the Blue Ribbon Kennel Program. Kennels with favorable inspection histories and in good standing with the state apply to the state for this status so that their puppies will be permanently identified as Blue Ribbon Puppies, originating in this outstanding kennel.

Twenty-two states, including the Southwestern states Arizona, California and Nevada, have recently taken a new, humane and legal approach to the puppy mill cruelty. By passing puppy lemon laws, purchasers of a sick animal will receive a monetary refund of its price, as well as incurred veterinary bills. This law was meant to be helpful in criminal court cases. Serious California communities such as West Hollywood and South Lake Tahoe as well as Lake Worth, Florida, have proactively taken the puppy mills/backyard breeders and their pet store partners by the tails and have enacted ordinances outlawing any stores selling live pets.

To further curtail illegal breeding, state sterilization laws of all companion animals should be strict and enforceable, but surprisingly 20 states are not serious enough about the over-population of dogs and cats to enact such statutes. This is such a vital issue to impacting the overpopulation of companion pets that it should not be left to the whim of individual communities or counties to enact.

The strongest sterilization statute comes from Rhode Island, with an excellent check and balance system. Texas laws dictate cross reporting between inspection and law enforcement agencies and require that all breeds obtain licensing for breeding on premises, of which inspections will be performed every 18 months. They require cross reporting between inspection and law enforcement groups.

Thirty states, including New Mexico, Arizona, California, Colorado, Nevada and Texas, require sterilization, or promise to sterilization with a deposit, in order to adopt companion animals from municipal or private shelters or rescue organizations.

New Mexico's 135,000 yearly private and public kenneled dogs and cats, kittens and puppies are live reminders that the pet overpopulation problems in our state are worsening. These facilities were unable to place 65,000 adoptable companion animals, which were euthanized. According to APNM, the more pets who are spayed or neutered means fewer animals die and, from the business/fiscal standpoint, millions of New Mexico dollars are saved…yearly.

Andi was firm. *The strength of any law depends on the resources and commitment of its enforcement and community. Our county and local ordinances have enacted a few precautions to provide some feeble stop-gaps for irresponsible breeding and puppy mills. They include Breeder Permits, Intact Permits, Litter Permits and Multiple Companion Animal Permits. These are safeguard measures used by communities to make it more difficult for backyard breeders/puppy mills, the epitome of animal cruelty.*

Citations were issued in the cruel, calloused and heartless cases we speak of in this chapter, all of which are considered only to be misdemeanor offenses and all of which left hundreds of animals suffering and dying in repulsive, filthy conditions. How can most of our nation's statutes, laws, ordinances and codes consider these acts against loving and innocent beings as mere misdemeanor offenses?

As Andi closed this session, she cautioned her audience. *Puppy mill stories, each as if not more horrific than the one last week, will continue to headline the news, because the estimated number of puppy mills operating, legally and illegally, in America, tops 5,000, each housing an average of 100-150 dogs. The solution is simple: tighten legislation and establish examining boards, with the commitment of sufficient resources to strictly enforce these laws.*

I firmly agree with one North Carolina deputy, who, after his tenth puppy mill bust in the past 18 months, complained, "Until strong dog breeding legislation is passed, our law enforcement agencies will encounter yearly hundreds upon hundreds of sick, infected and dying dogs from unlicensed breeding facilities and their owners will only be charged with misdemeanors."

IMPLICATIONS OF BACKYARD BREEDING AND PUPPY FARMS ON PUBLIC SAFETY

Irresponsible breeding by puppy farms, backyard breeders, hobby breeders and careless pet owners have resulted in dangerous and overcrowded animal care facilities throughout America. The health, sanitation and environmental issues raised by these unlicensed, uninspected sites include the distinct possibility of their spreading diseases for miles into the surrounding areas.

Laws to correct these public health and public safety issues are paramount. States must pass stronger laws requiring closer enforcement of required state sterilization laws of all companion animals. And states must become proactive by contributing heavily to low-cost, no-cost spay and neuter clinics. According to the Minnesota Legislature, each $1 invested in low-cost sterilization, an unchosen animal is spared, bringing a $35 savings to communities in animal control costs (receiving, capturing, housing, feeding, possibly euthanizing, maintaining facilities, investigating) over a future ten-year period. That is an unbelievable return, monetarily, as well as for the community's well-being.

CHAPTER FIFTEEN
TRAINING: "THE UNCHOSEN"

"We can't solve problems by using the same kind of thinking we used when we created them."

– Albert Einstein, theoretical physicist,
Nobel Prize 1921, Theory of Relativity

The plight of the abused animal highlights each of these chapters. However, even though the pages in this chapter, "The Unchosen" do not pertain directly to the responsibilities of law enforcement; they address the needless executions of a frightening number of innocent animals...those chosen to die. Their deaths are the result of indifferent and inadequate laws and enforcement which we must work to change. And it is the deaths and suffering of all of our animals that this book is attempting to lessen.

Rescued pets make the best pets because their reactions reveal that they have seen the "other side" of life. They are more appreciative, more attentive and loving, less demanding. Odds are that rescued pets will carry baggage of their previous life (most likely of their mistreatment and neglect): anger, distrust, possession, dietary and health issues, cowering, fear of a long list of everyday sounds, lack of socialization or training...just to mention a few. Still, they are where my heart is, and my experience makes me aware of the untold, heartbreaking difficulties faced by those many volunteers who give their souls to a rescue group, all in the name of love. Giving them more responsible care is the crux of BCACT; our efforts are dedicated to the rescuing of those whose lives have been so bleak.

The ever-increasing proliferation of unwanted dogs and cats (in one word, overpopulation) is recognized as the largest challenge to today's already over-burdened public and private shelters. The majority of these "petable" residents of the over-crowded shelters are there because the spay and neuter laws in localities and states are either lax or not actively enforced. These communities must be held accountable for these needless deaths and "fix" their laws.

Six to eight million dogs and cats a year become wards of animal shelters according to HSUS, and it is through the dedicated energies of shelter employees and rescue volunteers that many are reunited with their owners or are adopted into new caring homes. The "unchosen": those healthy companion animals who are the "left-overs" number 2.7 million a year. Each year, 5,000 plus animal control facilities are forced to euthanize thousands of adoptable companion animals, "throw-aways," about 1 every 13 seconds.

Midland, Texas Animal Shelter, through the use of progressive marketing and partnering with PetSmart Charities and Adoptables, a foster-based rescue group, lowered their shelter euthanasia rate for seven consecutive years. However, that entailed closing the shelter during specified periods for intake of animals left wandering and needing professional intervention.

In 2009 New Mexico became the 18th state to ban the use of gas chambers to euthanize pets. Passage of this legislation was due mainly to the perseverance of Yvette Dobbie, who was horrified that the city officials in Clovis, New Mexico, the location of one of the state's largest shelters, accepted the chambers as "humane" and felt lethal injections were more expensive. Clovis Mayor explained their opposition to lethal injection was due to the community's confusion about cost and a "we'll-do-it-our-own-way" cantankerous attitude prevalent throughout Eastern New Mexico.

Mary Martin, Santa Fe Humane Animal Shelter and Humane Society director, had an emotional comment concerning Clovis's death boxes. "We need to own up to the fact that these animals in our possession are our responsibility. You can't just put them in a box and kill them. It takes courage; it takes a courageous staff to care for the animals to nurture them and then have to put them down."

Acting on Mary's assessment of the cruel means of euthanasia in Clovis, a Santa Fe woman organized a rescue which saved more than 150 pets from the Clovis shelter and is helping the city with a transfer program that that area's unwanted pets to transport them out of state for adoption.

The link between high euthanasia rates, overcrowded city shelters and the high rates of euthanasia is, by necessity, carved in granite. It is not a secret; it is common sense, an easily reached deduction.

2014 statistics reveal that Portales, New Mexico, a university community, was forced to euthanize 85% of its shelter animals. This city shelter, along with the nearby Clovis shelter reflected an attitude of calloused indifference. They had instigated no proactive measures, no firm sterilization codes, no up-to-date changes in their animal care ordinances, no transporting their surplus pets to other nearby communities with a need for more adoptable companion animals. They had not set up any sterilization clinics, low-income or senior, had not proposed county or city taxes to be ear-marked for sterilization, nor had they organized a city drive to educate and fund sterilization programs.

Finally, in 2015, a few caring and serious individuals in the Clovis-Por-tales area began investigating and asking the right questions, surveying other state shelters and analyzing the data. Their Animal Task Force Ad Hoc Committee found specific programs for operating a city-run animal shelter which should increase their pet adoptions. Neither community had not one of these, but recently have begun implementing them with imme-diate results.

- ♦ No one had ever applied for grants. They had to go out of town, out of state to find help offering low cost spaying and neutering clinics. They teamed up with Soul Dog in Colorado to sterilize more than 60 Clovis animals and demand for this service has the next clinics booked to capacity.

- ♦ Working with a local rescue, they are now transporting hundreds of dogs and cats out of state to communities in need.

- ♦ The shelter now has Saturday and extended hours, hosts adoption events, trains volunteers to socialize the pets, and offers discounted or free adoptions for non-profits or seniors.

- ♦ Revisions for their animal ordinance are being written and submitted, including spay and neuter policies, breeders' licenses and micro-chipping.

Until early 2015, North Carolina shelters were allowed the routine use of gas chambers as regular method of euthanasia of their "unchosen." An ALDF petition led to the ban on pet gassing in that state.

This continuous stream of innocent deaths can be "fixed" by respon-sible ordinances and educational programs in states and communities by providing adequate funding to "fix" companion animals. Enforceable and firm community sterilization codes coupled with free or low-cost spaying and neutering programs, having secured grant or government monies ear-marked for this purpose, have proven to save thousands of lives, yearly…in a single shelter. And local veterinarians need to take an active role in allevi-ating these crowded conditions. Such a program is strongly urged by most animal national, state and city humane organizations, including American Humane Association, Animal Rescue Foundation, ASPCA, AVMA, Best Friends Animal Society, DogFinders, HSUS, PAWS, PETA, and PetFinders.

Successful sterilization programs such as that in Jacksonville, Flori-da, should be researched for feasibility in states with overcrowded shelters and thus high euthanasia rates. This Florida city with a population exceeding 900,000, was battling with a euthanasia rate comparable to that of New Mexico's current statistics.

Approximately 135,000 dogs and cats enter New Mexico municipal and county shelters yearly and almost 50% are euthanized because there is not enough kennel space to hold them and not enough families wish to adopt them. A government sponsored 2002 sterilization program launched in Jacksonville, Florida, drastically changed their intake and euthanasia within months. Currently this compassionate city of 900,000 does not euthanize healthy or treatable companion animals and hails its efforts as "No-Kill" for space facility, with a 90% live release rate.

Still, the public should be wary of many shelters touting the "No Kill" banner, as some are misrepresented and have become the problem rather a temporary answer. Those shelters that turn-away those needy pets (who will probably be "Unchosen") have given the owners little choice. Rejected by "No Kill" shelters, those pets are often put on the streets by their calloused owners or owners who can no longer financially or emotionally care for a pet.

Cost and accessibility of spaying and neutering are two of the main barriers to mandatory spaying and neutering (MSN) laws. Studies indicate that shelter intake is greatest from areas where human poverty levels are high, increasing the possibility of euthanasia from these low income communities.

Rated 49th worst in poverty statistics and touting the highest rate of child poverty in the United States, New Mexico covers 121,593 square miles of land, most of which is sparsely populated, so it is not unusual for residents of Cibola (4,542 square miles), Catron (7,000 square miles,) Sierra (4,236 square miles) and Hildago (3,445 square miles) Counties to face a 100 mile drive for licensed veterinarian care. But each of these counties offers a publicly funded spay/neuter program. Funding for these desperately needed sterilization programs in New Mexico requires political commitment (a service the public demands), as communities lack the knowledge and monies to successfully sponsor these programs on their own. They instigated new state 2015 program allows income tax payers to utilize a check-off box on their forms to dedicate funds for state spay and neuter programs, the program is complicated and un-marketed...almost useless as a tool to fund much needed spaying and neutering services throughout the state.

A required sterilization program alone is not the solution to the high euthanasia rate in our country if it is without low cost or free spay and neuter programs. Evidence one of our country's strongest laws on pet sterilization in <u>California's</u> Los Angeles County. It required most dogs and cats to be spayed or neutered by the time they are four-months-old, hoping to reduce the thousands of needless euthanizations occurring in Los Angeles' animal shelters every year. Its goal was admirable: the eventual elimination of the euthanization of adoptable pets. The ordinance provided exemptions for those that have competed in shows or sporting competitions, guide dogs, animals used by police agencies, and those belonging to professional breeders. Owners with older unneutered pets and newcomers to the city with animals were also required to comply with the ordinance. "The best laid plans of mice and men..." This ordinance, which reads so well was not just a failure, it was a disaster because the city lacked the funds to offer low cost sterilization services and had developed no plan for enforcing the ordinance. It was discontinued in 2011, after experiencing an increase in intakes and in the percentage of pets who were euthanized.

Other cities enacting mandatory spay/neuter laws for pet owners include Dallas, <u>Texas</u> and Las Vegas, <u>Nevada</u>. Thirty states require sterilization or a promise to sterilize in order to adopt an animal from a pound, animal shelter, or pet animal rescue. Most state and local require higher licensing fees for intact animals and mandatory sterilization for dangerous or vicious dogs.

The ordinances of Rio Rancho and Bernalillo County, <u>New Mexico</u> still do not require sterilization of their companion animals, although the county, according to Officer Patrick Trujillo, Field Supervisor, offers their SNAP (Spay, Neuter, Assistance Program). It provides free spaying or neutering for pet owners with addresses within the unincorporated area of the county, is not income-based, but does place a limit on the number of animals eligible for SNAP per household.

Is it not enough that we are so indifferent in our respect of life, that we brutally kill (not euthanize) these innocents, these "Unchosen?" According to PETA, there still exist community shelters in which "The Unchosen" are not even granted a peaceful death. They are shot, poisoned, electrocuted, gassed, or placed in decompression chambers...yes, today, in the 21st century. This, of course, is through vigorous objections of the policies of American Veterinarians' Association, firm in their belief that the kindest means is the intravenous injection of sodium pentobarbital by a trained professional.

The responsibility to end inhumane types of death in our kennels is not that of law enforcement personnel, but of those concerned citizens, who respect dignity in both life and death, to investigate, ask pertinent questions and to learn the truths about their community shelter. Only stronger laws, adequate funding and stronger enforcement can undo the injustices facing today's "unchosen."

"All great civilizations have crumbled due to their lack of respect of life. You do not have to be a parent of a child nor an owner of a pet to respect life, but you must have self-respect before you can respect all life."

– Anonymous

CHAPTER SIXTEEN

TRAINING: INTERVENTION FOR THE ANIMALS

"I have found that in my more than 15 years in animal welfare, throughout the country, that it is less about the ordinances and more about the people who are charged with enforcing them. If you have people who are compassionate, committed and, frankly, there for the right reasons, they will find a way to be a voice for the animals."

– Matt Pepper, president, CEO,
Michigan Animal Humane Society

Andi concurred. *Animals are the heart, the reason of BCACT. This collaboration of caring deputies and experienced animal care officers takes seriously its charge to uncover and halt animal abuse.*

Although my sheriff deputies and BCACS officers will be conducting these unannounced sweeps jointly, these classes will better prepare you for your mission: arming you with the necessary knowledge and training to protect the animals in all of Bernalillo County, specifically our South Valley, where animal abuse calls and incidents are highest.

A brief history of pets in America will aid our understanding in why our animal abuse rates are excessive. DNA suggests man's best friends, dogs, split from wolves and were bred up to 40,000 years ago. Fast forward to World War II, after which the owner-pet relationship changed substantially when most of the population shifted from rural to urban. In this pre-war era, most animals were accustomed to living outside and were treated more like livestock, so house-training and behavior mattered less. The 20th century changed the role of pets from guard dogs and barn yard pets to that of important, live-in companions. America's society and their laws are slowly evolving toward a more ethically and morally humane attitude and treatment of our animals. And these, in turn, hopefully produce kinder interactions between animals and humans.

In addition, our changing lifestyles in these new decades reveal that:

- The majority of the present American adults are single and rely on their pets for friendship.
- More homes have pets than children.
- A child is more likely to grow up with a pet than a father.

Pet owners of our 21st century hold images of obedient pets. But the lack of pet ownership education and animal humane laws and enforcement by our communities have greatly weakened this dream. Now stir into these households some self-serving traits attributed to today's youth: failure to accept responsibility and the lack of respect of life, and pet ownership is doomed. Pets require training, veterinarian care, time, patience and money. Failure of today's pet owners to grasp these realities of conscientious pet ownership has resulted in our present situation: the likelihood of abandonment, abuse and neglect of domesticated pets.

And those conditions necessitate trained and compassionate municipal animal care officers and shelters to house and protect these animals from this abuse, neglect and abandonment. They require cooperation and intervention between their government agencies. Because of the overwhelming number of these throw-aways and abused, Bernalillo County is grateful to rely on a large assortment of animal rescue organizations staffed by eager and devoted volunteers. We are among those states fortunate to have sanctuaries in their states that will also assume lifetime care for these rescued animals.

However, since our South Valley is mostly rural and farming, most of our domesticated animals still live outside, and are still considered as guard dogs or livestock. Protective aggression is rewarded with praise by their owner, turning their pet into another ingredient in a fast increasing picture of violence. Particularly in America's unincorporated areas, many animals (including livestock), exist in deplorable conditions, in which food and water are offered, when remembered or at a whim. Neglect is a form of abuse that often begats violence.

Phil Arkow Coordinator of the National Link Coalition—the National Resource Center on The Link Between Animal Abuse and Human Violence—broadens the public's concern about public safety to recognize the significance of animal abuse. "Historically, animal cruelty laws have been enacted because these crimes are seen as a crime against society. Today, the public and many different professional groups are appropriately redefining animal abuse as not just a crime against animals, but an important link to many other types of family and community violence. Our law enforcement personnel need to keep in mind that animal abuse is also a societal issue which often indicates and predicts crimes against the human members in our communities."

When answering a call to visit a property for possible animal abuse, abandonment or other county violations involving animals, you must adhere to your training and official guidelines, for your safety as well as that of the animal, the family and the nearby residents. Although your call may be concerning a different complaint/incident not involving an animal, you need to be on alert for a dog on the property and be aware of the following safety measures.

APPROACHING A PROPERTY*—*First…always check for signs of a dog: 'Beware Of" signs, shelter, feces, dog chains, toys, food and water dishes.*

- *Entering property without a warrant or consent:*
  1. *Requires that you must have a reason, such as a complaint.*
  2. *Necessitates you make an attempt to contact property owner.*
  3. *Is allowable in order to check the welfare of an animal.*
  4. *Does not allow you to photograph or take property unless it is exigent for the wellbeing of people, animals or property.*
- *Make sure you checked prior records on this address for deputy notes about their pets and property layout.*
- *Park your vehicle inconspicuously.*
- *Check for signs (lights, music, open doors, automobiles) that the homeowner is on property.*
- *When approaching a yard or house, make noises so that you do not startle the dog/s. The sound of keys is familiar to most dogs, whereas knocking could be a sound of an intruder.*
- *You are entering the dog's property. Do not challenge the dog by staring at him.*
- *Slowly (all movements, if possible, should be cautious and not jerky) turn sideways and assume a relaxed stance.*

- *Keep your eyes on the dog at all times. Never turn your back on a dog.*

- *Toss a stick or a ball or even a dog treat. Attempt to establish some rapport.*

- *Do not yell at the dog or be assertive. Speak softly in a tone the owner would most likely use.*

- *Secure the area. Close all gates once you enter the property. You do not want to release a vicious or injured dog onto the streets. And you do not want a neighborhood dog (unknown quantity) entering the property you are approaching in response to the cries or barks of those dogs.*

- *Stay calm. Our stress levels affect our judgements.*

- *Most important of all: under no circumstances should a deputy compromise his personal safety or that of his partner.*

RECONSIDER YOUR INTENT AND OPTIONS

- *Have I attempted to contact the owner (doorbell? phone?) and ask him to lock-up the dog?*

- *Is the owner possibly hiding?*

- *Can I work around or remove this dog without having an encounter?*

- *Do I have the time to request an animal control officer?*

- *Is it possible for me to use a garbage can, lid or another available item to shield myself?*

- *Can I use a fire extinguisher?*

- *Would using my bite stick be helpful?*

- *Do I have quick access to a water hose?*

- *Should I resort to an OC or a TASER?*

- *Keep in mind that because OC, a pepper-spray, does not penetrate deeply the skin of a furred animal, it usually does not take a dog long to recover and possibly come after you.*

- *Have I checked for other animals on the property which could attack, such as other dogs, cats or geese?*

ANIMAL TALK—*You can't just eyeball a dog and guess whether it is dangerous. Observe and interpret these warning signs given out by the whole dog.*

A dog's demeanor can change—from negative to positive—according to whether you are on or off property, whether you represent a threat or not. Dogs who are territorial or aggressive or serve as guard dogs are usually, through their body language, telling the deputy that they are near/on their property, which I am protecting. Aggressive dogs speak to you through body language. They try to appear large and intimidating by standing erect, hackles raised, tail raised and rigid, head held high, ears up and forward and an intense stare. Their lips are curled over snarling front teeth and their muzzles are wrinkled. The sound they make might be a low growl or a threatening bark. A wagging tail is not an indication of happy. And keep in mind that some dogs are still unknown quantities as they can immediately turn from friendly to deadly at the command of their owner. <u>Head these warning signs and err on the side of caution.</u>

If you are bitten by a dog, <u>do not pull away</u>. If possible, push in towards the dog's mouth to lessen the severity of the injury. This should force him to let go and back away, a natural instinct for the dog. Immediately consult a physician if animal's rabies tags are not current.

LETHAL FORCE—*It's time we tackle a problem that is troublesome and embarrassing within law enforcement agencies, and which must be met with training so that it will occur in much smaller numbers.*

And, we will try to do just that…through education and understanding. I am speaking of a deputy shooting and killing someone's pet: when it is justified and when it is not justified. These tragic incidents are on the rise. According to the U.S. Department of Justice (USDOJ), even though no reports exist of a law enforcement officer killed in the line-of-duty by a dog, law enforcement officers shoot more than 10,000 dogs per year. Most of these canine victims are family pets (all sizes), not large, snarling, aggressive dogs trained to attack. And most experienced officers and attorneys agree that these deaths are avoidable through mandatory training of the officers.

Warranted or not, today's dog owners become very emotional, unreasonable and possibly violent in such a tense situation. Most deputies respect dogs and do not wish to confront the litigation, media, or possible discipline for using deadly force on a hostile, snarling animal. Sadly, some such encounters using deadly force are justified, and some of this blame and responsibility must be accepted by the owners.

What brings the most ire, and usually deserved, from homeowners, are when the dog is killed by officers during encounters that are considered to be routine, such as false burglar alarms at homes, calls about nuisance barking or following up on reports or investigations. The repercussions from the press releases on 'puppy-cides' have caused community riots, anonymous hacking and shutting down of the city's internet server, hundreds of angry calls that tied up the municipal phone system for days. Lawsuits against such shootings have been very successful. Six figure damages are not unusual. Juries awarded $990,000 against Santa Clara County, California, and $800,000 against San Jose, California.

Because companion animals are considered by most courts as "personal property," cash awards to the owner of an officer-killed-canine are usually based by considering the damages to the owner, measured by the market value/purchase price of the animal, not on the resulting harm or suffering to the companion animal. Most do not take into consideration the wrongful death of the companion animal or the resulting anguish and stress for the owner. However, Tennessee law has a provision which allows suits for emotional distress damages due to the wrongful death of a companion animal. Several cases in Alaska, Florida, Hawaii and New York have also taken into consideration this emotional trauma for the owner.

OWNER PRECAUTIONS—*In the interest of safety for your dog as well as for the public and law enforcement officers, ALDF has helped to compile a list of suggestions for dog owners.*

- *Before contacting a law enforcement agency, crate your dog.*

- *If law enforcement is in your area or neighborhood, crate your dog.*

- *Keep your dog isolated away from law enforcement and others during periods of discord or stress.*

- *All fences, gates, screens and doors (including doggie doors) must be secure to prevent your dog from escaping or leaving the property.*

- *It is the law: dogs cannot roam unleashed.*

- *Do not leave your dog outside, unattended, or in an unfenced outdoor area of your property.*

- *If anticipating a visit from law enforcement, leash your dog in his kennel or a safe place away from others. Dogs are easier to control if leashed.*

Because of a grueling media attack and lawsuits, <u>Colorado</u>, <u>Illinois</u>, <u>Tennessee</u> and <u>Texas</u> have adopted statutes which require its law enforcement personnel to attend canine encounter training. These highly specialized classes in animal behavior will teach the law enforcement officers to differentiate between threatening and non-threatening canines in order to prevent unnecessary shooting of dogs in line of duty.

Some class instructors suggest the use of alternative equipment such as catch-poles, nets, batons, usually standard equipment for animal control officers. Because the BCACT team is also composed of these officers, their expertise, knowledge and training with this equipment will be invaluable to our deputies. Our inter-agency communication within BCACT will reduce wrong addresses and help us to cooperate when determining protocol and procedure.

SEARCHING THE PREMISES—*Always remain in contact with your partner. Remain mentally and physically alert: inquiring, curious and cautious. The unknown surrounds your search.*

The only legal justification, to enter and search personal property without a search warrant is eminent danger, as per the advice of the legal advisor for BCSO. Include in your search warrant statements of facts which support such and an affidavit with a description and items that may be searched or seized.

HELPING AND SEIZING THE INJURED ANIMAL— "If the situation with the animal gives you pause and doesn't seem right, it probably isn't."
– Matt Pepper

Matt continued, "I have trained police officers in four states, primarily in animal behavior on the field and animal cruelty. I always tell them that you might feel as if you are not the correct department to investigate something; which doesn't seem right; perhaps you feel unsure about it or not knowledgeable enough on the issues. Request that information from the people who do investigate animal cruelty rather than ignore it. Take it seriously and get it into the right hands even if those hands aren't yours."

Exercise extreme caution when searching premises where an animal might be abused, ill, in danger or dangerous. There are some specific animal behaviors which can be met with a positive response, and other movements which might require a defensive tactic. Dealing with abused, abandoned or starved animals requires extreme caution, not bravado. An animal in pain reacts to his pain, and he is frightened. And his reaction is often protective aggression. Do not approach an animal that is behaving in a threatening manner. Keep your face away from the animal, and do not move in an assertive manner, but cautiously…no quick movements. Move slowly and speak softly and calmly as you approach.

Possibly tossing a treat will act as a peace offering. Determine if the animal is mobile. If the animal can safely be rolled onto a towel or blanket, you can wrap it around the animal. Wear protective leather gloves because the animal is frightened and might bite or scratch. If you think a muzzle is necessary, be sure that the pet can breathe. This is where two six-foot soft leashes with a ring on one end and a loop on the other would be helpful. Use one to make a muzzle or harness from a leash wrap and the second will loop and act as a leash or collar. Beware of other animals on the property misinterpreting the cries of the injured animal. It may be necessary to create some type of barrier to prevent the animal or others on-property from running into secured areas, off-property or into the road.

Human safety is the priority. Make certain that you are not in any danger from the unpredictable behavior from a frightened or injured animal. Remember, they do not know how to communicate where and how much they hurt. They do not know that you are trying to help them.

Be aware! The risk is not limited to the animals. You can present danger to and from not only the abused animal but also his owners. All your senses should be set on high alert when working with an abused animal's owner and family members. If an individual can harm an innocent animal, they are certainly capable of harming a human, particularly one who is confronting them about their treatment of their animals. Be aware of non-verbal cues. Use your training to de-escalate any volatile situation. Be safe.

DOCUMENT: *video, photograph, diagram and sketch the entire property, all buildings including the residence, and all animals and their conditions, their food and water bowls, their veterinarian records and all medications*.

Secure and seize all evidence: animals are considered as property, so keep a chain of custody by giving each animal an identification number. It is a good strategy to allow the defendant to view and comment on evidence seized. And, take more notes than you need. They will be invaluable during court hearings.

NMDOG coordinates with BCACS for safe transport and delivery of the injured/abused animal to a county-approved veterinarian or volunteer rescue association or a municipal shelter. National statistics reveal that shelter euthanasia of "the unchosen" is the leading cause for deaths of healthy dogs and cats in America. More than 2.7 million healthy, adoptable pets (the "unchosen") are euthanized by our shelters each year, 1 every 13 seconds. This is 64% of the animals entering a shelter.

The majority of dogs rescued by Bernalillo County and Albuquerque are variations of the Pit Bull breed, and we are fortunate that NMDOG accepts as many as her current boarding situations dictate. Not just in our area, but nationwide most municipal and volunteer-operated shelters are cautious about accepting—some even excluding—Pit Bull Terrier-crosses.

DANGEROUSLY HOT VEHICLES*: *It is illegal in the county and city to leave an animal in a hot car. If such is reported to you, you should check the animal for these danger signs of a heat stroke:*

- *Excessive panting*

- *Dark or bring red tongue and gums*

- *Sticky or dry tongue and gums*

- *Staggering*

- *Stupor*

- *Seizures*

- *Bloody diarrhea or vomiting*

- *Coma*

If the animal is suffering from the heat inside a locked vehicle, then take necessary steps to free the animal. If the suffering animal can be heard but not seen through a glass window or door, consider breaking the lock.

REPORT ACCOMPANYING REMOVAL OF ANIMAL

Once you have removed the animal from the vehicle, and contacted animal care services to transport the animal to the veterinarian, this check list is helpful for your report.

- *Check existing weather including heat index, temperature and humidity.*

- *Search vehicle (obtain a search warrant if necessary) to determine if pet tried to escape: claw marks, chewing, scratching.*

- *Search vehicle for bodily fluids.*

- *Photograph car as to condition of shade on car, position of windows.*

- *Interview the perpetrator as to whereabouts and obtain receipts and video surveillance to show how long animal was left in car.*

- *Obtain from perpetrator all of animal's veterinarian records and licenses.*

- *If the animal lives, it may suffer from a long list of health issues related to this incident.*

SERVING WARRANTS*—State law allows peace officers, such as sheriff deputies, to apply to courts to obtain warrants to seize those animals (including livestock) who are suspected of being abused.

If you observe the animal cruelty occurring, consider entering the property because a crime is being committed in your presence and exigent circumstances exist.

According to United States VS MCConney, 9th Cir. read, "Those circumstances that would cause a reasonable person to believe that entry (or other relevant prompt action was necessary to prevent physical harm to the officers or other persons, the destruction of relevant evidence, the escape of a suspect, or some other consequence improperly frustrating legitimate law enforcement efforts."

Keep in mind these exigent circumstances are interpreted by judges whose insistence for a warrant is uncompromising. Be well versed in how the law interprets exigent circumstances.

- *Animal shows signs of being near death.*

- *Animal is severely emaciated.*

- *Animal's collar is embedded in its neck.*

- *Animal displays numerous sores, wounds such as those that would be a result of fighting, stabbing, burning, disease, insect infestations, gunshot, infection.*

- *Animal appears to be suffering from exhaustion or is strained when breathing.*

- *Animal is whimpering, crying.*

- *Animal is crying out, possibly in pain or distress from behind a closed door.*

- *Animal is vomiting, has diarrhea and shows signs of not being cared for.*

- *Animal appears to be too undernourished, too weak or too sick to stand.*

- *Animal is unresponsive.*

- *Animal is threatened by the possible fire or flood of the building where he is located.*

- *Animal is suffering from heat stroke or suffocation inside a closed vehicle.*

- *Animal has no adequate shelter provided in freezing or below freezing temperatures.*

If any one of these exigent conditions exist, and it is possible for you to move the animal to safety, consider doing so rather than waiting for a search warrant. Then call BCACS to transport this animal to a veterinarian or shelter.

When exigent circumstances exist, but the suffering animal is not easily accessible, you should try to locate a witness, after which you should contact BCACS to transport the animal to a veterinarian.

According to the above guidelines, the cruelty case below represents a clear example of exigent circumstances, but, regardless, they were not upheld by the New Mexico judge. In 2012 Albuquerque City Family Services employee Tim was charged with three counts of animal cruelty and torture after animal control officers discovered three severely emaciated pit bull terriers, Cesar. Rockstar and Baby Bop, and entered the property to quickly remove them into *the capable hands of a veterinarian. Veterinarians and animal control officers and staff choked down their tears at the sight of these dogs, as there was not a bone in their starved bodies that you could not see.*

Evidence found on the property pointed to these dogs being groomed to fight. This was not the first time this dog owner had been reported and charged with abuse but AAWD's out-of-date tracking system could only find evidence of 11 other citations or charges, which resulted in the euthanasia of five of his dogs (Pit Bull Terrier crosses) because of aggressive behavior. AAWD presented more records indicating that both Tim and his father had previously surrendered dogs that had to be euthanized. When arrested, the owner whined to the authorities that he could not afford to feed his pets because of the depressed economy.

The response from one attending veterinarian, who was surprised that these dogs were even alive, exhibited controlled anger. "This is not acceptable under any circumstances, regardless of economy. Thank goodness that these tough dogs were survivors."

Because a warrant was not first obtained by the officer in this 2012 case, the judge dismissed the case, even though the prosecutor argued that the animal welfare officer had a good-faith belief that these animals were dying right then and there, and that he had to get them immediate medical care.

It would also serve to enlighten some of the judicial staff in counties, where, because they have no information bank on this individual's record of animal or human violence, allow them to plea-out to a misdemeanor: a less serious charge with provisions of school probation and surrender of animals. This occurs in almost 90% of the cases originally charged as extreme animal cruelty, a felony.

Care must be taken by the district attorney in assigning a prosecutor for any animal abuse case. This individual must understand the seriousness of animal abuse, not only as a crime alone but also as a red light for hidden, future violence. The charges should be treated in such a serious manner even when handling a busy case docket, and might require specialized pre-trial motions, civil bonding and forfeiture procedures as well as the housing of animal victims. Keep in mind that animal victims can't tell you what happened.

Diane Balkin, an ALDF attorney, advises that taking animal cruelty cases seriously achieves greater and earlier benefits in crime prevention, helps break cycles of violence, and assists courts in assessing criminal offenders' level of dangerousness. She advises, whenever possible to obtain written consent to search, which is important to establish probable cause.

ANIMAL CRUELTY*—*Incriminating evidence to identify, document, photograph and seize:*

"Where you see evidence of animal abuse, open your eyes: there is more."

– Matt Pepper

- *Dates of inoculation tags, licenses*
- *Appearance of animal: collar, halter, harness imbedded in flesh*
- *Appearance of animal: too thin, ribs, vertebrae and hip bones prominent*
- *Cleanliness of pet's space in regard to old feces, vomit or diarrhea*
- *Ear fungus detected by pungent odor*
- *Ear mite infestation*
- *Fighting scars*
- *Matted, listless fur*
- *Loss of fur*
- *Unattended or seeping wounds*
- *Tumors*
- *Runny nose*
- *Eyes inflamed or watery*
- *Congested breathing*
- *Chronic cough*
- *Rotten teeth*
- *Signs of diarrhea or vomiting*
- *Heavy chains*
- *Bloated stomach*
- *Evidence of recent surgery (ear or tail cropping) without proper veterinary medicines or care*
- *Evidence of body piercings*

- *Nails curled into flesh; tips of hooves turned upward due to excessive length*
- *Hooves spongy or emitting foul odor*
- *Sores, scabs or infections on body*
- *Tip-free clean water always available, nearby*
- *Tip-free clean food bowls nearby*
- *Appropriate shelter from elements*
- *Overcrowding*
- *Excessively aggressive or fearful*
- *Listless or unresponsive*
- *Self-mutilation, destructive scratching or biting at self*

Guidelines in this publication are not to be construed as providing legal or official police, sheriff or animal control policy.

*As recommended by <u>Investigating Animal Cruelty in New Mexico, A Field Guide for Law Enforcement Officers,</u> NMDPS, APNM, HSUS

CHAPTER SEVENTEEN

TRAINING:
RECOGNIZE AND REPORT

"The world is a dangerous place to live, not because of the people who are evil, but because of the people who don't do anything about it."

– Albert Einstein, Theoretical physicist,
Nobel Prize 1912 Theory of Relativity

Beware: Violence against animals is not just violence. It is usually synonymous with a history of violence against society and/or an indicator of future acts of violence against society. As the eyes and ears of their community, law enforcement personnel rely on that knowledge to protect their citizens.

We must sharpen our senses of observation and train ourselves to recognize evidence of the LINK, the Deadly Link, between animal, child, elder and domestic abuse. These are situations we encounter routinely. For the future safety of all family members in the reported residence, our observations must be shared with appropriate agencies.

Phil Arkow, Coordinator of the National Link Coalition, explains this in depth. "Violence takes many forms, and often it is linked to crimes of interpersonal violence. In the world of the LINK, we see this manifested as bullying, animal fighting, elder abuse, intimate partner violence, child abuse, animal cruelty and neglect. Traditionally, all of these forms of violence were considered separate, but research now confirms that the causes of one form of violence are often similar to those of the others—it's all about the perpetrator's need for power and control."

These types are not individual issues unto themselves, but are closely linked together by the proven fact that one begets the other. Where there is one, most likely the others await. Violence on any scale to anyone can have long-term effects on everyone involved, not just the victim. And the Deadly Link underlines the importance of cross-reporting between city, county and state entities as well as cross-reporting internally. This communication helps crimes of violence to be more easily detected and more proactively enforced through the cooperation of governmental agencies.

But who reports what to whom, termed cross-reporting, varies from state to state. A summary of laws to help law enforcement walk more easily through that confusing maze was published in 2015 in two resource charts on the National Link Coalition website. Cross-reporting has become a rewarding policy of our newly-formed inter-governmental task force, BCACT. It serves as the foundation of National Coalition on Violence Against Animals (NCO-VAA), inspired by the National Sheriffs' Association.

The International Association of Chiefs of Police was in agreement. "This last decade has seen growing recognition of the connection between the commission of acts of cruelty to animals and other serious crimes against people and property...the incorporation of animal cruelty response into mainstream community policing and the development of new approaches to the investigation, documentation and prevention of animal abuse and neglect."

An example of the importance of observing a household for evidence of the Deadly Link (this time it was child abuse which served as the red light for ongoing animal abuse) occurred late 2014 while a deputy and I were on the scene of a multiple child abuse call. Upon arrival we found the condition of the house to be deplorable, endangering the health of the five small residing children, all infected with lice and scabies. Child welfare was notified.

While we were waiting for an ambulance to provide safe medical transport for the children, I noticed a very tiny Chihuahua resting on the floor behind the front door. While the mother was being removed from the home in handcuffs, under arrest for numerous counts of felony child abuse, I questioned if the dog belonged to this household. Over cries of the children, "Our doggie" the mother loudly denied ownership: she found him "running the streets." A quick call by a BCACS officer revealed no reports of this dog being lost or found.

The seemingly lifeless dog had no collar, no tags, and a scan showed no microchip: no registered owner. This was a no-brainer. This lil' pup needed some TLC while waiting for BCACS. Wrapping him in a warm blanket from the trunk of my vehicle, we visited a nearby grocery store, purchased puppy food and more warm blankets (it was a freezing 12 degrees outside). When we finally arrived at my office, I scooped a handful of puppy food into a small bowl, and the little guy came alive, scoffing it down as if this was the first meal he had ever eaten. His tiny tail started to wag so hard I thought he might take off into flight! As he ate, I inspected his small body. I could count each rib, and his skin and small patches of fur were covered in scabs, raised red blotches and open cuts. I suspected that he might also be infected with scabies and suffering with mange. I would name him Clancy after the sad, hobo clown.

The more he ate and the warmer he became, the more appreciate and loving he became. I felt badly that I could only handle him with the barrier of gloves and the blanket, fearing that I might come in contact with his diseased skin. Once BCACS arrived at my office to take Clancy into custody, he suddenly lunged forward and licked my face feverously: lunge licks.

After receiving a few days of much needed medical intervention, Clancy was released to NMDOG, who had no trouble in finding him a happy life with responsible owners. I wish it were this easy to find new and caring homes for abused and mistreated children.

Recognizing, rescuing and placing abused children and animals was also difficult more than 150 years ago when America's first Society for the Prevention of Cruelty to Animals (SPCA) was formed in conjunction with a Society for the Prevention of Cruelty to Children (SPCC). These wise organizations recognized these linked vulnerable populations who were unable to protect or advocate for themselves. When animals are abused, people are at risk. When people are abused, animals are at risk.

But the FBI, until recently did not recognize The LINK. As a result their compilations did not include animal abuse as a separate category, and this crime was filed away under 'miscellaneous crimes,' along with a variety of lesser offenses. Reported occurrences of animal cruelty were almost impossible to locate, much less track or enter into statistical data or studies.

Finally, October 2014, the FBI officially acknowledged this very important connection/link that animal abuse holds in today's ever-violent environment. Their up-dating information is a tedious task: collecting up-to-date, detailed statistics on animal cruelty and its case-by-case connection to human violence and crime, state by state. The FBI's National Incident Based Reporting System (NIBRS), effective January 2016, re-classifies the crime of animal cruelty as a 'Group A Felony,' with its own category, much the same as the felonious crimes of arson, assault and homicide. The FBI is confident that their new requirement for the filing of animal abuse information with its more serious classification upgrade will be instrumental in aiding their attempts to root out these abusers and other undetected domestic and child abusers before their behavior worsens. However, it is approximated by the FBI that it will take three years of gathering this data for helpful patterns to emerge. Thirty-four states are certified to participate in the NIBRS. New Mexico, a state with one of the largest accountable statistics of animal abuse is not among those.

Harbor no misconceptions. This new directive does not imply any animal cruelty investigation by FBI agents, and it does not re-classify animal cruelty as a federal felony. Hopefully, it will lend additional clout to the crimes of animal abuse in our states and communities. Hopefully it will pressure legislators, commissioners and councilors to introduce harsher penalties for crimes of animal cruelty across America, so that prison sentences for extreme animal cruelty will become the norm not the exception.

Anticipating the inclusion of animal cruelty crimes in the FBI's NIBRS, the National Sheriffs' Association's Annual Conference, June, 2015, featured a symposium on animal abuse, Pause for Paws. One of the expert speakers, Martha Smith-Blackmore, a forensic veterinarian, conducted a workshop entitled Crimes Against Canines: Animal Cruelty from a NIBRS Perspective. The conference also featured a board meeting of the National Coalition on Violence Against Animals, which is in the process of developing a standardized training curriculum on animal abuse for law enforcement training academies.

Andi saw the new FBI policy as a challenge to better their department. *We at Bernalillo County Sheriff's Department, and especially my members of BCACT, are pleased with this new dictate by the FBI and will ready our deputies and officers for a new duty: to sort their animal cruelty arrests into four categories: simple or gross neglect, intentional abuse or torture, organized abuse to include cockfighting and dogfighting, and animal sexual abuse.*

Again, it is our duty, when involved in BCACT encounters, not to look upon the crimes of animal abuse, cruelty and neglect as isolated incidences but as linked to family violence, thus the need for cross-reporting, making our observations known to the appropriate agency. They serve as a red flag, an alert to law enforcement officers that other family members may be in danger.

Remembering that animal abuse is a proven indicator of related family or community violence could possible save the life of a family member. Deadly Link statistics reveal:

- A recent survey revealed that in homes of pet-owning families charged with child abuse, 88% of their animals were also being abused.

- Abusers can be even more aggressive if pet cruelty is also involved. A threat by the abuser to mutilate or kill pets is one of top three indicators that a woman will be killed by her batterer.

- New Mexico's ranking in domestic homicides is usually within the worst three in the nation as exampled by its 77 domestic violence homicides between 2006 and 2010.

- New Mexico reports 21,000 incidents of domestic violence each year. Research revealed in two separate studies that between 71% and 88% of women victims of domestic violence reported that their partners had also abused or killed a family pet/s.

- 80% of American households consider their pet as part of their family. Batterers often use this relationship to exercise power or fear over their victims, half of whom will delay leaving home because of concern for the safety of their companion animals. It is a common occurrence for the victim to be intimidated by their abuser's threats, that if they tell or call for help, their beloved pet will be tortured or killed.

- Very few New Mexico domestic shelters for family abuse have accommodations for a pet. Most New Mexico animal shelters, due to constraints of time and space, are unable to hold and care for pets for a prolonged period of time.

- 85.4% of women and 63% of children reported incidents of pet abuse after they were safely relocated to domestic violence shelters.

- Animal abuse is present in majority of homes where child abuse has been substantiated. This is an indication of poly-victimization, the reason why 18-45% of domestic violence victims and children delay escaping their abusive situations.

But family pets are only one of many reasons why battered partners remain in their abusive situations: economic or emotional dependence, threats and fears of repercussions, concerns about becoming homeless, embarrassment, lack of self-worth or not being believed. If they are undocumented citizens, they fear that they will be turned-in by their abuser. Actually many still have feelings for their abuser and believe that they will change. And some victims of domestic violence actually accept their situation, believing that they themselves must make specific behavioral changes to please their abuser and then he/she will stop; they deserve their punishment. Lastly is their frightening incognizance of their abusive situation: they do not realize that what is happening to them is domestic abuse, a criminal offense, and there exist laws in our nation to protect victims of against domestic abuse, both physical and psychological.

Recently 28 states have passed laws which include pets in domestic violence protection orders. Some others have legally defined animal abuse as a form of domestic violence for the purposes of enhancing the penalty for domestic violence. The "Model Law For Protective Order For Domestic Violence" can be referenced at the website of ALDF Resource Center.

For example, Colorado's legislation is inclusive. "Domestic violence also includes any other crime against a person, or against property, including an animal, or any municipal ordinance violation against a person, or against property, including an animal, when used as a method of coercion, control, punishment, intimidation, or revenge directed against a person with whom the actor is or has been involved in an intimate relationship."

Other states with similar LINK laws include Arizona, Indiana, Maine, Nebraska, Nevada and Tennessee. The Native American Humane Society President and CEO, Diana Webster is attempting to form a LINK organization, but Native Americans are not monolithic; there is a unique culture for each tribe. She is firm that "recognition and prevention are the beginning to safer tribal families and communities."

Other countries with LINK coalitions include Australia's Lucy's Project, Spain's GEVHA (Grupo para el Estudio de la Violencia Hacia Humanos y Animales), Brazil's Lar em Paz, Portugal's O Elo—Link Violencia Humana-Abuso Animal: Uma Realidade Mundial. Several European nations have formed the European Link Coalition and have sent their brochure to appropriate members of the European Parliament.

LINK training is available in all states and schedules appear in monthly issues of LINK-letter, an online publication of the National Link Coalition. Florida's Sheriff's Office magazine, All Points Bulletin, Winter 2016 issue devoted several pages to training procedures for The LINK. Noting the differences between intentional animal abuse and equally devastating cases of animal neglect, the magazine outlined 39 specific physical and environmental signs to look for that suggest abuse, neglect, animal fighting, animal hoarding and puppy mill operations.

FBI's new policy should also provide considerable credence to those law enforcement officers and social service workers whose responsibility it is to deal with those children who have shown aggressive behavior toward animals. Now animal cruelty crimes will be brought to the attention of all law enforcement personnel every month for required crime reports.

According to internationally recognized American cultural anthropologist, Margaret Mead, "One of the most dangerous things that can happen to a child is to kill or torture an animal and get away with it."

LINK researchers have connected children's acts of animal abuse with their being involved in such violent acts as bullying, corporal punishment, school shootings, sexual abuse, and developmental sociopathic. Also, when children are exposed to an environment filled with violence (as a witness, victim or perpetrator), they often, along with the abuser, become desensitized to violence and lose their ability to empathize with the victim.

Animal abuse was present in 60% of households being investigated for child abuse, and in 88% of homes investigated for physical abuse. One-third of these animal abuse happenings were attributed to children.

Thirty-one percent of our youth have been subjected to the horrors of dog-fighting. Child abuse convictions are nine times as prevalent among owners of high-risk, "dangerous dogs," who themselves were victims of animal abuse. The cycle is obvious. Animal abuse is but the tip of an iceberg of family violence. Family violence affects the public safety and public health of the entire community.

The National District Attorney's Association lists these reasons as some which cause a child to abuse an indefensible pet.

- ◆ *The child might feel powerless when they are abused by adults and, in retaliation, find their own victims over which to exert control, thus gaining a sense of power or possibly a sense of intimidation.*

- ◆ *Abuse of the innocent animal may carry a message of punishment for unwanted behavior from people or jealousy of someone's relationship with the animal.*

- ◆ *Children may abuse a pet of a sibling or peer for revenge or emotional maltreatment, or they might be caught up in the continuing atrocities within their home.*

- ◆ *Or the abuse may be for the shock value or to draw attention to themselves. Animal abuse is sometimes an initiation ritual for becoming a gang member or peer-group acceptance.*

To better protect our children, laws should increase the penalties for animal abuse in the presence of a child, designate that perpetrated or witnessed child abuse should be categorized as an adverse childhood experience and mandate cross-reporting that requires animal care officers report animal abuse to all child protection workers in their area.

In an effort to identify and rehabilitate adolescents who have been charged with animal cruelty before they have a chance to become violent toward people, FBI's new dictate of reporting of animal cruelty will make it easier to track and classify crimes of animal cruelty by both adults and children. By paving the way for required cross-reporting between agencies, their long-awaited policy will now provide considerable information to the law enforcement offi-cers and social service workers who are professionally involved with those children who have shown aggressive behavior toward animals.

"Animal abuse should never be excused as an acceptable stage of development. While some children may kill insects and harm animals in exploring through curiosity, intentional animal abuse motivated by an intent to harm suggests a need to intervene, to teach the child respect for other beings," cautioned Chris Risley-Curtiss, associate professor of social work at Arizona State University.

Laws must mandate cross-reporting that requires animal care offi-cers report animal abuse to all child protection and social service workers. Diane Balkin with the Animal Legal Defense Fund agrees and elaborates. "There's a link not only between animal abuse and human violence, but also among the agencies involved. We cannot make a dent against violence if we don't work together with a multidisciplinary approach."

Cross-reporting shared the hero spotlight when in Laurens County, South Carolina Sheriff Department, responding to a call of a concerned neighbor, discovered a badly beaten two-year-old boy in cardiac arrest along with two other toddlers. When their search of the premises revealed 90 animals, 75 of which were dead, animal control was immediately con-tacted. The 25-year-old mother, 36 weeks pregnant, was charged with only four counts of child abuse and cruelty to animals.

The FBI's new system of classifying animal cruelty still falls short of requir-ing life-saving regional and national cross reporting incidences of animal and human abuse in their national database registries, an ingredient in analyzing crime statistics. Studies have proven that downplaying an animal abuse case could be a serious mistake: recognition and cross reporting can reduce recid-ivism. It is important to monitor convicted/felony animal abusers because of their increased likelihood in continued and increasing violence towards ani-mals and people. It stands to reason: if the people who keep their dog chained outside without necessary care, shelter or sustenance, then they are probably more apt to also neglect his children.

The Mayor's Alliance for New York City's Animals has published a com-prehensive guide, *Helping People and Pets in Crisis Toolkit,* a first-of-its-kind LINK resource for those front line professionals.

The following quote from Phil Arkow, coordinator of the National Link Coalition carries a heavy, thought provoking punch. "If cross-reporting were required for all affected state, county and city agencies, we would have a communication solution that would result in a much more systematic approach to reducing most forms of family and animal violence through earlier, timelier, more preventive interventions."

The state of Connecticut began its successful cross-reporting program in 2015, requiring the sharing of pertinent abuse information between their Department of Children and Families and the animal control officers. Oregon's recent 2015 statute allows Department of Human Services to report suspected animal abuse with immunity for good-faith reporting. In 2016, ten states introduced similar laws to require cross-reporting between professionals, veterinarians, government, law enforcement, domestic violence, child and animal welfare agencies.

Referencing Mr. Arkow's professional assessment, our state legislators must recognize that any decision made is only as good as the information used to reach it. Thus, the importance of establishing a strong communication network between the county, city, and state, necessitates the networking of all judicial, law enforcement, animal control, social services, Children, Youth and Families Department (CYFD), veterinarians and those involved in field medical and elder care to make factual observations and notations of any suspected abuse of animals, children and family members. To ensure its credibility, these notations would then be reported in approved format of specially programed software, to one another on a timely basis. But to accomplish this sharing of information about convicted abusers, legislation at the appropriate level is necessary.

A Model Law for Animal Abuser Registry can be referenced at the website of ALDF Resource Center. Animal Humane Association of America (AHAA) also offers model legislation for cross-training and cross-reporting which is currently used by several states now requiring the reporting and sharing of animal abuse data. This well respected, national association urges that our cities must protect our companion animals from predators and abusers by the systematic tracking (cross-reporting) of national animal abuse data.

Several such national or municipal database registries are currently available now to those municipalities and states who are serious about saving lives through the use of such software. RegistryApp and National Animal Abuse Database, or Do Not Adopt Registry, created by the Animal Legal Defense Fund (ALDF) compile animal abuse conviction data into a single directory available nationwide. Adopted and successful in Suffolk County, New York, their abuser database law was named Justin's Law after a two-year-old, 19 pound Doberman rescued from the locked bedroom of a foreclosed home. This was followed by a 2014 New York City animal abuser database legislation. Orange County, New York passed a strong animal cruelty message with a $5,000 fine to any person providing an animal to a convicted abuser on their database list. Ulster County, New York followed suit with similar database requirements and legislation. Either of these two mentioned software applications can make a difference for many animals' lives. Another, different data-tracking system similar to CompStat was devised for ASPCA to help New York City animal abuse investigators spot, track and respond to trends such as co-occurring animal abuse and related domestic violence.

Animal abuse occurrences in New Mexico are alarmingly high, some of the highest in our nation. There exists no information, no database of animal abusers that will ensure rescue groups and shelters, both private and municipal, that the animal that they are entrusting to another's care will be treated with love and responsibility. Currently there is no system in place in our counties, municipalities or state that requires entering and sharing the names of those convicted of crimes of animal abuse. Thus, these abusers can go from one shelter to another to adopt and again abuse these innocent pets. Without such database, we have no laws to ensure that animals are not placed again and again and again into the hands of these convicted individuals, which have an exceptionally high rate of re-offending. (In one attorney's experience, 80% of animal abuse perpetrators re-offended within one year of a felony conviction.)

The reporting of animal cruelty and other LINK crimes just received a high-tech boost with the unveiling by the National Sheriffs' Association (NSA) of its new, free ICE Blackbox app. The application for smartphones allows users to stream videos of animals being abused in real-time to the NSA's control center, where they will then be forwarded to appropriate local law enforcement officers responsible for enforcing animal abuse laws in that jurisdiction. The goal of the app (not meant to replace calling 911), which turns smartphones into surveillance cameras, is not to just help animals who have been abused, but also to help anyone who has felt victimized to stop the crime. Relying on statistics demonstrating that a high percentage of animal abusers will commit another violent crime, John Thompson, NSA Interim Executive Director. "We think this is a game changer. It's going to protect communities all across the United States."

"We are asking citizens to get involved and be part of the eyes and ears for law enforcement to help root out this violence and cruelty from their communities," explained Michael Markarian of HSUS which helped develop the app.

IMPLICATIONS OF RECOGNIZING AND REPORTING ON COMMUNITY HEALTH AND SAFETY

"We cannot make a dent against animal abuse and human violence if we don't work together with a multidisciplinary approach."

– Diane Balkin, ALDF attorney

A history of animal abuse is one of the four significant risk factors of an individual's becoming a perpetrator of domestic violence. By observing and **recognizing** *the evidence on which The Link is based—that people are at risk when animals are abused—and* **reporting** *this to appropriate agencies, law enforcement, animal and social workers can be instrumental in preventing future occurrences of family violence. Recognizing and reporting reduces the risk this abuse poses to the health, safety and welfare of its innocent victims: the children, the elderly, the family and their pets.*

CHAPTER EIGHTEEN
READY TO MAKE A DIFFERENCE

"Understand, our police officers put their lives on the line for us every single day. They've got a tough job to do to maintain public safety and hold accountable those who break the law."

— President Barack Obama, 44th United States President, first African American to hold this office

At the end of each training session, Andi addresses her final congratulatory comments to all the BCACS officers and new BCSO deputies. *"Now you possess the training and the knowledge. You represent power which must never be misused. We, as law enforcement officials, must use this knowledge to educate our communities and act as examples to these citizens we serve. Are we ready to make a difference?*

I speak proudly of the outstanding achievements of Bernalillo County's animal cruelty task force since its inception in 2012. Because it was the successful collaboration of the two law enforcement departments, BCACT was not only a new entity to New Mexico government, but, more important, it continues to become an effective enforcement tool that impacts harmful and violent behaviors directed towards our county animals. Our state, our county and our sheriff's office are very proud of BCACT and its dedicated, compassionate members.

For those of you who do have an interest in being a part of BCACT and our sweeps (when schedules can be coordinated), BCACT sign-up sheets are located at my table; I will contact you when we have our next unscheduled sweep through neighborhoods chosen because of their high-call volume of animal neglect and abuse complaints.

As you employ these newly learned skills and knowledge about animal abuse in Bernalillo County, I know you will find them to be very beneficial yet rewarding, on and off the job. Congratulations and welcome!

Before leaving the lectern, an exhausted but elated Andi added a post-script. *This training was certified by The State of New Mexico Department of Public Safety, who will issue continuing education credits, meeting an in-place continuing education requirement for the deputies and officers of Bernalillo County.*

It is important that each of you realize that ASPCA provides grant funding to law enforcement jurisdictions to offset the costs incurred during animal cruelty cases, to support continuing education and skills training or to purchase equipment that can enhance and improve an agency's response to animal abuse cases. For more detailed instructions about animal cruelty incidents, I suggest:

- Investigating Animal Cruelty in New Mexico, A Field Guide for Law Enforcement Officers, created as a collaborative project by the New Mexico Department of Public Safety, Animal Protection of New Mexico, and the Humane Society of the United States. Its information will strengthen local inter-agency investigations of animal cruelty.

- Five, free, short videos which were jointly produced by The National Canine Research Council, Safe Humane Chicago and the Department of Justice Community Oriented Policing Services. These instruct law enforcement in the key points they need to know about how to approach dogs and their options for less-lethal force. They reveal the correct and safe way to assess a dog's body language, tactical operations for dealing with dogs and the potential legal ramifications of shooting dogs.

- The Problem of Dog Related Incidents and Encounters, published by DOJ COPS and available free to law enforcement agencies.

- The "Model Law for Humane Canine Response Training Act" at the website of ALDF Resource Center.

Following the graduation ceremonies, Andi continued to fascinate the new deputies with more courageous incidents of the task force.

After the completion of the first sessions of BCACT's 16-hour training in 2012, 27 enthusiastic deputies enrolled. Not only was I very proud of these men and women, but I admired their new-found dedication and compassion. Because of their success, BCACT continues its mission every year to change the lives, for the better, of countless animals in Bernalillo County.

I am especially pleased that those BCACT deputies who later accepted beats outside the South Valley continue, whether on or off duty, continue to carry dog treats in their pockets, slip leads, leashes, collars, dog and cat food, water bowls, toys and blankets in their vehicles.

In 2013 Deputy Duran was cruising after hours down a South Valley road. As bold as brass was a sign, "For sale cheap puppies." He stopped, explained about the illegalities of selling roadside puppies, seized them, and called Angela. All of the little snickerdoodles, only three-weeks-old, were immediately placed in those NMDOG's foster homes specifically for puppies. Deputy Duran chose one of those lucky guys, Russell, as his own BFF. After necessary veterinarian care and training, Russell had a special responsibility and the title to go with it: South Valley Sub Station Deputy Therapy Dog, bringing a sense of calmness and warmth to his BCSO family.

The strong partnership that developed between the BCACT deputies and BCACS officers was an unexpected bonus for the South Valley. It integrated the resources, experience and knowledge of Animal Care Services with the authority, training and connections of the Sheriff's Department. It was gratifying that deputies were developing strong interest and concern over their animal abuse cases, checking on the condition of the abused animal and the legal disposition of that abuse case.

Angela of NMDOG recognizes the successes of individual BCACT members with her own unique ceremony. When deputies, sergeants or detectives go above and beyond their normal duties to ensure the safety and rescue of an animal, and arrest and aid in the prosecution of the abuser, this individual has earned the position of Team Leader on sweeps.

At the beginning of each sweep, Angela patiently waits for me to finish our safety and operational briefing. Then Angela stands in front of the team to recognize the accomplishments of the chosen team member and place a high quality, handmade slip lead around their neck. This "donning of the leash" ceremony reminds me of a person being knighted. Cheers and hugs accompany the bright red blush of the honored team member.

Law enforcement officers are by nature a humble group, never expecting accolades or thank-yous for what they do. When they receive their slip-lead, that deputy, detective or sergeant has officially become a member of Angela's "Dog Mob." They are now expected to be ever-vigilant and aware for any signs of animal abuse or suffering and use their new equipment (lead) to save the lives of our four-legged citizens. It is the members of the "Dog Mob" that I designate to assist me in responding to any animal cruelty call, tip or need, outside of boots-on sweeps. It is a huge responsibility and these deputies never disappoint. Because of their selfless service, the community is safer.

My leadership philosophy is to discover what motivates my deputies to be proactive and point out their achievements. In the case of BCACT deputies, detectives and sergeants, their motivation for proactive excellence is something as simple as a lead and the slobbery kisses of a grateful animal.

Andi ended her 2015 training session only weeks before she was promoted to Captain, BCSO. *Part of the training that you deputies underwent included a block in trauma medical care for those life threatening injuries often seen in law enforcement during violent encounters. Each of us were provided medical equipment to deal with such injuries. This kit saved the life of a loving dog on an incredibly beautiful June evening in 2013.*

The call came in that a stranger had tried to kill a man and his dog, who was bleeding to death in the middle of a South Valley road. Indeed, it looked like a massacre when my deputies arrived and were met by a man covered in blood. Assuming it was his blood, the deputies began checking him for wounds, but he pulled away and shouted that the blood was not his, but that of his beloved dog, a male Pit Bull, Bro.

The dog's owner, Mik, explained that some man, a stranger, walked into his yard and began yelling at him, trying to start a fight. When he did not respond, the man pulled out a knife and tried to stab him. Although Bro, a muscular and fiercely loyal dog, placed his body between the two men, the stranger was intent on harm, so as he charged, Bro jumped on him and brought him to the ground. The man jumped up and ran off. Mik had past difficulties with the law, so he did not report this incidence to the sheriff's office.

About an hour later, both Bro and owner were still in the yard, kicking back on a summer evening, when the stranger reappeared and ran at the dog, kicking him hard in the face. In retaliation, an angry and growling Bro lunged at him; the stranger pulled out a machete type knife and began relentlessly stabbing him. A badly injured Bro gave chase, but as the stranger ran away, his wallet fell in the road.

When my deputies summoned me to the scene, I was prepared for the worst, but what I saw brought joy to my heart and tears to my eyes. The deputies were using their issued trauma bags and tourniquets to stop the bleeding on Bro's extremities, placing trauma wound seals on those places where Bro had the deepest punctures. They wrapped him in sterile packing and gauze everywhere they could as the owner cried for them to please, save his dog's life.

BCACS had been notified, but the estimated response time was significant. Totally absorbed in the urgency of the moment and confronted with an opportunity to save this brave pet's life, my deputies requested permission to transport the dog to the emergency vet clinic, with warning lights ablaze and sirens howling. This was probably the only chance Bro had to live as he had lost so much blood, and although it was not policy, sometimes the heart takes over.

In the arms of a deputy, Bro, had a speedy transport in my patrol car to the 24-hour clinic, where his life-saving care began.

His ex-con owner, whose past was peppered with criminal activities, was shocked at our compassionate response. But like so many who had struggled in life, he finally found the strength to turn his life around; Mik had found peace and meaning in living a positive life, providing love and nurture to a dog who was as misunderstood as this man was.

Because of the humane and valiant efforts of my deputies, Bro made a full recovery and has returned to his normal happy routine, including riding in Mik's car, which now sports a special license-plate-cover that reads, "Bernalillo County Sheriff's Department saved my dog's life."

The crazed, knife-wielding perpetrator was sentenced for extreme (felony) animal cruelty and ordered responsible for Bro's extensive veterinary expenses.

All of the deputies involved in that incident had undergone this inter-agency animal cruelty task force training, and I believe it was this knowledge that brought forth that compassion that saved Bro's life. It also changed our department's public image and gained a loyal and staunch supporter of our BCACT, Mik. This was a win-win situation for life.

She closes with a quote from Matt Pepper, former director, BCACS. "During my many years in animal welfare, I have been witness to the increasing impact that animals have on our lives: reducing stress, encouraging social interactions, exercise, laughter and affection. Their impact on our lives is immeasurable. Unquestionably, they give more to us than we could ever give to them."

It is our duty to protect these remarkable innocents.

CHAPTER NINETEEN
CONNECTING IN THE COMMUNITY

"Coming together is a beginning. Keeping together is progress. Working together is a success."

— Henry Ford, American industrialist, engineer, creator of Ford Model-T car, 1908

We were totally unprepared. Our March 2012 animal cruelty task force had organized its first official but unannounced South Valley sweep, during which specific high-call, high activity neighborhoods would be checked for animal welfare code violations: cruelty, neglect and chaining. Our deputies would also check for outstanding warrants. BCACT's first sweep was not only an over-whelming success, it was a statement.

Twenty-five of us: Angela Stell from NMDOG, 15 sheriff deputies, one sergeant, six animal care officers and one animal care supervisor along with Matt and I, walked in groups, cautiously going door-to-door, checking-out surrounding areas of possible concern. This small, old paved road served residents of mostly one story, single family homes, predominately stucco with a few adobe and a few manufactured mobile homes. Ranging from 1/3 acre to sizeable lots, some properties back up to a Rio Grande drainage ditch, which also runs through the middle of the residential road. The confusing numbering system of homes located on this road is erratic and follows no numerical or block pattern; neighbors on the same side of the street sported both odd and even number, an impossible situation, even with a GPS.

Many homes were surrounded with chain link fences and locked gates. Vegetation in this area consisted mostly of weeds and old partially dead cottonwood and elm trees, which provided us little shade from the bright sun as the day's temperature reached 75 degrees and the sweep extended into eight tiring hours.

As we went from one home to another, often knocking on doors with questions, the team was shocked at the large number of violations they encountered, and they were amazed by the many pet-friendly residents who eagerly supplied team members with nearby specific households to check for possible ongoing abuse of animals. We explained that they, as responsible residents, must serve as our eyes and our ears. If they hear or see something suspicious, it is their duty to ensure a safer neighborhood, to let us know, and providing information about where and animal abuse complaints can be filed. We were exceptionally pleased with their positive attitudes and their desire to help those neighborhood animals in need.

What a shocker when, the first hour of our sweep, we issued 12 citations for animal violations to a single household. This action, coming so soon in our sweep served as an example. This small area of close knit South Valley residents would quickly learn how serious BCACT was when this first animal abuser was handcuffed and taken away to jail for animal cruelty by our new unit. People noticed. People were surprised. People talked. And now, the people knew. Bad news travels fast. If you chain, harm, neglect, abandon, violate, or refuse medical aid to any animal in your care, there will be consequences.

Four deputies and two animal control officers approached the adjoining, sizeable property, which was not just littered but covered completely with trash; rusted automobile parts including two cars in various stages of dismantlement adorned the dirt and weeds. Visible were three mixed-breed dogs, chained with thick logging chains, only two to three feet in length. Each dog had carved out into their feces-ridden area of confinement a half circle path. Five-gallon paint buckets, cut in half with sharp, uneven edges, were bone dry, with no semblance of ever having contained either food or water. These starving dogs had no county license stipulating that they had been vaccinated for rabies; they had not been neutered. They were taken for immediate veterinarian care, then placed, by BCACS into protective custody at AAWD.

Neglected horses were tethered in stalls that appeared not to have been cleaned for years, so a misdemeanor citation for negligent animal cruelty (maintenance and care) was issued to the owners. No food or water were observed. Within an hour, bales of hay and supplemental food was dropped off by BCACS. Matt and I conducted a follow-up on this property in two weeks; the stalls were found to be clean, and the horses had been groomed and ferried; food and water were available.

The most gruesome site was several yards further into the yard where lay a magnificent white adult stallion, with sad, suffering azure eyes. A month prior his leg had been bitten by a rattlesnake and his owners, instead of seeking veterinarian care, had wrapped the injured leg with silver duct tape. This once-beautiful animal was obviously experiencing a lot of pain, and could not put any weight on his injured leg, now swollen to gross proportions.

As I turned away quickly from this sickening site and its permeating odor of decay, I felt a sudden, sharp pain in my left calf. Yikes! This could be a joke if it didn't hurt so much! I was being attacked by an angry, weirdly shaped mutant-fowl, emitting shrill, high pitched screeches similar to the screams of a dying animal. Feathers of brown and white, this bird was as large as a goose but bore the small bill of a duck; its too-long neck was grossly disproportionate with the body. Although none of the unit made light of my injury from a "guard goose" those not present in this operation assumed it to be a badge of valor, representing a vicious encounter during the sweep with a biting dog. I corrected their preconceived notion so that it wouldn't heighten any fear of dogs they might already harbor.

My internet search taught me that geese naturally understand that any person not living on their property is an 'intruder' and are used to stand guard at police stations in rural China, whiskey warehouses in Scotland, and were used to secure the periphery of U.S. bases in Vietnam.

These animal owners were convicted of three misdemeanors and one felony. Because it was their first conviction, they were placed on an 18 month probation. The snake-bitten stallion was too ill to save and was humanely euthanized by a county-contracted veterinarian.

As the day grew on, the atrocities against companion animals increased, so much so that most of the banter that was previously the part of the unit had ceased, and we walked, in silence, dreading the next scene of animal abuse that we might discover.

We joined forces, all 25 of us, for what we thought would be the last few yards of this first sweep. Still checking out homes in the same vicinity, our unit came across another chained dog, a Shepherd-cross, violently pulling, jumping, growling and barking loudly inside the confines of the ten-foot high chain-link fence encircling the property. Something else caught our attention...something that should have been reacting to our presence and was not. Huddled in the shadows, quietly under the carport of the small white stucco house was a small, brown Pittie, who appeared to be too ill or too injured to acknowledge our presence by raising his head for even a bark. We rattled the fence and gate and used our loudspeaker to gain the attention of the residents, without avail. We agreed and made the call that this Pit was an exigent circumstance due to the potential life threatening situation. Six deputies and I utilized the telescoping properties of our ASP batons to scale the fence, armed with treats and a leash. We immediately began yelling out greetings, identifying ourselves and knocking on the doors and windows of the house, but without response.

We cautiously approached this seemingly stationery dog. We whistled and called to him, so we could observe his reaction acknowledging our presence, but there was no movement. We began to throw treats to him, and although they remained untouched where they landed, we could hear the sounds of his tail pounding on the concrete block floor. Soon we were close enough to observe remnants of food and water in his bowls. As we came closer we could see that his back legs were broken, laying immoveable at unnatural angles in what appeared to be weeks of dried feces. His skin was bright red and looked infected and infested with mange, ticks and other insect infestations. He seemed to be struggling to reach our treats, but could not seem to lift his body from the ground. No doubt: this animal was in critical condition. This call was a no-brainer: break into the property, back up a pick-up truck, load the injured dog and take him ASAP to a veterinarian, who later estimated his conditions (hip injuries and two broken legs) and a nasty case of demodectic mange to be at least weeks, if not months old.

So, one of the deputies jumped back over the chain link fence, cut the chain around the eight foot gate to allow vehicle access, and backed in the pickup truck. As I reached towards him, to muzzle and load his almost motionless body, I was truthfully frightened that he still could be aggressive. I was emotionally unprepared for his reaction. He must have sensed we were his salvation. He licked my hand and my heart. We agreed that the most appropriate name for this brave canine, whom we would later adopt as our mascot, was "Sheriff."

His owner was just pulling up as we were leaving his property, heading for the veterinarian's office. Two deputies stayed behind to question him and further investigate this crime of extreme animal cruelty. He admitted that the dog had been recently hit by a car, but he lacked funds to seek medical care for his dog. The neighborhood eyewitnesses had seen the dog run over by a vehicle from the owner's household. A BCSO background check of the owner had revealed that he had previously been charged with violence against a person. Both the woman and man residing on the property were arrested and charged with extreme animal cruelty. Their untruthful statements and attitudes were indicative of apathetic individuals, oblivious to the suffering of their dog.

This abused canine's tragic and touching story was highlighted on Albuquerque's KOAT TV five o'clock news, after which his veterinarian's office received a barrage of care packages addressed to "Sheriff." This 18-month-old dog had touched the hearts of hundreds of animal lovers and now had enough treats to last him years and enough leashes to last him many miles of happy trails. Sheriff was adopted by his foster parents' roommate, and both were present, mascot and owner, at our 50 year celebration of the Bernalillo County Sheriff Department. One year later as the roommate and his shadow Sheriff were traveling in their Jeep on NM Hwy 215 and Interstate 25, they were involved in a rollover, a one-car accident. The driver/roommate had dozed off. Luckily, both walked away unharmed. Called to their rescue were deputies from Bernalillo County Sheriff's Department...small world.

The red tint of the Sandia Mountains to the east signaled sunset as we were nearing the last property of the sweep. All of us were both emotionally and physically drained after encountering the animal abuse, house after house, hour after hour. This was an uncommon reaction for deputies conditioned for emotional resilience. Our discussions carried a gloomy undertone as we recounted how defensive and untruthful these people were about the neglect of their animals, resorting to spinning tales, denying ownership, inventing excuses, and other dishonest and manipulative measures. We were also surprised that, as violators were cited, most quickly quieted their own guilty conscience for animal cruelty by supplying the names of their neighbors whose animal violations were they judged to be greater. The almost complete lack of black animals reinforced the still-strong presence of superstitions, stigmas, myths and animal folklore still practiced in so many South Valley homes. They have yet to recognize that superstitions have only the power that you attribute or give to it.

Our conversations quickly came to a halt when a Chihuahua-cross, dragging his hind legs, pulled himself into the road, where a passing truck barely avoided hitting him, not only because the driver was speeding but also because the dog was, of course, laboriously slow and small. His filthy fur, the same color as the dirt road, did not make him easy to see, either. We scooped him up and approached the nearest home, the last home. The residents, his owners, were not particularly upset that he was out of their fenced property. When one of my deputies inquired about his physical condition, they, matter-of-factly explained that he had been hit by a car three years prior which resulted in his losing the use of his hind quarters.

"So," as one of the calloused owners challenged, nervously shifting his weight from foot to foot, "the dog drags himself? It's good enough. He doesn't need to see a vet."

The years of being forced to drag his misshapen, broken body in whatever contortion caused the less pain had re-shaped his spine into a curve so severe that it resembled a "C." Because this case was considered by state statute

30-18-1-A1 *to be an example of negligent, not intentional/willful animal cruelty, we could only arrest for a misdemeanor, but we were able to legally seize, under Statute* **30-18-1.1,** *the animal and whisk the little guy off to the veterinarian. The judge gave the owner two years' probation and charged $500 in fees. It was also stipulated that he could never again own an animal.*

When an owner decides to legally surrender a dog, they sign over ownership of the animal to the County so that they no longer own the dog. Surrendered dogs cannot be reclaimed by the owner.

Another of the same owner's dogs, a Chow Chow-mix, was also seized, as evidence, by officers in our unit, because he was chained and starving, without any water or food bowls present. After veterinarian exams and care programs, both dogs were adopted to new forever homes through Lap Dog Animal Shelter.

Because of the wording of current New Mexico statutes regarding animal cruelty and extreme animal cruelty, these owners were arrested and charged only for a misdemeanor. If the New Mexico statutes for animal cruelty were stronger, these owners could have been charged, instead, with a fourth degree felony, which carries stricter penalties. Present laws in this state accept that our animals are nothing more than personal possessions: objects to buy, trade and dispose of with no acknowledgement that they are living, breathing, giving creatures.

Although this was but our first sweep, the team efforts certainly made known their no-nonsense policies to protect South Valley animals. Encountering 45 house contacts, they were responsible for 183 citations, 5 extreme animal-cruelty related arrests, 6 unrelated arrests. The deputies uncovered 2 drug trafficking issues, 3 individuals with outstanding warrants, one for assaulting a sheriff's officer, and 1 arrest for child abuse, discovered after deputies engaged the family members about the condition of the pets. Other violations cited included conspiracy, tampering of evidence, zoning violations, fire code violations. (Bernalillo County Fire Department has made inquiries about also being included in our sweeps). This sweep was also helpful in identifying gang-affiliated houses and validated numerous gang members. We were very busy being successful.

Fourteen dogs including seven puppies were seized. NMDOG took protective custody of two, and the remaining were taken into custody by BCACS. We had only covered a quarter of our planned sweep, and our unit, though exhausted, was eager to continue, but New Mexico law requires that the paperwork for felony charges and arrests must be filed the day of, so my deputies were forced to return to the South Valley substation to complete the required documentation. Because our deputies always work in pairs, they divide their responsibilities to book the offender, photograph the crime scene, and write the report, a narrative averaging four pages. Follow-up and court appearances related to the investigation are usually a dual effort.

That phenomenal number of citations, violations to the Bernalillo County animal code, included the illegal chaining of an animal, lack of spaying or neutering without an intact permit, failure to inoculate, license or chip, improper care and maintenance, lack of necessary veterinary care, lack of basic care, shelter and nourishment, running-loose off property, lack of warning signs identifying an on property dangerous dog, and exceeding number of animals without multiple animal permit. One red tag was placed on a residential building, deemed uninhabitable.

Current New Mexico statutes read that only after a fourth conviction for animal cruelty (a misdemeanor charge) is it considered a felonious offense. With the exception of a few states including California, Illinois, Michigan, Maine and Oregon, most statutes are so antiquated and inhumane that they hang like a yoke around the neck of any individual involved in animal rescue. **NM House Bill 224** and **Senate Bill 83** were sponsored and introduced in the 2013 legislative session to strengthen this statute and to stipulate that extreme neglect, when it leads to great bodily harm or death of an animal, would be reclassified as a fourth degree felony. These legislative rewrites, if voted into law, would call for harsher penalties in the cases such as that of the seized Chihuahua with the broken back, the stallion with the rattlesnake bite or the seized Pittie, unable to move because of two broken legs. In none of these cases had the extremely negligent owners sought any veterinarian care.

These bills were proposed because prosecutions of some animal cruelty cases were hampered by the current wording of the statute, making it exceptionally difficult to obtain felony convictions in animal cruelty and extreme animal cruelty charges, such as dehydrating and starving an animal to death, abandoning an animal or recklessly mistreating an animal resulting in great bodily harm or its death. Both of these proposed bills stated amendments to the current statutes that would make the above mentioned conduct, when it leads to great bodily harm or death, punishable as a fourth degree felony.

APNM is a non-profit organization, and is well respected by the New Mexico legislature as a balanced, forceful and effective animal rights advocate. It has been challenging historic and wide spread animal cruelty throughout our state since 1979. Through their organized efforts, they built unprecedented support and organized testimony for these two bills,

HB 224 and **SB 83.** A powerful coalition composed of a cross-section of New Mexico citizens: individual ranchers, farmers, veterinarians, animal activists, shelter owners and volunteers, sportsmen and representatives of national animal organizations as well as determined community members, many who traveled long distances, attended and gave compelling testimony at numerous hearings. Their attendance, compassion and commitment were instrumental in the passage of the **SB 83** through two committees unanimously and the passage of **HB 224** through two committees and a contentious House floor vote of 34-29.

All that effort by these individuals who had genuine respect for animals, all those positive votes that were cast for the change to strengthen our animal cruelty laws could not require the Senate majority leader to present this favored House bill for a full Senate vote. So this humane bill which would have changed the lives of so many innocents died at the hands of one, inhumane, calloused legislator, who refused to take the time to protect those animals who are not adequately protected by our current, ineffectual laws.

Today's headlines scream that it is not an uncommon occurrence for politicians in all states to blatantly misuse and abuse power, disregarding the wishes of their constituents and let their politics interfere with public safety. Our communities are safer and better places to live when our laws support keeping animals safe from harm. The link of animal abuse to human violence is an undisputed fact.

It is the responsibility of concerned citizens to continue to take necessary steps, educating neighborhoods and urging their community to enact stronger laws or incorporate animal cruelty teams, such as BCACT which will lessen all violence, both animal and human.

CHAPTER TWENTY
S'MORE SOUTH VALLEY SWEEPS

"When it is all over, it's not who you were, it's whether you made a difference."

– Bob Dole, United States Senator
and member of House of Representatives

As our randomly scheduled sweeps by BCACT continued, South Valley residents with animals became more aware: aware of Bernalillo County animal codes, aware of penalties for infractions and aware that this team did not only address animal code violations, but was interested in family abuse, building code infractions and health and sanitation concerns. By the seriousness of our detail and by our unannounced re-visits, "just to check," the neighborhoods had no doubt that BCACT's undertakings demanded respect and justice for all victims, both two-legged and four-legged in Bernalillo County. They were so successful and had such a positive impact on the neighborhoods that BCACS, NMDOG and BCSO made a commitment that BCACT would be a permanent unit.

As 35 mile-an-hour winds chilled the March 2013 morning, we bundled up and stomped our high boots on shimmering hoarfrost covered weeds and debris as we began this new and fulfilling sweep. We made 45 house contacts resulting in 80 citations, three animal care related arrests, six un-related arrests, one child abuse arrest, three adult dogs and seven puppies seized and one very damaged Pit Bull Terrier cross, Bianca, was euthanized.

When we discovered a caged Casey, it was difficult for team members to register that this was a dog, alive, un-groomed for his lifetime, and covered with fur so thick, heavy and matted with feces and debris, that his encumbered legs could barely move, much less walk. His entire body emitted a noxious odor. No doubt that this long-neglected dog was definitely in need of immediate veterinary care. His unbelievable condition required two tender and separate shavings, both with sedation, to free this criminally neglected Lhasa Apso mix of his accumulated 2.4 pounds of fur, infested with lice and mange. Salves and ointments were gently applied to his bright red, infected skin. Our veterinarian diagnosed him with Laryngeal Paralysis, a progressive condition in which larynx does not open and close properly, making it difficult to breathe or eat. While Casey was recovering from his skin ailments, re-growing his champagne colored fur and gaining weight, a Casey Club formed from press releases of his dilemma. His fans sent a variety of Casey donations: checks to be applied to his large veterinarian bill, leashes, collars, soft and cuddly toys, and a colorful assortment of light weight shirts to protect his hairless body from sunburn. Casey also required behavioral modification training and socialization. His required expensive and complicated surgery for his larynx was successful, and, after all his medical issues were resolved, this brave and handsome 12 pound lad was re-homed with a family that continues to shower him with constant attention and care.

Owners of Casey and Bianca were charged with felony animal cruelty, but maybe the cruel life both endured could have been shortened by neighbors or passersby who cared enough about animals to alert or report, anonymously... or maybe neither atrocities would have occurred if the owners thought they would face serious jail time and large fines...maybe.

Nearly 90% of all abuse cases are the result of a report from a caring neighbor or friend, or by cross-reporting from another government or social welfare agency. Such was the situation of Sven, a young Min Pin whose life was saved by concerned neighbors who reported animal cruelty during one of our sweeps. The investigation of their calls resulted in BCACT deputies and officers seizing multiple dogs, injured, starved and abused. Their owners were charged with two felony counts of extreme animal cruelty, lack of veterinary care. One of the injured was an adorable, but very sick pup, Sven, whose festering and open wounds had not been sutured. After proper veterinary and follow up care, Sven is an active, happy puppy, enjoying his new home and the attention of his new loving owners.

Our October 2013 surprise sweep was conducted in the cool early morning hours and under the backdrop of brightly colored hot air balloons, hovering over our targeted location. They were part of our yearly International Balloon Fiesta in Albuquerque, where more than 100,000 spectators and visitors flock their launching pads to view the ascension and maneuvers of 700 of these wonders, flown by 1,000 pilots from all over the world. One fiesta visitor appropriately termed this mass ascension of balloons as a "Desert Kaleidoscope."

We gathered, discussed our routes and fanned out in a little-known impoverished, immigrant neighborhood located on the time-forgotten Pajarito

Mesa. Not even platted on the city map, it acted as a temporary refuge for indigent immigrants trying to make a go of their new life in America, one way or another, within or without the confines of the law. It had all the signs of a neighborhood under siege. The land on both sides of a man-made, carved, narrow dirt road was littered with rusted machinery, automobile parts and discarded construction materials, sub-standard buildings, ramshackle mobile homes and shelters. The dirt yards contained remnants of broken toys and very little hope.

Most buildings were adorned with multi-colored gang graffiti. One of the first we visited housed tragedy: a severely emaciated horse and six sick dogs, their health in such danger that they were immediately surrendered by their owner and transported to a veterinarian. One, a Pit Bull Terrier cross did not survive the transfer, but the others, five Chihuahuas, under the care of NMDOG volunteers, found new and nurturing homes.

Before this sweep, BCACT officers, deputies and volunteers were made aware of the reputation this vicinity held for holding dogfights and cockfights and for breeding of dogs for that barbaric and illegal form of amusement. So we were not shocked at the inhabitants of one backyard but surprised at the sheer number: 100 roosters, many with their combs and wattles removed, a sure sign of cockfighting. When confronted, the mother explained that they were 'pets for her daughter and the neighborhood children.'

When we entered the residence, we agreed that it was so filthy and insect infested and unsanitary that the small daughter living there with her mother was in a dangerously unhealthy environment. After notifying Child, Youth and Families Department (CYFD), she was placed in their temporary protective custody. The mother was arrested and charged with child abuse, various zoning, health and sanitation violations, breeding of animals for fighting and owning such animals as well as seven counts of animal abuse.

The housewife of the home next-door had witnessed our visit, seizures and arrests, and was now on pins and needles, waiting outside their residence, for her husband to return and answer the anticipated questions and concerns. Before long, he arrived and took us on a tour of his large stables, housing well-tended-to horses, all Quarter horses racing at the Albuquerque Downs.

In a back stall lay a nursing Bulldog with her two puppies and flyers advertising their price at $500 each. Three citations were issued for lack of litter, intact and breeding permits. The search for the sire took only a few more steps. He lay, panting, injured and sick in the dark corner of the small tack room. His bloodied head and leg wore filthy, foul-smelling old bandages. His food bowl was live with insect activity. The stench was overwhelming. The *owner's excuse was that these injuries were due to a coyote attack, and the dog had been taken to a veterinarian for care. We suggested that the injured and sick dog would recover more quickly inside the warm home with more attention given to cleaning his wounds and bandages.*

After citing a few more homes for illegal breeding of Pit Bull Terrier crosses and possessing dogfighting paraphernalia, we come across a lot, no residence, on which more horse stables (a loose definition) had been put together with ill-fitting, differing lengths and widths of warped pressed board and plywood. Amazingly, the stalls were clean, attended to by a stable hand, who when questioned about why the horses' mouths were tied shut, replied, "They have a race tomorrow."

Although dogfighting is clandestine, its presence was obvious at the next property we visited. Five Pit Bull Terrier crosses lay hurting in the mud, bleeding from unattended open puncture wounds, teeth broken, legs fractured. They were seized and put into the care of NMDOG for immediate veterinary care. As we surveyed the rest of the property, we discovered one other dog who appeared to be bleeding and emaciated, but was not moving. As we approached her, we could see that she was protecting the three puppies she was nursing. Her condition was worse than we had thought as most of her fur had been lost to mange; she was freezing. She and her puppies also accompanied Angela to the veterinary hospital. Within another ten minutes, we discovered two more puppies, eight-week-old Ringo and Starr, both shivering and frightened, hiding in piles of trash. Owners argued that none of these dogs required medical attention, but relinquished ownership when they were reminded that deputies were leaving, only to return with a warrant; charges would be immediately filed. The owners agreed that it would be in their best interest to surrender the dogs.

As we moved throughout the neighborhood, we encountered many chained dogs. After explaining the new chaining ordinance in the county, we issued citations to those whose dogs showed evidence of neglect or abuse and issued warnings to those whose dogs appeared otherwise healthy. NMDOG followed our warnings and citations by volunteering to construct strong, safe fences or dog runs to interested owners. Other volunteers from NMDOG made sure these dogs and cats had proper nourishment. They handed out food, collars, leashes, bottom-weighted food and water dishes. Along with those pet supplies came educational talks from Angela as she elicited promises to be more responsible from the cited or admonished owners. To those who wish to obey the no-chain ordinance of the county, she sets dates for her volunteers to construct strong and safe dog runs and fences on their properties. As we left, I reminded those owners of chained dogs that I would return intermittently to check on the treatment of their animals. And so I did, the following week, and issued seven citations to those whose dogs were still chained, reminding them, "BCACT cares about these dogs and I will always schedule a follow-up visit where questions remain."

BCACT's last sweep before this book was written was sensationally successful, its positive results making evening news headlines statewide. We walked our assigned routes, making contact with 100 neighbors, not just pet owners, to inquire if the citizens had any particular issues or concerns that our Bernalillo County Sheriff's Office could address or improve. But the atmosphere of this sweep was entirely different. Instead of finding the majority of the dogs on a chain or trolley system, their dogs unexpectedly greeted us, tails wagging, from their newly constructed fences or runs. What a wonderful sight! This was a positive result we could see, hear and feel. Our enforcement of the new tethering ordinance had made a very positive difference in the treatment of the animals in Bernalillo County!

It was a busy eight hour sweep as we checked 50 dogs for wellness and compliance with licenses and inoculations; 3 were seized for neglect. We also inspected 40 roosters, 2 horses, 1 pig, 15 goats and 2 kittens. Fifty-five county animal care violations were issued. One of our 5 arrests for animal neglect-cruelty resulted in 40 misdemeanor animal cruelty charges. A follow-up search warrant brought about an additional seizure of 7 dogs and the arrest of 2 animal cruelty offenders. Through cross-reporting, county zoning was given referrals of 3 homes for investigation. And the rewarding moments of these sweeps were not only the unexpected compliance of the chain ordinance by so many dog owners, but the gratitude and the smiles on the faces of those needy dog owners to whom we gifted 400 pounds of kibble. BCACT has and will continue to make a difference!

CHAPTER TWENTY-ONE

YOUR COMMUNITY'S ANIMAL CRUELTY TASK FORCE

"Never doubt that a small group of thoughtful, committed citizens can change the world. Indeed, it is the only thing that ever has."

– Margaret Mead, cultural anthropologist,
women's right activist, author

Law enforcement officers encounter more community interest, public out-rage, media exposure, and communications on animal abuse cases than any other service, according to statistics released by the National District Attorneys' Association. Some district attorney offices in the United States have responded to the significance and complexity of animal cruelty cases by assigning a special prosecutor, in charge of these cases. Nicoletta Caferri of Queens, New York, who holds that position, noted the public safety implications of her position. She intends to make a difference.

♦ Animal abuse is a direct contradiction of a civil society whose basic human decency demand humane treatment of living, feeling beings.

♦ Animal abuse is the responsibility of all prosecutors, as they are charged with the task of enforcing all laws.

♦ Animal abuse signals sociopathic trains, so early intervention could potentially prevent or limit future violent crimes against people.

♦ Animal abuse cases are useful in uncovering domestic abuse and can prevent or limit future domestic violence.

♦ Animal abuse cases also uncover other crimes, such as gambling, money-laundering, narcotics, weapons offenses and gang activity.

Another example of a new and better approach to fighting animal abuse is the brainchild of the Albany, <u>New York</u> County District Attorney's new Animal Cruelty Task Force. They introduced a website and its app as part of its multi-agency response to animal abuse. The website serves to alert the public that "Animal Abuse Prevention Starts with You." The download-able app from the New York State Animal Protection Federation includes all New York animal cruelty laws, a big help to law enforcement officers as well as those who witness the crimes.

My previous class training presentations outlined the necessary steps to create an inter-agency animal cruelty task force such as BCACT in your community which can considerably lessen the danger for your companion animals, thus providing a safer environment for your citizens.

And knowing how to interest, stimulate and involve those citizens in the formation of your animal cruelty task force can positively impact your results. Even after the formation of a community animal cruelty task force you can call upon these individuals with whom you have already developed rapport to ask for donations of food and animal care items, donations for emergency veterinary care, help in finding responsible fosters or adopters for abused animals, and even assistance in locating an animal abuse offender. Involved, interested, informed citizens are an asset to all community animal abuse task forces.

Our BCACT undertaking has demanded respect and justice for all animal victims. Since that date, (and we are just beginning) our well-meshed collusion has resulted in amazing statistics: 900 property contacts, 69 animal care related arrests, 30 unrelated arrests, hundreds of citations and violations involving companion animals, hoofed animals, goats, rabbits and roosters. And hundreds of abused animals have been seized and re-located in permanent, responsible homes.

Most important, each sweep found fewer infractions and, thankfully, more homes in compliance with the animal codes in our area. In order to analyze our impact, we recently installed a program to track our statistics.

Our formation of BCACT instilled a stronger sense of responsibility for our animals in both our deputies and BCACS officers, who, whether on or off duty, showed compassion in their heart-warming rescues of hundreds of our needy pets. These animals represent but a few in the hundreds who are still waiting for us. But although they are just a few, our intercession was a life-call for the animals rescued.

BCACT successfully continues its mission of blowing the whistle on animal cruelty. We are hoping that our compassion, proactive approach, educational advise, honesty and fairness in our enforcement will become the role model for the formation other inter-agency animal cruelty task forces, not just in rural areas or unincorporated areas in the Southwest, but in any community or county plagued by animal cruelty.

It is our team's desire to infiltrate America's communities with inter-agency animal cruelty task forces such as BCACT. If your community, sheriff's office or animal care services is interested in further information concerning the formation of a BCACT in their area, Bernalillo County Sheriff's Office Anti-Cruelty Task Force is prepared to provide information for your questions and help you to arrange presentations. Changing your community into a safer, more humane place to live will not happen overnight, but it can only begin with your interest, energies and efforts. We are here to help you.

I encourage any person in law enforcement, animal care services, a non-profit rescue group or any other goal directed towards community safety to seek out like-minded partners and never give up. I was fortunate to have Matt as a mentor and Angela as a talented and tenacious team member, working diligently to combine our strengths…for the animals. This book is also for the animals, and serves as a step-by-step instructional guide for law enforcement agencies to use in establishing their animal cruelty task force.

Another highly successful and recent coupling of agencies to fight animal abuse and abandonment was a recent union of Los Angeles, California Police Department with ASPCA, resulting in a 28% increase in animal cruelty arrests and 115% increase of abused animals treated by the ASPCA. Across America law enforcement and community councils are recognizing the value of animal cruelty task forces.

When a beloved cat, Charley, "best bud" of a local, special-needs eight-year-old, was discovered mutilated in St. Tammany, Louisiana in 2015, the ordered necropsy confirmed that his fatal injuries were caused by a person. Fearing that neighborhood juveniles were imitating similar crimes viewed online, a concerned Sheriff Strain retaliated by joining forces with humane officials to form an animal cruelty task force.

Fresno County, California launched in 2015 a specialized Animal Cruelty Unit to be staffed by several dedicated prosecutors working alongside local law enforcement including Central California SPCA humane officers who investigate approximately 1,200 animal cruelty reports yearly.

Richland County, South Carolina Sheriff's Department announced the 2015 formation of a multidisciplinary animal cruelty task force, a unit which will include the district attorney's office, animal control among other entities.

Virginia Attorney General Herring announced the organization of the nation's first statewide "Animal Law" to be composed of a few staff attorneys who will devote time needed as resources on animal welfare, fighting or abuse issues for local, county and state law enforcement agencies.

Port St. Lucie, Florida sheriff, after a national Link Conference, developed a LINK training program for deputies and detectives so they could work together in attacking the dangerous connection between animal abuse and family members.

A very unusual approach by the prosecutor's office in San Bernardino County, California won the 2015 Achievement Award from the National Association of Counties. Her program, ACT on Wednesdays, entails contacting animal control officers for addresses of "problem places," which she, with law enforcement officers will visit on ride-alongs, to introduce herself, say "hello" to the neighbors, and acquaint them with an anonymous WE-TIP hotline for animal fighting and animal abuse crimes.

2014 Training Keys released by the International Association of Chiefs of Police (IACP) focus on animal cruelty task forces launched by law enforcement agencies nationwide as well as national initiatives from the USDOJ, the National District Attorneys' Association, and the Association of Prosecuting Attorneys.

The National Law Enforcement Center on Animal Abuse newsletter hailed the many animal-friendly programs initiated by Albany County, New York. Sheriff Craig Apple was instrumental in establishing the nation's first registry of offenders convicted of animal cruelty, animal fighting or sexual abuse of an animal. His officers are also members in the Albany County District Attorney's Animal Cruelty Taskforce who introduced another example of a new and better approach to fighting animal abuse with their new website and its app as part of its multi-agency response to animal abuse. The website serves to alert the public that "Animal Abuse Prevention Starts with You." The downloadable app from the New York State Animal Protection Federation includes all New York animal cruelty laws, a big help to law enforcement officers as well as those who witness the crimes.

BE INFORMED—*Whether you are a concerned citizen, city/county councilor or a law enforcement agency, make a fair assessment of the animal cruelty environment in your area. Become familiar with animal cruelty laws of your area: city, county and state. Compare your statutes and ordinances with animal cruelty Model Laws written by ALDF or with the HEART Ordinance (see Appendix).*

- *What percent of intake animals in your local animal control shelter are euthanized?*

- *What programs does the shelter have for marketing these "unchosen?"*

- *What percentage of animal cruelty felony cases (state, county and local) resulted in convictions, jail time and fines?*

- *How were your state's animal cruelty laws rated by HSUS or by ALDF?*

- *What recommendations do those two respected organizations suggest to improve your ratings?*

MAKE LAW ENFORCEMENT CONTACTS, HOLD COMMUNITY MEETINGS, DESIGN YOUR ANIMAL CRUELTY TASK FORCE

Your first proactive step to a safer, more humane community is to present your assessment and ideas along with the information in this book to everyone concerned: your sheriff and police departments, neighbors, animal activists, and your elected councilors, officers and mayor. Our task force is available to speak to any audience interested in reducing their animal cruelty. Our Bernalillo County Animal Task Force is only a phone call away. Let us help you to be instrumental in protecting those four-legged creatures who do so much for us without ever saying a word.
Become their voice. Make a difference.

"It is beautiful to have dreams and to be able to fight for them."

– Pope Francis, 9-27-15

Bernalillo County Animal Cruelty Task Force
ATTN: Capt. Andrea Taylor,
Bernalillo County Sheriff's Department

400 Roma, NW
Albuquerque, New Mexico 87102

ataylor@bernco.gov
505-468-7621
www.bernco.gov

Start-up presentations may also be scheduled at 505-298-8048

APPENDIX (HEART)

ARTICLE 2: HUMANE AND ETHICAL ANIMAL RULES AND TREATMENT ORDINANCE OF THE CITY OF ALBUQUERQUE

PART 1: GENERAL PROVISIONS

9-2-1-4 DEFINITIONS.

CHAINING or TETHERING. Confining an Animal when unattended by an individual with a tether, rope, chain, or other device to a doghouse, stake, tree, structure or other stationary object.

CRUELTY. A person intentionally killing an Animal without Lawful Justification or mistreating, injuring, maiming, disfiguring, tormenting, torturing, beating, mutilating, burning, scalding, poisoning, attempting to poison or otherwise unnecessarily causing an Animal to suffer physical or emotional harm. Any of the following is a separate act of Cruelty: failing to provide necessary sustenance to an Animal under that Person's Custody or control, failing to provide Adequate Shelter, failing to provide Potable Water, failing to provide palatable, nutritious food of adequate quantity, taunting an Animal, dyeing, or artificially coloring an Animal under the age of 12 weeks, transporting an Animal in an open vehicle without proper restraints, leaving an Animal in a vehicle when the temperature is such that it could cause pain or suffering to the Animal. Abandonment or Neglect of an Animal is Cruelty. Inaction of the Owner toward an Animal in need of Basic or Emergency Medical Care is Cruelty. Surgery by a Veterinarian is not Cruelty but ear cropping, de-barking, tail docking or Alteration by an individual who is not a Veterinarian is Cruelty. Euthanasia by a Veterinarian or a Euthanasia Qualified Employee of Albuquerque Animal Care Center (AACC) shall not be deemed Cruelty provided it is carried out by methods specified in this article or by other generally accepted methods. The application of pesticides or rodenticides by a properly licensed professional is not Cruelty.

EXTREME CRUELTY. A Person is guilty of Extreme Cruelty to Animals if a Person intentionally or maliciously tortures, mutilates, injures or kills an Animal, or if a Person poisons an Animal. Extreme Animal Cruelty is governed by §§ 30-18-1 NMSA 1978 et seq. and is a Fourth Degree Felony, punishable by a fine up to $5,000 and 18 months imprisonment.

PART 2: CARE, MAINTENANCE, HOUSING, RESTRAINT AND TRANSPORTATION STANDARDS

Any person who violates a provision of this article shall be deemed guilty of a petty misdemeanor and, upon conviction thereof, shall be subject to the penalty provisions set forth in § 1-1-99 ROA 1994. Every violation of this article shall be a separate misde-meanor. Every day this article is violated shall be considered a separate offense. Upon receipt of a citation, the person cited must appear in court.

9-2-2-1 REQUIRED CARE AND MAINTENANCE FOR MAM-MALS AND BIRDS KEPT ON RESIDENTIAL PROPERTY

G) *PERMANENT IDENTIFICATION.* All Companion Animals shall be Permanently Identified by a Microchip or Tattoo. Microchipping shall be available for free at AACC for Low Income Persons and Seniors. It is the Owner's responsibility to contact AACC for information regarding using a Tattoo as a Permanent Identification.

9-2-2-2 HOUSING AND RESTRAINT STANDARDS FOR MAM-MALS AND BIRDS KEPT ON RESIDENTIAL PROPERTY

(D) OUTDOOR- SECURE FENCE
(3) *Chaining, when not accompanied by a Person.*
(a) Chaining is prohibited as a means of outdoor confinement for more than one hour during any 24 hour period.
(b) No Chain shall weigh more than 1/8 of the animal's weight.
(c) The Chain must be affixed to the animal by the use of a non-abrasive, well-fitted harness.
(d) The Chain must be at least 12 feet long and fastened so the animal can sit, walk, and lie down using natural motions.
(e) The Chain must be unobstructed by objects that may cause the Chain or the ani-mal to become entangled.
(f) The Chain shall have a swivel on both ends.
(g)The Chained animal shall be surrounded by a barrier sufficient to protect the Chained Animal from At Large animals. The barrier shall be sufficient to prevent chil-dren from accidentally coming into contact with the Chained animal.

9-2-2-6 TRANSPORTING ANIMALS IN VEHICLES: When trans-porting Animals they must be kept safe.

(A) *Pickup Trucks.* Animals that are transported in the bed of a pickup truck must be humanely restrained or Crated to prevent the possibility of the Animal falling out, protected from extreme temperatures and provided with a non-metal surface to sit or stand on.

(1) *Humanely restrained.* The Animal must be attached to the truck by means of a Harness, not a neck collar, in a way to insure that the animal cannot jump out of or fall from the truck or be strangled. There must be two fixed point fastening locations at least two feet apart to attach the harness to in order to prevent the Animal from strangling or falling out.

(2) *Crate.* If an Animal is put in a Crate or other enclosure, the Crate or enclosure must be securely fastened to the bed or sides of the truck so that the Crate or enclosure cannot turn over or fall out.

(3) *Protection from weather.* No Animal shall be left in the bed of a truck whether in a Crate or not when the weather is such that the Animal will be exposed to extreme heat, cold or rain.

(B) *Cars, Vans and RVs.* Animals riding inside vehicles that are not in Crates or other enclosures must not be allowed access to a window opened wide enough for the Animal to jump, fly or fall out. Animals left unattended in cars, vans or RVs must have adequate ventilation to prevent the temperature in the vehicle from rising high enough such that any reasonable Person would know that the Animal would suffer from heat exposure. During the warmer months, no amount of ventilation will keep the car from getting too hot. If the Mayor determines that an Animal in a vehicle is in immediate danger, the Mayor may enter the vehicle by whatever means necessary, without being liable to the owner of the vehicle, and seize the Animal.

(C) *Transporting more than one Animal.* In addition to all other regulations in this article, Animals should never be overcrowded when being transported. If the Animals are Crated or kept in any enclosure, they may be allowed to share a Crate but each Animal should be able to stand up, move around, lie down and stretch out naturally. If Crates or enclosures are stacked, they must be attached securely to prevent the Crates or enclosures from falling or turning over. If Crates or other enclosures are stacked, it is important that no urine or feces are passed between Crates and enclosures.

PART 3: REQUIRED LICENSE AND PERMITS

9-2-3-1 REQUIRED ALBUQUERQUE COMPANION ANIMAL LICENSE.

(A) *Albuquerque Residents.* All residents of Albuquerque who own Companion Animals shall have a current annual Albuquerque Companion Animal License for each Companion Animal they own that is over the age of three months.

(B) *Non-Resident.* Any Person who lives in Bernalillo County or the surrounding counties of Valencia, Cibola, Sandoval, Torrance or Santa Fe and is not a City resident but who keeps a Companion Animal in the city for more than 15 consecutive days or an aggregate of 30 days in any year shall obtain an Albuquerque Companion Animal License.

(C) Companion Animals must have a current Rabies Vaccination and be Microchipped or Permanently Identified before the Owner can be issued a License.

(D) Low Income Persons, Seniors, and Owners of Service Dogs must obtain an annual License for their Companion Animals but are exempt from the annual License fee.

(E) *Impounded Companion Animals.* Any Person who lives in Bernalillo County or the surrounding counties of Valencia, Cibola, Sandoval, Torrance or Santa Fe who owns a Companion Animal that has been impounded by AACC shall obtain a City License.

(F) *License Tags.* A License Tag shall be issued with each License.

(1) Any Companion Animal outside the Owner's real property shall wear a collar or a Harness with a current License Tag and an Anti-Rabies Vaccination Tag attached to the collar or Harness, even if the Companion Animal is Microchipped.

(2) A collar or Harness with the required tags attached may be removed from the Companion Animal temporarily for medical care, training, grooming, or when the Companion Animal is in a Bona Fide Animal Show.

9-2-3-6 INTACT COMPANION ANIMAL PERMIT OR ICAP.

Owners of dogs and cats over the age of six months that have not been Altered shall obtain an Intact Companion Animal Permit for those Animals.

(A) All Intact Companion Animals must be Licensed and Permanently Identified by a Microchip or other identification method acceptable to the Mayor before an ICAP can be issued.

(B) No Person shall have more than four Intact Companion Animals in any Household.

(C) The Household shall be secure against ingress by Companion Animals of the same species or egress of the Companion Animal for which the ICAP is issued. The Household shall meet the standards of a Secure Facility or a Secure Fence.

(D) If an Intact Companion Animal that has been issued an ICAP is impounded twice by AACC, the ICAP will be automatically revoked and the Intact Companion Animal will be required to be Altered. If an Intact Companion Animal is Impounded twice and must therefore be Altered, the Permit Holder shall pay AACC to Alter the Companion Animal.

(E) If an ICAP Holder wants to breed an Intact Companion Animal or if a female Intact Companion Animal has been impregnated, the ICAP Holder must obtain a Litter Permit prior to the birth of the Litter.

9-2-3-7 COMPANION ANIMAL LITTER PERMIT.

(A) Owners of female intact Companion Animals must obtain a Litter Permit prior to the birth of a Litter or within one week after the birth of the Litter.

(B) All female Intact Companion Animals must have an Intact Companion Animal Permit and be Licensed and Microchipped or otherwise Permanently Identified before a Litter Permit will be issued.

(C) No Person shall apply for or obtain more than four Litter Permits per Household in any consecutive 12 month period.

(D) No Person shall apply for or obtain more than one Litter Permit per female Companion Animal per Household in any consecutive 12 month period.

(E) Litter Permits expire six months from the date of issue.

(H) The following Care and Disposition requirements regarding Litter Companion Animals are in effect whether or not the Owner of the Litter possesses a Litter Permit:

(1) Puppies and kittens shall have at least the first in any series of required Vaccinations and be de-wormed by a de-worming treatment consistent with the size and age of the Animal before being transferred to a new Owner or otherwise separated from the mother.

(2) Puppies and kittens shall be microchipped or otherwise Permanently Identified prior to being separated from the mother. Proof of Permanent Identification must be provided to AACC.

(3) The Litter Permit Holder shall upon transfer or conveyance of the kitten or puppy, deliver a complete Vaccination record to the new Owner.

(4) The Litter Permit Holder shall document and retain for inspection the name and address of each recipient of any Litter Companion Animal once owned by the Litter Permit Holder.

(5) The Litter Permit Holder is liable for the medical costs, including medicine, for any puppy or kitten that is diagnosed as sick by a Veterinarian within one week from the date of sale. The Litter Permit Holder shall reimburse the new Owner the costs associated with the sick Animal, up to the amount of money the puppy or kitten was purchased for. The new Owner shall be allowed to keep the puppy or kitten even if the Litter Permit Holder pays the medical costs. The new Owner or the Litter Permit Holder may appeal to the Administrative Hearing Officer if there is a dispute as to the fact of the Illness or the amount of the charges. If the Litter Permit Holder does not prevail on appeal, the Litter Permit Holder shall reimburse the costs of the appeal to the new Owner.

(6) A Litter Permit is required to advertise any Companion Animal under the age of six months old for sale, gift or other transfer or conveyance, in any local periodical or newspaper of general circulation. The Litter Permit number must be included in any advertisement.

(7) Failure to advertise without including a valid Litter Permit number shall be a violation of this article. Any Person who advertises a Companion Animal and purports in the advertisement to reside outside the city limits or lists a telephone number outside the city limits and is subsequently found to maintain Companion Animals inside the city limits or is found attempting to sell Companion Animals in the city limits is in violation of this article. Each day of possession of each said Animal will constitute a separate offense.

(8) Puppies and kittens can only be sold, given as a gift or other transfer or conveyance from the location listed on the Litter Permit. Puppies or kittens being sold on public property or commercial property even with the Owner's permission are in violation of this article and the puppies and kittens may be seized.

(9) Puppies and kittens shall not be sold to a Pet Store, Animal Broker or other Animal dealer.

(10) Puppies and kittens shall not be released from the Permitted Premises prior to eight weeks of age.

9-2-3-8 MULTIPLE COMPANION ANIMAL SITE PERMIT OR MCASP.

Any Person intending to exceed the maximum limit of six Companion Animals, no more than four of which are dogs, in a Household shall obtain a Multiple Companion Animal Site Permit (MCASP).

(A) All Companion Animals at a Multiple Companion Animal Site shall be Licensed, Microchipped or otherwise Permanently Identified. Fostering a pregnant Companion Animal and her eventual offspring is a temporary exception to this rule.

(B) A MCASP will only be granted to applicants in a Residential Zone.

(C) Any adjoining property owner may petition the Administrative Hearing Officer for revocation, modification or suspension of a MCASP if the adjoining property owner is reasonably aggrieved by any effects of the Multiple Animal Site.

(D) No Person shall keep or maintain more than 15 Companion Animals at any MCASP site, no more than four of which can be Intact. This limit may be exceeded under special circumstances determined by the Mayor.

9-2-3-10 GUARD DOG SITE PERMIT OR GDSP.

Any Person wishing to operate a Guard Dog Site shall obtain a Guard Dog Site Permit (GDSP).

(A) Any Person wishing to operate a Guard Dog Site shall have a Tax ID number and be registered under the Albuquerque Business Registration Ordinance before applying for a GDSP.

(B) The Owner of the Guard Dog must have an Intact Companion Animal Permit for each Intact dog.

(C) The GDSP attaches to the real property and the GDSP Holder may not transfer Guard Dogs to a separate site lacking a GDSP.

(D) A GDSP will not be granted for property in a Residential Zone or within 250 feet of a school.

(E) When a Guard Dog is on duty outside of a building, the premises must be enclosed by a Secure Fence.

(F) The escape of a Guard Dog from a Guard Dog Site is a violation of this article and can constitute a basis for revocation of a GDSP and seizure of the dog.

(G) If the Mayor determines it is necessary to control noise at the Guard Dog Site, the Mayor may require the Owner of the site or GDSP Holder to construct a barrier which breaks the Guard Dog's line of sight to the exterior and adequately buffers the noise.

(H) The doors, windows, and all other openings to the outside of a building where a Guard Dog is on duty must be secured to prevent its escape.

(I) The Guard Dog Site shall be posted with warning signs that are at least 12 inches by 12 inches.

(1) The warning signs shall state "Guard Dog" and "Guardia" and shall show a picture of an aggressive dog.

(2) The warning signs shall be posted not more than 50 feet apart on the exterior of the fences or walls surrounding the site, and shall be posted at all exterior corners of the site and at every entrance to the site.

(J) Vehicles used to transport Guard Dogs shall be secured so the public is protected from Injury, shall be constructed or modified to ensure that the Guard Dog is transported in a safe, humane manner and that does not violate §§ 9-2-2-6 et seq., and shall be posted with warning signs on each side of the vehicle.

(K) A GDSP Holder shall not apply for a Litter Permit or Multiple Companion Animal Site Permit for the Guard Dog Site. No breeding of Animals is allowed at a Guard Dog Site.

9-2-3-16 LICENSE AND PERMIT FEES.

(A) There is hereby created a Humane and Ethical Animal Rules and Treatment (HEART) Ordinance Fund; 60% of all net License and Permit fees collected under the HEART Ordinance shall be deposited in the HEART Ordinance Fund. HEART Ordinance Fund monies are dedicated exclusively to programs for the free microchipping and the free spaying and neutering of Companion Animals for Low Income Persons, Moderate Income Persons, Seniors and when possible, the general public. All fees listed in this article are a minimum fee amount and may be increased administratively by the Mayor.

PART 4: PROHIBITED ACTIVITIES

9-2-4-1 CRUELTY TO ANIMALS.

Nothing herein shall be construed to preclude a conviction for Extreme Cruelty under state law.

(A) Cruelty is any act or inaction that causes, is known to cause or is calculated to cause physical or psychological pain, injury, damage or harm to an Animal.

(B) Any Person, including employees of AACC, may be cited for Cruelty hereunder whether or not said Person owns the subject Animal.

(C) Cruelty is applicable to all Animals within the city limits of Albuquerque.

(D) Personal observation of Cruelty by an ASO, Reserve ASO or Police Officer is not required and such officers may issue citations, file criminal complaints or assist any other Person in filing a criminal complaint if an Animal has been treated cruelly. A charge of Cruelty under this article is not a lesser included offense for a charge of Cruelty under state law.

(E) In addition to criminal charges for Cruelty, the city may avail itself of the remedies of Seizure, Confiscation and Protective Custody provided under this article.

(F) Any Person who treats an Animal in any way that would lead a reasonable Person to conclude that such Animal has been subjected to harm without Lawful Justification is guilty of Cruelty.

(G) Any charges for medical care paid by the city for an Animal suspected of being a victim of Cruelty shall constitute a municipal lien against the Animal.

9-2-4-2 SPECIFIC ACTIVITIES THAT CONSTITUTE CRUELTY TO AN ANIMAL.

Any Person who acts intentionally, willfully or maliciously is guilty of cruelty when engaged or attempting to engage in the following behavior:
(A) Killing or attempting to kill an Animal. Exceptions include:

(1) Humane Euthanasia performed by a Veterinarian, a Euthanasia Qualified Employee or a Euthanasia Authorized employee of AACC or the Animal Humane Association;

(2) Killing a bird if such bird is Poultry owned by that Person and will be used for food;

(3) Killing a rabbit if such rabbit is owned by that Person and will be used for food;

(4) Killing mice or rats that are not a Domestic Animal or otherwise claimed as a pet by any Person; and

(5) Reasonably necessary taking of Animals by a governmental entity or contractor of a governmental entity for bio-disease management including, without limitation, selection of birds to determine the existence of or monitor the spread of avian flu.

(B) Poisoning, attempting to poison or allowing an Animal access to poisonous substances such as antifreeze, baiting any Animal with any substance soaked, treated or prepared with any harmful or poisonous material unless such actions are undertaken by a licensed professional exterminator.

(1) There is no justification for poisoning Animals in the city.

(2) A Person may use poison to kill mice and rats, but only within a Person's own enclosed structures.

(3) Except when applied by a licensed exterminator, no poison may be used outside, even on a Person's own property, or in any way in which a poisoned animal, including mice and rats, can consequently poison other Animals.

(C) Abusing an Animal which includes, but is not limited to, maiming, disfiguring, torturing, beating, having sexual contact with, hurting, burning, scalding or cruelly setting upon any Animal.

(D) Using a prod, stick, electrical shock, chemical, physical force, starvation, pain or discomfort on an Animal in order to make it perform for entertainment purposes.

(E) Generally accepted methods of animal training that do not cause undue physical and emotional suffering, including the training of Livestock, Companion Animals, Guard Dogs, hunting dogs, police dogs and Service Animals shall not constitute Cruelty.

(F) Using a whip or riding crop in a manner that causes injury to the Animal.

(G) Chaining an animal to a stationary post, pole, or other immovable object by means of any instrumentality or other extension device including, but not limited to, a chain, tether, coil or rope and leaving such animal unattended for more than one hour in a 24 hour period.

(H) Any owner who reclaims an Injured Animal from AACC for the purpose of obtaining treatment by a private Veterinarian and who subsequently fails to provide written proof of treatment to AACC within five days.

(I) Abandonment of an Animal. Any Person who relinquishes possession or control of an Animal in a location where any reasonable Person would know the Animal has little chance of finding food, Potable Water, and shelter is guilty of Cruelty. Abandonment also includes dumping or releasing an Animal anywhere or leaving an Animal behind when a Person moves.

(J) Use of a Spring Loaded Trap. Spring Loaded Traps are absolutely prohibited in the city unless used on mice or rats inside a Household or inside a commercial property.

(K) Improper use of a Live Trap. Any person who leaves an Animal in a Live Humane Trap for more than 6 daylight hours or 12 nighttime hours.

(L) Overworking an Animal.

(M) Animal Fighting. No Person shall promote, stage, hold, manage, conduct, carry on, train for or attend a game, show, exhibition, contest or fight in which one or more Animals is injuring, killing, maiming or destroying itself or other Animals or attempting to injure, kill, maim, or destroy other Animals or people.

(1) Any Person who attends or observes any Animal fight is vicariously criminally liable under this article, whether or not that Person paid for entry to the event.

(2) The owner of any premises used for Animal fighting is in violation of this article.

(3) Any Person who profits in any manner from an Animal fight, including but not limited to on-site vendors or purveyors of illegal gambling concerning an Animal fight, is in violation of this article.

(4) Any person who sells, receives, possesses, transports, loans or gives away any Animal used for fighting or Animal Fighting Paraphernalia is in violation of this article.

(5) No Person shall provoke or entice an Animal from the property of its Owner for the purpose of engaging the Animal in an Animal fight.

(N) Teasing or Taunting Animals. No Person shall tease or taunt any Animal with the intent, purpose or effect of provoking a reaction from the Animal.

(O) Artificially coloring an Animal. No person shall dye or artificially color an Animal under the age of 12 weeks or use any dyes or coloring substance that could be harmful to the Animal.

(P) Any Person who violates any provision of § 9-2-2-1 except (F) and (G), § 9-2-2-2, § 9-2-2-3 except (F) and (G), § 9-2-2-4, § 9-2-2-5 or § 9-2-2-6 is guilty of Cruelty and shall be cited for Cruelty. The failure to restrict an Animal by use of a leash or the use of a leash that is longer than eight feet is not Cruelty.

(Q) Failing to report an Injury to an Animal caused by a Motorist. A Motor Vehicle Operator who strikes or runs down an Animal shall immediately call 311 and provide the facts regarding the accident and, if possible, the injuries sustained by the Animal. The Motor Vehicle Operator may elect to transport the Animal to AACC, a Veterinarian or VEC for Emergency Medical Treatment.

9-2-4-3 ANIMAL LIMITS AND RESTRICTIONS.

(A) INTACT COMPANION ANIMALS. No person shall own or possess an Intact dog or cat over the age of six months old without a valid Intact Companion Animal Permit except as provided herein.

(B) BREEDING COMPANION ANIMALS. No Person shall own or possess a pregnant female Companion Animal without obtaining a Litter Permit.

PART 8: SAFE-HAVEN

9-2-8-1 CREATION OF SAFE-HAVEN.

To increase every Animal's chance of being adopted, this article hereby creates SAFE-HAVEN. Safe-Haven guarantees every adoptable Animal at AACC at least ten days, including two weekends, without the possibility of being euthanized.

REFERENCES AND RESOURCES

"1st-Grader Honored After Dog Attack," *Albuquerque Journal*, 11-08-15

"2011 Dog Bite Fatality: Four Pit Bulls Maul New Mexico Woman To Death," http://www.dogsbite.org

"2012 Dog Bite Fatality: Pet Pull Bull Kills 74-Year-Old Santa Fe Man," 05-08-2012, http://www.dogsbite.org

"Ag-Gag Bills At State Level," www.aspca.com

"Albuquerque New Mexico/Bernalillo—County—New Mexico," Wikipedia.com

American Humane Association's National Resource Center on the Link. http://www.americanhumane.org

"ALDF State Statutes Ranking Report 2014," www.aldf.org

"Animal Care Ordinance, BernCo, Chapter 6, Animals," *BernCo Animal Care Services*, 02-26-2013

"Animal Cruelty and Human Violence, a Documented Connection," Humane Society of the United States, www.humanesociety.org

"Animal Cruelty Laws State by State," www.aldf.org

"Animal Hoarding Case Study: Vikki Kittles," www.aldf.org

"Animal Protection Issues." THLN, Animal Protection Issues, Animal Protection New Mexico, www.apnm.org

"Animal Sheltering Board 2014, HB 147," www.apnm.com

"Animal Welfare Advocated Applaud Governor Hoseam for Vetoing Ag-Gag Bill," *HSUS All Animals*, 05-2013

"Are There Laws Against Animal Hoarding?" www.spca.org

"ASPCA and NYPD," *ASPCA Action*, Fall, 2015

"ASPCA Launches Ag-Gag Campaign: Open the Barns," www.aspca.org

"Assessing Shelter Dogs and Temperament Testing," www.paw-rescue.org

"Back-to-Back Raids Save More than 250 Dogs," *ASPCA Action*, Spring/Summer, 2015

"BCSD Deputies May Get Animal Abuse Training," KOAT Channel 7-ABC News, 05-13-2010

"BernCo Animal Care Director Matt Pepper Appointed to National Animal Care Association Board of Directors," 10-15-2015, www.BernCo.gov

"The Ban on Cockfighting But Tradition Lives On," *New York Times*, 07-06-2008

"Boy, 4, Mauled to Death by Dog in His NYC Home," *New York Times*, 05-29-2011

"Buyer Beware: The Problem with Puppy Mills and Backyard Breeders," www.paw-rescue.org

"Canines Help Deputies," *South Valley Ink*, 01-19-2013

"Celebrity Corner," *ASPCA Action*, Spring/Summer 2015

"Center for Disease Control Web-based Injury Statistics," nationalCanineResearchCouncil.org

"Chain-Free Las Cruces/Dona Ana County" http://www.Facebook.com/chainfreeLasCruces

"Chained Dog Cruelty Case Prompts Reward" 05-28-2012, Los Lunas, NM, krqe.com

"Challenging Animal Cruelty in September-CARE & the Link," www.apnm.org 09-23-2014

"Child abuse, neglect rates for South Valley," compiled from *New Mexico Community Data Collaborative,* 2007-2011

"Public Safety First at its Animal Shelters" staff editorial, *Albuquerque Journal*, 04-03-2015

"Companion Animal Rescue Effort," www.apnm.org

"County Commissioners Agree to Tax Increase," *Albuquerque Journal*, 05-18-2014

"Cruelty to Animals and Interpersonal Violence: An Update," *International Association of Chiefs of Police Training Key* 689, 07-2014

"Demand Maximum Sentence for Tim Chavez for Charges Animal Cruelty and Torture, Albuquerque, NM, 09-08-2012," https://Hand4Paws.wordpress.com

"Dog and Cat Spay/Neuter Program, HB 415, 2014," www.apnm.org

"Dog Attack Fatality in New Mexico," 01-02-2013, www.dogbitelaw.com

"Dog Killed by Pit Bull at Soccer Game" 05-25-2012, krqe.com

"Dogfighting Group Must Pay $2M" AP, Montgomery, Alabama, *Albuquerque Journal* 01-17-2015

"Dog Rescue: Why You Should Avoid Puppy Mills," *Cesar's Way*, www.cesarsway.com/dog-rescue

"Domestic Violence and Animal Abuse: A Multi-disciplinary Approach in Illinois," *Community Policing Dispatch,* 03-20-2010, http://cops.usdoj.gov

"DNA Research Suggests Dogs Bred Up to 40,000 Years Ago," *Los Angeles Times*, 05-26-2015

"Father, Girlfriend Charged in Boy's Mauling Death," http://miami.cbslocal.com

"FBI Ranks Animal Cruelty as Top Tier Felony," *Detroit Free Press*, 10-01-2014

"Field Investigations and Responses," www.aspca.org

"Fight Against Backyard Breeding," *Bosque Beast*, 08-28-2013

"Happy Ending In Animal Torture Cases," krqe.com 08-04-2012

"Health Benefits of Pets," www.Helpguide.org

"Home Burglary Prevention Advice," *Bottom Line Personal Publications*, 09-2008

"HSUS Releases Annual Ranking of State Animal Protection Laws," 01-2013, 2014, humanesociety.org

"It's Not Rocket Science: With More Spays and Neuters, Fewer Animals Die and Communities Save Money," *Our Programs in Action*, Animal Protection of New Mexico, 04-2015

"It's the Law in New Mexico: Synopsis of the Felony Animal Cruelty Law" *Petroglyphs*, 2001

Investigating Animal Cruelty in New Mexico, A Field Guide for Law Enforcement Officers, New Mexico Dept. of Public Safety, APNM, HSUS

"Judge Dismisses Animal Cruelty Charges Against Tim Chavez," *Albuquerque Journal*, 01-30-2013

"Laws That Protect Dogs in Puppy Mills," www.aspca.org

"Man Accused of Burning, Beating Dogs" August 7, 2012, KRQE, Roswell, NM

"Model Animal Protection Laws, 2010, www.aldf.org

"Mother and Her Son Arrested After Posting Photograph of Puppy in Plastic Bag," krqe.com 12-13-2013

"Multi-State Dogfighting Raid Saves 367 Dogs", August 26, 2013, www.aldf.org

"New Mexico Revamps Spay/Neuter License Plate Law," www.apnm.org

"New Rules for County Pet Owners," *Albuquerque Journal*, 08-16-2013

"No Punishment for Students, Staff," *Albuquerque Journal*, 05-19-2016

"NM Cruelty Statutes," Animal Legal and Historical Center, 2014, animallaw.info

"NM Gets a Poor Return on Your Hard-earned Dollars," editorial, *Albuquerque Journal*, 04-12, 2016

"NM Near Bottom in Financial Literacy," *Albuquerque Journal*, 04-01-2015

"Oregon's Felony Animal Cruelty Law—The Kittles Bill," www.aldf.org

"Pets in Protection Orders by State," National Link Coalition by Phil Arkow, arkowpets@snip.net

"Position Statement on Dangerous Dog Laws," ASPCA Policy and Position Statements, www.aspca.org

"Prevention of Cruelty to Animals Act: Model Legislation from No Kill Advocacy Center, 2014, www.nathanwinograd.com

"Public Safety and Humane Implications of Persistently Tethering Domestic Dogs," *New Mexico Department of Public Safety Report to Consumers of Public Affairs Committee*, 01-2008

"Puppy Mills-Animal Protection Issues," www.nathanwinograd.com 11-2010

"Puppy Mills," www.sourcewatch.org

"Puppy Mills and Backyard Breeders," www.dogster.com

"Roswell Mayor Bans New Mexico Rescue Groups in Response to Dog attack," KRQE News, Channel 13, 06-18-2014

"Safe Haven For Sophie: The CARE Program Provides Life-Saving Support for Victims of Domestic Violence," www.apnm.org

"Silver City Bans Chaining of Dogs," *Albuquerque Journal*, 08-28-2015

"Slow Road to a Quick Fix," *Bosque Beast*, 08&09-2015

"South Valley, Bernalillo County Early Childhood Report," *State of New Mexico Children, Youth and Families Department Early Childhood Services Division 2014*

"South Valley, New Mexico," wikipedia.com

"Sports Dog of the Year," *Sports Illustrated*, Scorecard, 11-02-2014

"Starved Dog Found at City Worker's Home," krqe.com, 08-03-2012

"State Advocacy:Victory! New Jersey Governor Signs Bill to Protect Pet Store Puppies," *ASPCA Action*, Spring/Summer 2015

"Study Reveals Increasingly Positive Outcomes for Pit Bulls in Shelters," *ASPCA Action,* Fall 2015

"Suspected Puppy Mill Shut Down: 600 Animals Seized," animallaw.info

"TAG: Pet Purchase Protection Act," http://www.animallaw.info

"The LINK-Letter," volume 9, number 2, 02-2016, www.nationallinkcoalition.org

"The LINK-Letter," volume 9, number 3, 03-2016, www.nationallinkcoalition.org

"The LINK-Letter," volume 8, number 11, 11-2015, www.nationallinkcoalition.org

"The LINK-Letter," volume 8, number 10, 10-2015, www.nationallinkcoalition.org

"The LINK-Letter," volume 8, number 8, 08-2015, www.nationallinkcoalition.org

"The LINK-Letter," volume 8, number 7, 07-2015, www.nationallinkcoalition.org

"The LINK-Letter" volume 8, number 4, 04-2015, www.nationallinkcoalition.org

"The LINK-Letter," volume 8, number 5,05-2015, www.nationallinkcoalition.org

"The LINK-Letter," volume 8, number 2, 02-2015, www.nationallinkcoalition.org

"The LINK-Letter," volume 8, number 1, 01-2015, www.nationallinkcoalition.org

"The LINK-Letter," volume 7, numbers 11-12, 11&12-2014, www.nationallinkcoalition.org

"Unchain New Mexico," http://www.facebook.com/unchainsand

"UNchain Santa Fe County," www.santafescoop.ning.com

"Understanding the Link Between Animal Abuse and Family Violence," American Humane Association, www.americanhumane.org

"U.S. Animal Protection Law 2014 Rankings," www.aldf.com

"TAG: Pet Purchase Protection Act," www.animallaw.info

"View Source for Puppy Mills," http://www.sourcewatch.org

"Viewers Outraged by Abused Kittens—Viewer Makes Generous offer" 06-27-2012, www.youtube.com

Village of Tijeras Ordinance #32, localtown.us/tijeras-nm

"View Full Version: "Roswell Mayor Bans NM Rescue Groups in Response to Dog Attack," www.pitbull-chat.com

"Walking With the Pet Patrol," *Bosque Beast*, 10 & 11-2013

"West's NM Statutes Annotated," Chapter 30, Criminal Offenses, Article 18, Animals, 01-14, www.animallaw.info

"What is the Link?" www.http://nationallinkcoalition.org

"Wilson County Puppy Mill Bust..Second This Month."*Durham County Examiner*, 08-24-2012

"Woman Killed by Pit Bull in Valencia County," *Albuquerque Journal*, 12-13-2013

"2012 Animal Protection Voters Scorecard NM State Legislature," www.apnm.org

"2013 Animal Protection Voters Scorecard NM State Legislature," www.apnm.org

"2014 Animal Protection Voters Scorecard NM State Legislature," www.apnm.org

"2015 Animal Protection Voters Scorecard NM State Legislature," www.apnm.org

2013 New Mexico Conference on THE LINK Between Animal Cruelty and Human Violence

2014 New Mexico Conference on THE LINK Between Animal Cruelty and Human Violence

Akers, Joshua M., The Transition From Unincorporated Community to Municipality in the South Valley, 2008, University of New Mexico, Bureau of Business and Economic Research, www.bber.unm.edu

Andrews, Barbara J, "AKC Inspected? The Cattle Dog Debacle," 10-2014, www.TheDogPress.com

Ankony, Robert C. and Kelly, Thomas M, "The Impact of Perceived Alienation on a Police Officers' Sense of Mastery and Subsequent Motivation for Proactive Enforcement," *Policing: An International Journal of Police Strategies and Management,* vol.22, no.2 (1999)

Applebone, Peter, "Series of Pit Bull Attacks Stirs a Clamor For Laws," *New York Times*, 07-08-1987

Arkow, Phil, "Forward: The Link Between Violence to Animals and People," Guide on Safer Communities, Safer Families and Being an Effective Voice for Animal Victims," March 2012, National District Attorneys' Association

Ascione, F.R. & Arkow, P. (Eds.) (1999) *Child Abuse, Domestic Violence and Animal Abuse: Linking the circles of Compassion for Prevention and Intervention,* West Lafayette, IN: Purdue University Press

Ascione, F.R. (2001) Animal Abuse and Youth Violence, *OJJDP Juvenile Justice Bulletin*

Barnard, Neal D, MD, "Animals Feel But Cannot Speak," Physicians Committee for Responsible Medicine, 09-2015

Bastian, Jon, "Cesar Millan: How Did Pit Bulls Get Such a Bad Rap?" 03-2013, www.cesarsway.com

Berry, Colin; Patronek, Gary; Lockwood, Randall, "Long-term Outcomes in Animal Hoarding," www.tufts.edu/vet/hoarding

Berry, Chris, "All 50 States Now Have Felony Animal Cruelty Provisions, 03-20-2014, www.aldf.com

Bittman, Mark, "Who Protects the Animals?" *New York Times*, 04-26-2011

Boat, Barbara, PH.D., "What Every Professional Should Know About the Link Between Child and Animal Abuse," 02-2015

Boetel, Byran, "Dangerous-Dog Policy Overhauled," *Albuquerque Journal*, 09-26-2015

"Bryan, Susan Montoya," Red.: Require Parents in Abuse Cases to Seek Help," *Albuquerque Journal*, 01-14-2015

Buel, Sarah M, "Fifty Obstacles to Leaving, Why Abuse Victims Stay," *The Colorado Lawyer*, 10-1999, Vol.28, No.10

Burkhart, Gabrielle, "Roswell Boy Attacked by Dogs Returns Home" KRQE News 13, 06-12-2014

Buzek, Aubrey, "Clovis Residents Take on Unwanted Animal Problems," *Clovis News Journal, Albuquerque Journal*, 03-20-2015

Clifton, Merrit, "Dog Attack Deaths and Maimings, U.S. and Canada, 09-1982 to 12-2013" www.DogsBite.org

Clausing, Jeri, "Debbie Swenerton, Animal Rescue Worker, Accused of Dognapping," *Huffington Post*, 12-04-2012

"Cruelty in New Mexico," *DVM 360 Magazine*, 04-29-2013

Dearden, Jason, "Dogfighting Thrives in Years Since Vick Case," *Albuquerque Journal*, 11-27-2014

Delea, Pete, "Authorities Raid Puppy Mill," *Daily News Record*, Harrison, Virginia, 02-07-2015

Delea, Pete, "Authorities Raid Puppy Mill," *Daily News Record*, Page County, Virginia, 07-03-2014

DiNuzio, Jeff, "Serial Dog Rapist on the Loose," *Pet News*, http://www.petfinder.com/pet-news/serial-dog-rapist-on-the-loose.html

Doren, Jenny, "*SPCA Seizes Animals Living in Horrible Conditions at Puppy Mill*," 10-31-2104

Duncan, Ashley, "Brief Summary of Laws Affecting Retail Pet Stores," Michigan State University College of Law, 2006, Primary Citation: Animal Legal and Historical Center, animallaw.info

Dunn, Lora, "ALDF Pursues Cat Killer," *The Animals' Advocate*, Volume 34, Issue 3, Winter 2015

Ellick, Adam, "A Ban on Cockfighting, But the Tradition Lives On," *NYTimes*, 07-06-2008

Evoncuk, Joanna, "Five Things to Do During a Dog Attack," 10-14-2014, https://multcopets.org

Fishman, Margie, "Delaware Pets: Pet Hoarding Hidden From View," *Delawareonline, The News Journal*, 03-30-2015

Fivecoat-Campbell, Kerri, "Five animal Shelter Practices That Should Make You Sick," 07-26-2012, www.Mainstreet.com

Fraga, Brian, "16-Month-Old Girl Killed by Family's Pit Bull in Las Cruces," 05-08-2012, *Las Cruces Sun-News*

Franklin, Frank, "The AKC:Worst in Show," www.humanesociety.org, 02-06-2015

Garcia, Clara, "Avid Runner Attacked, Injured," *Valencia County News Bulletin*, 10-18-2015

Gibson, Hanna, "Federal and State Dogfighting Statutes, Jurisdiction New Mexico," 30-18-2009, Michigan State University College of Law, 2014, Animal and Legal Historical Center, www.animallaw.info

Gleaner, Josh Cromer, "Kentucky Way Down the List in Animal Rights Laws," *Courier Post*, 01-26-2015

Gray, Roger, "East Texas Dogfighting," KYTX-CBS TV, 02-19-2014

Griffith, David, "Can Police Stop Killing Dogs?," *Police, the Law Enforcement Magazine*, Volume 38, no.10, 10-2014

Griffitth, David, "It's Not About the Dogs," *Police, the Law Enforcement Magazine*, Volume 38, no.10, 10-2014

Gutierrez, Joline Kruger, "Hoping for Best Friend's Return,"UpFront, *Albuquerque Journal*, 04-05-2014

Hayes, Victoria, "Detailed Discussion of Animal Hoarding," Michigan State University College of Law, 2010

Heild, Colleen, "City Puts Hold on Adoptions," *Albuquerque Journal*, 04-01-2015

Heild, Colleen, "City Report Upholds Criticism of Animal Welfare," *Albuquerque Journal*, 09-05-2015

Heild, Colleen, "Dangerous Dogs Being Released by City," *Albuquerque Journal*, 03-31-2015

Heild, Colleen, "Director Out at Animal Welfare," *Albuquerque Journal*, 10-02-2015

Heild, Colleen, "Dog Case Gets Pushed Back," *Albuquerque Journal*, 07-30-2015

Heild, Colleen, "New Mexico's Love Affair With Guns," *Albuquerque Journal*, 01-18-2016

Heild, Colleen, "They Killed Duncan," *Albuquerque Journal*, 05-14-2015

Heild, Colleen, "Team Advises Tougher Policy on Dangerous Dogs Adoptions," *Albuquerque Journal*, 06-25-2015

Jade, Ms,"Comprehensive Dog Bite Statistics," *The Dog Press Legislative Reporter*, 01-01-2015

Jennings, Elizabeth, "My View, Attorney General King Was Right on Cockfighting Ban," *Santa Fe New Mexican*, 07-27-2014

Kane, Paul, "Byrd on Michael Vick: Going to Hell," Washington Post Capitol Briefing, 07-19-2007

Kaplan, Elise, "I'd Like to do to Them What They Did to my Dog," *Albuquerque Journal*, 03-14-2015.

Kaplan, Elise, "Mauled Bodies of 'Bait-Dogs' Found," *Albuquerque Journal*, 02-06-2015

Kaplan, Elise, "Someone is Stealing Dogs in BernCo," *Albuquerque Journal*, 03-10-2015

Katz, Robyn, "Detailed Discussion of Commercial Breeders and Puppy Mills," Michigan State University College of Law, 2008

Kent, Alexander and Froblich, Thomas, "The Most Dangerous States in America," www.247wallSt.com

Kruger, Joline Gutierrez, "Nurse, Mauling Victim Reunited, 3 Decades Later," Up Front, *Albuquerque Journal*, 12-05-2015

Kuligowski, Kate J., "Creating a Less Abuse Society," *More Voices of New Mexico*, 2015

Layton, Lyndsey, "51% of U.S. School Students in Poverty," *The Washington Post*, 01-19-2015

Lockwood, Allie, "Why People Are Cruel to Animals," National District Attorneys' Association, 2014

Lockwood, Randal, Ph.D, Keynote address, 2014 New Mexico Conference on the Link Between Animal Cruelty and Human Violence

Ludwig, Jim, "Kennel Statistics by Jurisdiction 01-01-2014-12/31/2014, AAWD, Albuquerque, NM

Lynn, Colleen, "All dog Bite Statistics," www.Dogsbite.org

Manning, Sue of the Associated Press, "Pit Bulls in Training Service Dogs," *Albuquerque Journal*, 03-06-2015

Manning, Sue, "Fear Not Fido," Associated Press, *Albuquerque Journal*, 03-22-2013

Matlock, Staci and Roesler, Rico, "48 Dogs From Edgewood Home Stretch Shelter's Resources," *The New Mexican*, 04-03-2013

Matott, Sarah, "Students Build Dog Houses for Low-Income Families," *Carlsbad Current Argus*, 04-01-2015

Mayers, Amy, "ALDF-Backed Prosecutor Wins," *The Animals' Advocate*, Volume 34, Issue3, Winter 2015. ALDF

Mayers, Amy, "Dog Down," *The Animals' Advocate*, Volume 35, Issue 1, Spring 2016, ALDF

McKay, Dan, "Team Appalled by Conditions at Animal Shelters," *Albuquerque Journal*, 09-06-2015

McKinley, James C., "Dogfighting Subculture is Taking Hold in Texas," *New York Times*, 12-06-2008

McVeigh, Jim, "Study: Family Pet Often the Culprit in Dog Bites," Mayo Clinic Network, *Albuquerque Journal*, 06-08-2015

Megles, Suzana, "A Muddy Calf Rescue," *Life Arts,* 08-22-2012

Morrison, Jane Ann, "153 of Hoarder's Cats Euthanized Since 2010," *Las Vegas Review* Journal, 03-07-2015

Mullins, Alisa, "Animals Are Not Ours to Eat, Wear, Experiment on or Use for Entertainment or Abuse in Any Other Way," www.PETA.com/Chinese-fur-industry.htm

Murgado, Amaury, "Responding VS Reacting," *Police, the Law Enforcement Magazine*, Volume 38, no.10, 10-2014

Nathanson, Rick, "NM is 46th in U.S. for Child Homelessness," *Albuquerque Journal*, 11-18-2014

Nathanson, Rick, "NM Still Ranks 49th in Child Well-being," *Albuquerque Journal,* 07-21-2015

Nathanson, Rick, "Sick Dog Killer," *Albuquerque Journal*, 05-26-2015

Nelson, Sharon L. "The Abuse of Animals and Domestic Violence," *Animal Law*, a publication of Animal Legal Defense Fund, Vol. 17:369

O'Connor, Rebecca, "The Truth About Pit Bulls," *National Geographic Wild, Inside Wild*, 03-19-2013

Paul, Katherine and Cummins, Ronnie, "Shocking Reporting Factory Farm Abuses To Be Considered Act of Terrorism," *AlterNet*, 01-24-2013

Pederson, Lesley A. "Brief Summary of Fur Laws and Fur Production," 2010

Pepper, Matthew, "Partnering for Pets and People," *Animal Sheltering Magazine*, 07&08-2014

Pierce, Terri, "Throwing the Book At Abusers," *Bosque Beast*, August, September, 2014

Phillips, Allie; Lockwood, J.D.; Lockwood, Randall, "A Guide on Safe Communities, Safe Families and Being an Effective Voice for Animal Victims," National District Attorneys' Association, 2013

Phillips, Allie; Lockwood, J.D.; Lockwood, Randall, *Investigating and Prosecuting Animal Abuse,* National District Attorneys' Association, 2013

Pollard-Post, Lindsay, "Spaying, Neutering Key to Ending Euthanasia," 10-27-2014, www.PETA.org/Journal

Quigley, Winthrop, "Looking for Answers on New Mexico Poverty," *Albuquerque Journal Up Front*, 09-25-2014

Reed, Tom, "Is Trapping Doomed?" *High Country News*, 04-12-1990

Rodak, Jan, "Puppy Mill Bust," www.thebark.com/content/puppy-mill-bust

Ross, Brian, "Washington Keeps Cockfighting Legal in 3 States, 03-30-2014, ABCNews.go.com

Sanchez, Isabel, "Packed With Pets," *Albuquerque Journal*, 02-27-2015

Sanchez, Antonio, "Local Angels Give Rescue Dog Cubby New Life, Limbs," *Albuquerque Journal*, 05-23-2015

Scheideggor, Julie, "Ex-veterinarian Charged with 48 Counts of Animal Abuse," *DMV360 Magazine,* 05-16-2013

Sinclair, Leslie, Merck, Melinda and Lockwood, Randall, *Forensic Investigation of Animal Cruelty, A Guide for Veterinary and Law Enforcement Professionals,* 08-2006

Skrzycki, Cindy, "Fur Flies Over Use of Dog, Cat Pelts; U.S. Ban Approved," *Washington Post, 11-2011*

Staley, James, "Probation in Dogfighting Case," *Las Cruces Sun News*, 11-08-2013

Summers, Kathleen, "On the Front Line: The Fight to Stop Puppy Mills," *Colorado Dog Magazine*, Summer, 2008

Svartsman, Shulamit, "Suspected Puppy Mill Shut Down: 600 Animals Rescued," www.Lawyers.com

Swan, Ben, SFASHS, "Gov. Richardson Signs Bill to Ban Gas Chambers for Animals," SantaFeScoop.ning.com, 04-07-2009

Sweden, Jon, "Counting the Dollars at APS High Schools," *Albuquerque Journal*, 01-19-2015

Sylvester, Sandy, "Checklist for Puppy Mill Sites," *Investigating and Prosecuting Animal Abuse*, National District Attorneys' Association, 2014

Tassey, Eldine, "Breaking Cycle of Abuse Takes Time," *Albuquerque Journal*, 11-02-2014

Taylor, Andrea Lt. BCSO and Pepper, Matthew, Director, BCAC "Interagency Partnerships: Helping Animals, People and Community, 2013 New Mexico Conference on THE LINK Between Animal Cruelty and Human Violence

Taylor, Andrea, Lt. BCSO, "Animal Fighting and The Link," 2013 New Mexico Conference on THE LINK Between Animal Cruelty and Human Violence

Trager, Kevin and Barger, Kaitlin, "183 Animals Seized From Suspected Arkansas Puppy Mill," *USA Today*, 02-28-2014

The Public Safety & Humane Implication of Persistently Tethering Domestic Dogs, NM Dept Public Service and APNM, 02-2007

Walsh, F, "Human-Animal Bonds II: The Role of Pets in Family Systems & Family Therapy," ncbi.nim.nih.gov

West, Mary Ann, "Changing Puppy Mill Sales," *Huffington Post*, 07-30-2010

Westphal, D'Val, "Uncontrolled Breeding an Epidemic in NM," UpFront, *Albuquerque Journal*, April 10, 2015

Wigelsworth, Joel, "Up Front: Casa Q Gives LGBTQ Teens Support, Temporary Shelter," Albuquerque Journal, 07-31-2016

Wimsatt, Debbie, "Kentucky lax in Protecting Animals," *Courier-Journal*, 02-26-2015

Wisch, Rebecca F, "Table of State Dog Tether Laws," Michigan State University College of Law, 2014

www.aldf.com

www.aldf.org/police

www.animalfighting.org

www.animallaw.info

www.animalsandsociety.org/resources

www.apnm.org/campaigns/cockfighting

www.aspca.org

www.cdc.gov

www.bernco.gov

www.cabq.gov

www.aztecnm.gov

www.lasvegasnm.gov

www.dogsbite.org/legislating

www.dogster.com

www.edgarsnyder.com

www.hsus.org

www.Nationalcanineresearchcouncil.org/dogbites

www.ndaa.org/animal_abuse

www.nmdog.org

www.newmexico.hometownlocator.com › New Mexico › Bernalillo County

www.PETA.org

www.petfinder.com/pet_news

www.RedRover.org

www.registryapp.org

www.bernalillocountysheriff.com

https://vet.tufts.edu

www.thedogpress.com

www.wikipedia

ABOUT THE AUTHOR

A New Mexico native and graduate of University of New Mexico, Kate taught secondary education in New Jersey and New Mexico schools. She served for ten years as Education Director for Animal Humane Association New Mexico and Watermelon Mountain Ranch No Kill Shelter. Travelling the state with her assortment of performing blind and deaf dogs, she delivered her award-winning K-12 curriculums, You and Your Pet Are Forever to thousands of classrooms. Kate's recent writings have also appeared in various publications, including Bosque Beast, Petroglyphs, Pug News, DWAA Ruff Drafts as well as in More Voices New Mexico, third edition.

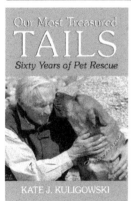

Her recent book, Our Most Treasured Tails, Sixty Years of Pet Rescue, was awarded the Maxwell Medallion by Dog Writers' Association of America for 2014 Best Book. It was also a Best Books USA finalist, and four-category finalist in NM-AZ 2014 Book Awards and received a five-star read from Readers' Favorite. After her book was honored by a 2015 New Mexico Legislature ceremony, she and her husband, Wally, and her families were recognized for their selfless efforts in rescuing New Mexico pets for more than a century.

She asks her readers to examine their own pet experiences and explore how to best use their resources and energies to fight animal cruelty by holding our legislators responsible for their votes on animal issues. In this book she asks her readers to unite two of their government resources to form an interagency animal cruelty task force. The underlying theme of all of Kate's writings is, "We can make a difference."

Our Most Treasured Tails, Sixty Years of Pet Rescue,

$16.99 + $3.00 S&H   255 page, hardcover including color photos
To order contact The Guys Publishing Company
905 Maverick Trail, SE, Albuquerque, NM 87123
wkkjk1027@gmail.com

ACKNOWLEDGEMENTS

Even after months of interviews, Andi Taylor continued to provide me with additional and updated information: her professional knowledge and experiences to compliment the chapters, photos and incidences during P.E.T. call-outs and sweeps. The strong dedication of an amazing Angela Stell of NMDOG is evident throughout the book. My interviews with Matt Pepper and Misha Goodman of BCACS gave me with insight into their P.E.T. responsibilities during the continuing and successful boots-on-the-ground sweeps. Matt, the most professional individual with which I communicated…constantly…was a font of information, ideas and resources. Bernalillo County animals miss him.

I felt honored to write of the selfless and brave efforts of their teams who continue to better the lives of hundreds of New Mexico Animals. I welcomed the professional inputs of Sheriff Manny Gonzales and his Undersheriffs Greg Rees and Rudy Mora, and admired their strong support of BCACT and its brave team members.

Several reporters for our local Albuquerque Journal kept our residents apprised of the misconduct of the AAWD administration. I was proud that they, too, respected the lives of our incarcerated animals as well as the safety of the potential adopters of unknown dangerous dogs.

Jim Ludwig, AAWD Animal Program Manager, was very helpful with department shelter statistics and with advice about how to best address some of the existing shelter situations. Desiree Cawley, Marketing Manager, was eager to supply me with requested information about the ongoing Pit Bull Terrier training classes. Several of my friends who are currently employed by AAWD have been most helpful in clarifying the present ordinance as well as internal and administrative policies.

Phil Arkow, coordinator for the National Link Coalition, and Lora Dunn, staff attorney with ALDF, both speakers at the 2015 Positive Links Conference, supplied pertinent information regarding the ratings and contents of city, county and state laws. They also supplied insight into where my emphasis should be in order to better influence my readers to become involved in pursuing stronger humane legislation.

Several occasions I required the time and expertise of fellow author, Loretta Hall of Southwest Writers in Albuquerque, an organization which has continually met the needs of both new and established authors.

This book would probably not have been possible without the talents and precious time of Julie Melton of The Right Type. She is a perfectionist who knows her trade, and because of this, she created a highly professional and easy-to-read book given a very short period of time. Hands down, Julie is the best.

My mother, Eileen Smyer Jacobson, was responsible for my learning the value of the written and spoken word, and my high school journalism teacher, Bess Booth, inspired my interest in writing. I have never stopped.

Because my husband and I have been involved in the animal rights and rescue work begun in the early 1900's by my New Mexico families, we view Andi's accomplishment, the formation of BCACT, as the realization of a dream for us and for all animal activists. Thank you, Andi. Thank you, BCACT members. I also salute the many thousands of animal volunteers who have given of their talents, resources, time and funds to continue this cause. By improving the world for animals, you have made our world a better world.

And as always, I rely on my well-read husband, Wally, a capable and kind critic. More important, he has always been there, not just for me, but with endless compassion for our many rescues, fosters and adoptees for 54 glorious years. We are blessed.

Kate J. Kuligowski

Silence Indicates Consent

TAKE THE TIME TO MAKE YOURS A MORE HUMANE COMMUNITY

1. Email or phone your U.S. Senators to ask for their support in animal protection legislation presently pending in Congress.

2. Email or phone your U.S. Representative to ask for their support in animal protection legislation presently pending in Congress.

3. Email or phone your state senator to ask for their support in animal protection legislation presently pending in your state.

4. Email or phone your state representative/s to ask for their support in animal protection legislation presently pending in your state.

5. Email or phone your town councilman to ask to sponsor animal protection codes in your town.

6. Email or phone your mayor to ask to sponsor specific animal protection codes in your town.

7. Email or phone your county representative to ask to sponsor specific animal protection codes in your county.

8. Write a letter to the editor of your community newspaper urging readers to support pending animal protection legislation, city, county and state.

9. Go online to the Humane Society Legislative Fund at www.hslf.org to find out how your federal legislators voted on animal protection issues.

10. Most states have similar humane websites with results of how state legislators voted on animal protection legislation. In New Mexico, it is www.apnm.com. Check online for your website.

11. If you see animal cruelty in your community, report it to the police/sheriff department.

YOUR INVOLVEMENT WILL LESSEN ANIMAL CRUELTY.

CPSIA information can be obtained
at www.ICGtesting.com
Printed in the USA
FSOW04n0024170816
23761FS

9 780692 759677